T0334020

ROUTLEDGE LIBRARY EDITIONS:
HISTORICAL SECURITY

Volume 11

# WAR AND STATE MAKING

Printed in the United States
By Bookmasters

# WAR AND STATE MAKING

## The Shaping of the Global Powers

KAREN A. RASLER AND
WILLIAM R. THOMPSON

LONDON AND NEW YORK

First published in 1989 by Unwin Hyman, Inc.

This edition first published in 2021
by Routledge
2 Park Square, Milton Park, Abingdon, Oxon OX14 4RN

and by Routledge
52 Vanderbilt Avenue, New York, NY 10017

*Routledge is an imprint of the Taylor & Francis Group, an informa business*

*British Library Cataloguing in Publication Data*
A catalogue record for this book is available from the British Library

ISBN: 978-0-367-61963-3 (Set)
ISBN: 978-1-00-314390-1 (Set) (ebk)
ISBN: 978-0-367-63645-6 (Volume 11) (hbk)
ISBN: 978-1-00-312009-4 (Volume 11) (ebk)

ISBN: 978-0-367-63653-1 (pbk)

**Publisher's Note**
The publisher has gone to great lengths to ensure the quality of this reprint but points out that some imperfections in the original copies may be apparent.

**Disclaimer**
The publisher has made every effort to trace copyright holders and would welcome correspondence from those they have been unable to trace.

# WAR AND STATE MAKING

The Shaping of the Global Powers

———

Karen A. Rasler
William R. Thompson

Studies in International Conflict,
Volume II

Boston
UNWIN HYMAN
London   Sydney   Wellington

Unwin Hyman, Inc.
8 Winchester Place, Winchester, Mass. 01890, USA

Published by the Academic Division of
Unwin Hyman Ltd
15/17 Broadwick Street, London W1V 1FP, UK

Allen & Unwin (Australia) Ltd,
8 Napier Street, North Sydney, NSW 2060, Australia

Allen & Unwin (New Zealand) Ltd in association with the
Port Nicholson Press Ltd,
75 Ghuznee Street, Wellington 1, New Zealand

First published in 1989

**Library of Congress Cataloging-in-Publication Data**

Rasler, Karen A., 1952–
  War and state making: the shaping of the global powers/
Karen A. Rasler, William R. Thompson.
    p.    cm.—(Studies in international conflict; v. 2)
Bibliography: p.
Includes index.
ISBN 0-04-445097-4
1. War—Economic aspects. 2. Geopolitics. 3. State The.
I. Thompson, William R.    II. Title.    III. Series.
HB195.R36   1989                                    88-26986
303.4′85—dc19                                            CIP

**British Library Cataloguing in Publication Data**

Rasler, Karen A.
  War and statemaking: the shaping of the global powers — (Studies in
international conflict; 2)
  1. War. International political aspects
  I. Title   II. Thompson, William R.   III. Series
  355′.02
ISBN 0-04-445097-4

Typeset in 10 on 12 point Garamond by Fotographics (Bedford) Ltd
and printed in Great Britain by The University Press, Cambridge

*To our parents, who all benefited from
the last global war — as did we*

# Contents

# Tables

# Figures

# *Preface*

Any book with the presumptuous title of *War and State Making* demands immediate qualification. Our focus does not emcompass all of the topics that might justifiably fit under the war and state-making umbrella. We spend little time on war making per se. In this study, we are interested in some of the consequences of, for example, Napoleonic warfare. How the wars were actually fought is a subject we leave to others. Moreover, we virtually ignore a large number of states that have been influenced by their participation in, or simply their presence near, warfare. For instance, we have little to say directly about Prussia, an excellent example of war-induced state making. We have even less to say about war-related political developments in the contemporary Third World.

Our primary excuse for these omissions is theoretical. We are not simply interested in the general phenomenon of war and state making. Rather, our interest is driven by the desire to test a decidedly macroscopic theory about the relationships between the ebb and flow of power concentration in the world system and global war. One assumption of this leadership long cycle theory is that all wars are not equally significant when it comes time to assess their consequences. Though they are fought only every 100 years or so, global wars, those intense struggles to determine who will have paramount influence in shaping how the world's political economy works, should be associated with unusually salient state-making consequences.

Although we are reluctant to limit the scope of these state-making consequences to the principal war participants, it is clear that only a few, very powerful states have fully competed in the deadly bouts of global warfare. Thus, this book mainly concerns the state making of the system's elite state actors of the past several hundred years—the global powers Portugal, Spain, France, England/Britain, the United Provinces of the Netherlands, Russia/the Soviet Union, the United States, Germany, and Japan. Indeed, our argument in brief is that the states of these countries, to a considerable extent, are the products of war making. It took warfare to create these states in the first place.

At the same time, developing the capability to wage more war was frequently a primary reason for creating the states. Once created, preparing for future wars, as well as waging wars more than occasionally, remained a primary function of the state organization.

Historically, global power state making, therefore, has been predicated predominately on developing war-making organizational machines. We do not think this facet of politics has changed much in our more complicated current era. Throughout the past 500 years, nevertheless, global wars have increasingly distinguished themselves as a major shaper of global power state making. This generalization provides our central focus. We test in various ways the distinctive state-making consequences of global wars in comparison to the effects of other types of war. In most instances, global wars are more significant than are non-global wars.

We think these findings help clarify how *specific* types of war have influenced *specific* types of states in a *specific* historical era. Too often, war- and state-making arguments are couched too specifically (as in the single country–single war context) or too generically (war in general influences state making in general). By focusing on maritime- and territorial-oriented global powers and comparing global wars with non–global wars, we aim for something in between the too specific and too generic. We also seek support for the leadership long cycle theory. To the extent that we are able to demonstrate that impacts of global wars are special, we believe we have produced additional validation for a theory designed to explain systemic oscillations and processes. That it also sheds light on the external sources of internal state-making oscillations and processes is a bonus.

To accomplish these ends, we bring together and discuss whatever evidence seems pertinent. We present empirical evidence as concretely as is feasible for an inquiry that spans nearly a millennium of bloodletting and state making. One of the most tangible types of evidence, in our estimation, is produced by statistical analysis of the impacts of war on long data series. Because this form of war-impact analysis does not occur until midway through chapter 4, the sudden appearance of Greek symbols and statistical tests of significance in the midst of what appears to be a more conventional historical analysis will startle some readers. We considered trying to make our case without the statistical analyses so as not to repel the statistically squeamish. But the statistical outcomes were too important to our argument to dispense with them. Although they remain an integral part of our analysis, we have tried to report them so that their technical nature would present few obstacles to the statistically uninitiated.

We are indebted to a number of institutions and individuals for their assistance at several junctures in the production of this study. Between 1982 and 1985, the National Science Foundation, through grants to both authors, provided the financial underpinnings for this project. Various chapters have been read and commented on by Richard Eichenberg, Richard Farkas, Suzanne Frederick, Jacek Kugler, Pat McGowan, George Modelski, Manus Midlarsky, David Rapkin, Robert Rood, Mark Rupert, Charles Tilly, Frank Zagare, and Ekkart Zimmerman. Naturally, these individuals are not responsible for any errors of interpretation. Nor do they necessarily agree with any or all of our conclusions.

Earlier versions of the following chapters were published in journal format: chapter 4—"Global Wars, Public Debts, and the Long Cycle," *World Politics*, 35 (July 1983), 489–516, © 1983 by Princeton University Press, reprinted with permission of Princeton University Press; chapter 5—"War Making and State Making: Governmental Expenditures, Tax Revenues, and Global Wars," *American Political Science Review*, 79 (June 1985), 491–507, reprinted with permission; chapter 6—"War and the Economic Growth of Major Powers," *American Journal of Political Science*, 29 (August 1985), 513–38, reprinted with permission of the publishers, University of Texas Press; and chapter 7—"War, Accommodation, and Violence in the United States, 1890–1970," *American Political Science Review*, 80 (September 1986), 921–45, reprinted with permission. Our thanks to *World Politics*, the American Political Science Association, the Midwest Political Science Association, Princeton University Press, and the University of Texas Press for permission to reprint this material. Figure 1.1, "Tilly's War-making–State-making Model," is reprinted with permission from Charles Tilly, "War Making and State Making as Organized Crime," in *Bringing the State Back In*, ed. P. B. Evans, D. Rueschemeyer, and T. Skocpol (Cambridge: Cambridge University Press, 1985).

# 1
## Global Wars and Global Power State Making

War and the expansion of the state are difficult phenomena to disentangle. Indeed, it is difficult to imagine tracing the historical development of the world system's most powerful states without frequent reference to the interactions of war-making and state-making processes. This observation may seem to be a phrase that can go without saying. Curiously, it is still not yet a fully accepted axiom for students of political science, political development, or the state.

Most studies of political development are relatively silent on the impacts of war. One obvious reason for this silence is that contemporary studies of political development have been preoccupied with Third World cases. The prevailing assumption seems to be that even though wars may once have been important for the development of the older states, the post–World War II era is somehow different. Third World wars are thought to be less frequent, briefer, and less consequential affairs than, say, the wars of sixteenth-century Europe.

Assumptions such as these may explain why one influential source on political development makes only a passing reference to "threats from the international environment" as being an important cause of political change. Even so, the external threat category appears to be restricted to primitive and traditional systems (Almond and Powell 1966: 306). To what extent such assumptions are warranted remains to be determined. Clearly, exceptions exist. Egypt, Jordan, Syria, Iraq, Iran, Pakistan, India, South Korea, Vietnam, Laos, and Paraguay come quickly to mind as Third World states that are not strangers to the consequences of war.[1] If we were to extend our purview to internal wars as well, the list of prominent exceptions would no doubt grow longer.

Whatever generalizations about war and development in the Third World turn out to be appropriate, our immediate interests concern the development of the older states. We are especially interested in the powerful states that have served as models—for better or worse—for the many, less powerful states that have emerged more recently.

Analysts are prepared to recognize the state-making impact of war as a historical fact for the older, more powerful states. Yet the developmental preoccupation with the Third World is not very helpful in explaining why these same analysts are content to restrict these influences to a time several centuries past. Another equally influential study of political development provides a useful and representative illustration of this tendency. At one point, Huntington (1968) seeks to explain why political modernization in the United States differed from the record established in Europe. Specifically, he seeks to explain why political participation preceded the rationalization of authority and the differentiation of political structures in the American case, whereas the reverse sequence characterized European cases.

> In large part, [the differences in political modernization] are directly related to the prevalence of foreign war and social conflict in Europe as contrasted with America. On the Continent the late sixteenth and the seventeenth centuries were periods of intense struggle and conflict. For only three years during the entire seventeenth century was there a complete absence of fighting on the European continent. Several of the larger states were more often at war during the century than they were at peace. . . . War reached an intensity in the seventeenth century which it never had previously and which was exceeded later only in the twentieth century. The prevalence of war directly promoted political modernization. Competition forced the monarchs to build their military strength. The creation of military strength required national unity, the suppression of regional and religious dissidents, the expansion of armies and bureaucracies, and a major increase in state revenues. . . . War was the great stimulus to state building. (Huntington 1968: 122–23)

Regrettably, Huntington (1968) has little more to say about the stimulating effects of war on state building in what is nearly a 500-page and wide-ranging study of political development. A reason for this absence of follow up, presumably, has something to do with the verb tense used in the passage cited above: war *was* the great stimulus to state building. Although we acknowledge the accuracy of the generalization as far as it goes, it is too restrictive. War was a great stimulus to state building, and it continues to be, if not a great stimulus, then at least a major factor. In particular, war making continues to be a major influence on the powerful states that ushered in the modern era of state making (roughly post-1500). These states have also been the principal political organizations responsible for trying to shape the nature of political arenas—their own and those of other peoples.

This study has several objectives. First, we seek to promote further the idea that war and state making have been and continue to be closely and reciprocally intertwined endeavors. This is hardly new territory. Both Skocpol (1985) and Mann (1986) point to the long European tradition in this vein, perhaps represented best by the work of Hintze (1975).[2] Focusing more on war's impact on social change, Wynn (1986) notes that the devastating effects of World War I in particular brought a number of British writers (Marwick 1965, 1974; Emsley 1979; Milward 1979; Best 1986; Bond 1986; Winter 1986) into what previously had been a central European camp. The United States, again according to Wynn, remains the major holdout in adopting a strong appreciation for the impacts and consequences of war.

> There still exists in America, despite considerable evidence to the contrary, a popular view of history and of twentieth century history in particular that depicts the United States as having a peculiar ability to fight (and win) total war with little social effect or disturbance at home. The impression remains of a nation with such enormous resources and reserves of power that it is able to beat plowshares into swords and swords back into plowshares with considerable ease and few lasting consequences. This reflects both American optimism and the nation's actual experience of history. So, while military and diplomatic aspects of war might be fully explored, the domestic, social, economic and political effects tend to be overlooked: wars are regarded as temporary interruptions or deviations from the main thrust and development of American history. (Wynn 1986: xiv)

The United States has indeed led a relatively charmed existence in avoiding the least desirable consequences of major-scale warfare in the twentieth century. This fact, coupled with Wynn's cultural allusion to American optimism, goes some way in clarifying why Americans under-appreciate the consequences of war. Nevertheless, dents are being made in this resistance.

General treatments, such as those developed by Modelski (1972), Bean (1973), Tilly (1975), Ames and Rapp (1977), Stein and Russett (1980), Gilpin (1981), and McNeill (1982), have helped legitimate the idea that preparing for, and participating in, war has influenced state formation processes. More specific studies of war's impact on the United States (Blum 1976; Stein 1978; Hawley 1979; Kennedy 1980; Higgs 1987) have also contributed.

Highly complementary is the movement primarily within American social science circles toward giving increased emphasis to the roles of internal and external crisis in interrupting institutionalized patterns and processes and in bringing about political change (Binder et al. 1971; Almond et al. 1973; Grew 1978; Trimberger 1978; Skocpol 1979; Block 1980; Krasner 1984; Gourevitch 1986). The cognate interest in "bringing the state back in" to the analysis of politics (Evans et al. 1985) is another notable reinforcing element.

Thus, the notion that wars have punctuated American and other people's sociopolitical and economic equilibriums on occasion is not novel. What is relatively novel about our approach are the theoretical distinctions concerning, and the empirical evidence relating to, the impacts of different types of wars, which we highlight in this analysis. Some wars simply are more important than others. Yet it is not enough to accept the premise that World War I may have had some influence on social welfare in Britain, women's voting rights in the United States, or the tenure of the Czarist regime in Russia in ways that the Boer War, the Spanish-American War, or the Russo-Japanese War could not and did not have. The point stressed here is not merely that some wars are more destructive than others and therefore more consequential; such a point is hardly controversial. Rather, one point of departure is the contention that wars represent disputes about how best to manage politico-economic problems and policies at various levels of interaction.

Most wars are restricted to disputes of interest primarily to only one or two states. Civil wars, at least prior to outside intervention, are the prototypical single-state war. The Chaco War fought between Bolivia and Paraguay over possession of largely desert territory provides a good example of a two-state case. Some wars assume regional significance when their issues and outcomes have enough importance for proximate states that participation quickly or gradually escalates within the area of interest. The Thirty Years War offers a seventeenth-century example. Some, but not all, of the Arab-Israeli wars since 1948 provide more recent illustrations. Even more rare are global wars. These complicated wars are fought over disputes about fundamental policies and rules for the transoceanic, global political system. Participation can become quite widespread given the planetary implications of these affairs. The extent of major-power participation tends to be complete. The high rate of elite-state participation, in turn, is a function of the perception that a global war's issues and results are too important to sit out. Whoever wins a global war is able to establish the all-pervasive framework of the postwar political and economic order. World Wars I and II, taken independently, or preferably as two phases of one extended war, represent the most recent example(s) of global war.

The statement that war influences state-making processes is a rather sweeping proposition. One way to improve the specificity of such statements (something we think is highly desirable) is to identify which wars are most likely to affect whose state making. Our primary thesis is that global wars are most likely to influence the state-making processes of the principal contestants in these watershed events. The specificity implied by this statement is underscored by the numbers involved. We are talking about a half dozen or so wars, occurring roughly a century apart during the past five hundred years, that have been primary shapers of the state-making activities of fewer than a dozen states. Moreover, in the temporal vicinity of any specific global war only some fraction of the historical set of leading powers actually possessed systemic elite status. The maximal set of fewer than a dozen states thus translates into something closer to a half dozen at any given time.

Several hundred political entities since the year 1500 might fit someone's definition of a state.[3] During that time hundreds of bloodletting events might fit someone's definition of a war. Hence, the scope of our present theoretical undertaking is quite restrictive. Yet we hasten to point out that our restrictive scope encompasses the last half-millennium's most important wars and most powerful states.

Even more important is the related argument that the impacts of global wars are more than merely a string of intermittent shocks to state makers and state making. Global wars are some of the more dramatic milestones in a long-term process of power concentration and deconcentration in the world system. Much of the state making of the systemic elite is a by-product, and a largely unintended by-product at that, of the ebb and flow of this systemic concentration rhythm. The urge to rise to the top within the initially European elite subset has caused a number of changes in organizational format, scope and scale, resource extraction, and domestic political alliances or accommodations that encompass what we refer to as political development and state making. Yet there is no need to overstate our case. The urge to improve or safeguard one's external position has not been the sole source of state-making changes by any means—but it has been one of the most significant and enduring sources.

Other points also need to be made. We would like to see fewer distinctions drawn between what is internal to the nation-state and the realm that is external. Too often, this habit of convenience gets in the way of theoretical and empirical analysis. When examining the effects of interstate wars on the states that fought them, the distinctions often serve little real purpose.

In general, we prefer to see fewer states compared simultaneously in cross-national analyses, but we also like to see them compared over longer periods of time. To be sure, the number of units and years that need to be analyzed will always depend on the question at hand. Even so, the practice of extracting much information from observations on very large cross-national aggregations measured at one point in time seems to be coming to an end. Our focus is restricted to a handful of important states (the global powers of England/Britain, France, Spain, the Netherlands, Russia/the Soviet Union, the United States, Germany, and Japan). Temporally, most of our analyses are confined to the past few hundred years. However, some chapters journey back as far as the eleventh and twelfth centuries.

Another special interest concerns the issue of testing and supporting generalizations about war and state making with whatever evidence and analytical techniques that are both available and appropriate. Our biases become apparent in later chapters. Questions concerning long-term changes demand long data series to track and assess the nature of the changes that are hypothesized to have taken place. Very few of these series—data on such subjects as wars, expenditures, revenues, and economic growth—are readily available. Nevertheless, pertinent data can be assembled, even though considerable labor may be anticipated.

Once assembled, the data series can be analyzed using techniques ranging from the ostensibly simple, such as the venerable and indispensable "eyeball" inspection, through calculating percentages, to more esoteric varieties of sophisticated statistical approaches. We use the gamut of these techniques as necessary to test our hypotheses about the impacts of war.

Internal-external distinctions, the number of units of analysis, and sophisticated statistical techniques, admittedly, are fairly abstract topics. We therefore reserve our discussions of these matters to later pages where, in the proper context, they are easier to follow. Here, it is best to focus on clarifying the principal connections between war making and state making. In the end, we draw a map of these connections (see figure 1.4).

Before we present our model, which serves as a structural armature for the analyses in chapters 2 through 7, some discussion of how we developed the model is warranted, especially since the core of our war-making–state-making model is highly derivative. Indeed, our model's core, subject to some alterations, is based on a model first developed by Charles Tilly (1985). Thus, to elucidate our model, we first need to review Tilly's argument and then to explain the reasons for altering the core relationships and making more explicit the geopolitical-economic context in which these relationships are firmly embedded.

### Tilly's Four State Activities Model

Tilly (1985) has suggested that the historical process of European state formation can be reduced profitably to a consideration of the interdependencies among war making, state making, extraction, and protection. In many respects, Tilly's model is an appealing simplification of historical reality and thus a good model. Yet several characteristics of the model are both representative of other approaches to the connections between war making and state making and, we think, much in need of reconsideration. Hence, we will exploit the Tilly model as a vehicle for advancing certain criticisms that apply to it and other kindred analyses. Despite our criticisms, though, the Tilly model still has much to recommend it. In the end, we incorporate a slightly modified version of it as the core of our more complicated map of the multiple linkages between war making and state making of some of the world's most powerful states.

Tilly begins the development of his model by recapitulating the argument on the provision of state protection as a profit-making business put forward by the economic historian and a leading scholar of Venice, Frederick Lane (1966). One first reduces the actors in a political economy to one or more competing rulers and various sets of subjects. The logic of the situation for a predatory, if rational, ruler amounts to keeping protection costs well below the proportion of state income extracted from the subjects who receive some measure of protection at home and abroad. The difference between protection costs and tax-generated state revenue, a form of tribute, becomes the ruler's profit margin. Presumably, a fully nonaltruistic ruler would wish to maximize this profit.

In other types of political systems, however, the governing logic at stake might operate along different principles. If the subjects or some group among them, such as merchants, controlled the state, they would probably be interested in maximizing protection rents. Protection rents are created for group A when groups A and B receive the same protection but group A's taxes or protection fees are lower than those of group B. A merchant oligarchy-controlled state would therefore prefer efficient solutions—obtaining the most competitive protection benefits at the lowest cost possible. Contrarily, a state controlled by bureaucrats is likely to seek to maximize bureaucratic salaries—thereby keeping protection costs high.

Various types of political systems are thus apt to behave differently in terms of the protection provided, the preferred level of protection costs, and the rents enjoyed by the state's subjects. This interpretation should also help explain why different types of states, for example, low versus high overhead types of regimes, came into being in such places as Venice and the United Provinces of the Netherlands as opposed to France or Spain.

Viewing the fundamental process of state building as a form of protection racket may be more appealing than some of the other more benign, contractually oriented perspectives on how and why states have come into being. Nevertheless, Tilly contends that states do other things besides provide protection. These other activities—war making, state making, and extraction as defined in table 1.1—are equally important to comprehending the

**Table 1.1**
*Tilly's Four State Activities*

1. War making: Eliminating or neutralizing their own rivals outside the territories in which they have clear and continuous priority as wielders of force
2. State making: Eliminating or neutralizing their rivals inside those territories
3. Protection: Eliminating or neutralizing the enemies of their clients
4. Extraction: Acquiring the means of carrying out the first three activities—war making, state making, and protection

*Source:* Tilly (1985: 181).

organizational forms assumed by states and the different ways in which state-monopolized violence is applied. For instance, the variable interaction of each of the four types of activity (counting protection) is said to have produced the specific types of organizations (e.g., armies, treasuries, police, courts) that gave the resultant states their distinctive organizational formats.

At the root of Tilly's discussion, however, is the following general principle: "the more costly the activity, all other things being equal, the greater was the organizational residue" (Tilly 1985: 181). Putting aside the possible meanings of "organizational residue," this apparently simple conclusion turns out to be quite complicated. In the process of elaborating the underlying reasoning, a number of variables enter the state formation equation. In addition to the initial four main governmental activities (war making, state making, extraction, and protection), two ostensibly different although interrelated dependent variables (the costs and the size of government) and six independent variables (power concentration, cultural heterogeneity, military organization, physical range, resource endowment, and the extent of an economy's commercialization) receive brief discussion.

The generalizations relating some of these factors are fairly easy to follow on a statement-by-statement basis. Fragmented power and cultural heterogeneity increase the costs of expansionary state making. Protection costs escalate the farther away from a home base the protection is provided. The poorer the resource endowment and the less commercialized the economy, the greater the difficulty of collecting taxes. The more difficult it is to collect taxes, the more extensive the fiscal apparatus needed to perform the collection task. The smaller the population and the larger the standing army, the more bulky the bureaucracy that develops to support the army.

Other generalizations are also advanced. However the ones cited in the previous paragraph illustrate that whereas the individual statements are reasonably straightforward, their interconnections are multiple and complex. They are also difficult to diagram. It may seem churlish to complain about the awkwardness of mapping someone else's causal argument, but verbal causal arguments should be mappable if they are to be reproduced, analyzed, and tested. The mapping exercise often reveals problems in the nature of the argument that are less apparent in the verbal expression.

This complaint, however, is not our major quarrel with the Tilly war-making–state-making perspective. The chief purpose of mentioning the dozen variables is to hint at the richness of Tilly's synthesis even though the full parameters of his model remain unspecified. For our immediate purposes, we must acknowledge the potential explanatory power because we propose to focus on what are revealing and representative problems associated with Tilly's sketch of the major interconnections.

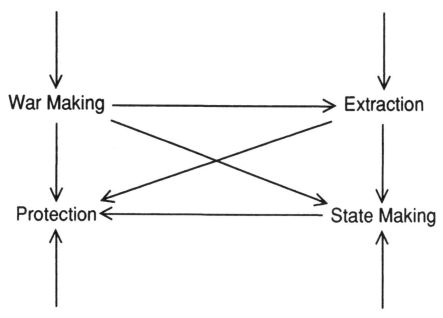

**Figure 1.1.** Tilly's War-making–State-making Model
*Source:* Tilly (1985: 183).

Figure 1.1 is Tilly's summarization of the model we have been discussing. The interdependencies among the four primary activities of the state are described as follows:

> In an idealized sequence, a great lord made war so effectively as to become dominant in a substantial territory, but that war making led to increased extraction of the means of war—men, arms, food, lodging, transportation, supplies, and/or the money to buy them—from the population within that territory. The building up of war-making capacity likewise increased the capacity to extract. The very activity of extraction, if successful, entailed the elimination, neutralization, or cooptation of the great lord's local rivals; thus, it led to state making. As a by-product, it created organization in the form of tax-collection agencies, police forces, courts, exchequers, account keepers; thus it again led to state making. To a lesser extent, war making likewise led to state making through the expansion of military organization itself, as a standing army, war industries, supporting bureaucracies, and (rather later) schools grew up with the state apparatus. All of these structures checked potential rivals and opponents. In the course of making war, extracting resources, and building up the state apparatus, the managers of states formed alliances with specific social classes. The members of those classes loaned resources, provided technical services, or helped ensure the compliance of the rest of the population, all in return for a measure of protection against their own rivals and enemies. As a result of these multiple strategic choices, a distinctive state apparatus grew up within each major section of Europe. (Tilly 1985: 183)

This explicit description of European state building is a nice summary of the role played by warfare in shaping the state. What is said implicitly, or not at all, is another matter, however. Specifically, we call attention to the following five aspects of figure 1.1 with which we disagree:

1  the unidirection of the causal flow,
2  the exogenous status of war making in the overall process of expanding states,
3  the absence of distinctions about the types of war and their variable consequences for extraction and state making,
4  the need to subordinate the role of protection to more general considerations related to the coalition-making activities of states and their managers, and
5  the absence of geopolitical-economic context.

### Unidirectionality and Exogeneity

The first two observations are closely intertwined. The Tilly model depicts war making as influencing extraction, state making, and protection. Extraction impacts on state making and protection. State making affects protection. The circle may appear to be closed in figure 1.1, but that is not really the case. There is no feedback, nor is any influence on war making identified.

Another way of looking at this problem entails redrawing the relationships summarized in figure 1.1. As executed, figure 1.2 is virtually identical to figure 1.1. The only difference is the absence of figure 1.1's four arrows signifying unstated influences. Disregarding this minor difference, figure 1.2

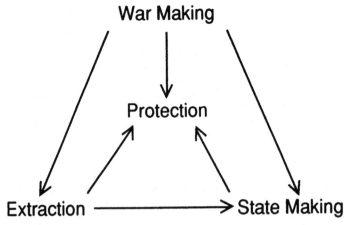

*Figure 1.2.* A Different View of Tilly's Simplified Model

emphasizes the dominant role of war making in the four-factor model. War making influences the other three factors. The possibility that the other three factors influence war making is not considered.

The absence of feedback and/or unidentified influences on war making may simply reflect the analytical shortcuts typically taken in constructing parsimonious models. Reciprocal influences, after all, are messy. The exogeneity of the war-making activity, on the other hand, may merely reflect habit as well as convenience. When one discusses state-building processes, it is customary to focus on domestic, internal, or national forces, as opposed to external forces or factors that can be left to other types of specialists.

Whether figure 1.1 is to some extent a function of habit or convenience is not important. What is significant is that many of the one-way relationships expressed in figures 1.1 and 1.2 are likely to be reciprocal. Extraction, protection, and state-making activities have all affected war making. Indeed, if one fully accepts the idea that war made the state and the state made war, drawing the directions of the causal arrows becomes highly problematic.

Consider the following assertions. War making clearly made increased extractive efforts necessary. Yet when these extractive efforts were successful, war making could be executed on a more intensive and extensive basis. War making exposed various groups of people to more dangers and threats. Crops and farmlands could be destroyed by invading forces. Towns risked being sacked. Merchants could expect to be attacked away from their home markets. These dangers and threats, particularly acute during times of war, made some form of protection more attractive.

Whether gaining some form of protection meant that the clients of the state were actually safer than they might have been in a protection-free environment is debatable and, no doubt, varied from place to place. Yet the fact that states acquired clients to protect also gave those states more interests to pursue, more disputes to resolve, and, consequently, more wars to fight. As for Tilly's internal rival suppression version of state making, it is often difficult to discern the boundaries between the suppression of internal revolts or sources of threat and external warfare with foreign allies of the rebels or internal sources of threat. One form of activity often led to the other as dissidents sought protection where they could find it. War makers, too, sought opportunities for further weakening their rivals at times of domestic vulnerability.

The notion that the relationships between war making, extraction, protection, and state making need to be viewed as reciprocal is not difficult to defend. The idea that war making should not be viewed as an external and exogenous deus ex machina may seem more dubious. What we have in mind, in part, is the need to evade the old internal-external trap in which analysts feel comfortable relegating activities that fall into one category to a residual backdrop in favor of the activities on which they prefer to focus. Some divisions of labor are only natural. Yet there are definitely times when they interfere with analysis and explanation. Students of state making may acknowledge the stimulative effects of external warfare, but they usually stop short of extending their theoretical inquiry to the purposes of the warfare. It suffices that warfare, as either a generic category or a specific event, contributes something to the internal behavior of state entrepreneurs and managers.

Much the same observation applies to students of warfare. Domestic repercussions of external combat may be duly noted. Unless they represent an extension of the fighting—as in one of the forementioned cases of foreign assistance to an internal revolt or persecuted minority—domestic reverberations are not likely to compel much attention. The operating principle in this analytical division of labor is to leave the homefront implications to analysts who specialize in domestic processes.

The problem with these divisions of labor is that although foreign-domestic behavior may not always resemble a seamless whole, few analysts will object to the contention that this type of conceptual pigeon-holing is inherently artificial. If this statement can be accepted as not all that controversial, the real question is whether the artifice is constructive. There is no need to condemn the genuine advantages of specialization, nor to weigh the advantages and liabilities of the internal-external dichotomy once and for all. There are reasons, however, for questioning the value of maintaining the internal-external distinction when pursuing questions related to the state-making consequences of war. A prime example of the liabilities involved is the tendency to treat all wars as more or less equal representatives of a single class of behavior.

### Global Wars

It has become customary in some international relations circles to define interstate wars in terms of violence between two or more similar national entities that surpasses some minimal level.[4] We have no quarrel with this sort of operational definition. Some minimal thresholds must be established to inventory or at least sample the universe of violent events in world politics. How else are we to separate the sabre-rattling exchange of verbal threats, the brief border skirmishes, and the full-scale, legally anointed, and bloody confrontations of nations? If $x$ number of battle deaths helps to distinguish the level of violence, so much the better. Only when we move away from the lower-level question of establishing minimal, if arbitrary, conventions for what an interstate war is do some of the more common operational indicators begin to impede analysis.

Battle deaths provide a good example. They are certainly not the only indicators of how warlike one war is compared to others; they have the disadvantage of overlooking civilian casualties. Yet counting battle deaths is a seductive way of indexing warfare. Somehow, the more soldiers who died, the more significant the war must have been. Despite the attractions of this reasoning, it has serious problems, some of which are hinted at in table 1.2. Table 1.2 lists the ten most deadly wars in which great powers have been involved since 1495. Deadliness is indexed by great-power battle deaths alone.

**Table 1.2**
**The Ten Most Deadly Great Power Wars Since 1495**

| Rank | War | Battle deaths |
|---|---|---|
| 1 | World War II | 12,948,300 |
| 2 | World War I | 7,734,300 |
| 3 | Napoleonic Wars | 1,869,000 |
| 4 | War of Spanish Succession | 1,251,000 |
| 5 | Thirty Years War—Swedish-French Phase (1635–48) | 1,151,000 |
| 6 | Seven Years War (1755–63) | 992,000 |
| 7 | Korean War (1950–53) | 954,960 |
| 8 | War of the League of Augsburg (1688–97) | 680,000 |
| 9 | French Revolutionary Wars (1792–1802) | 663,000 |
| 10 | Ottoman War (1682–99) | 384,000 |

*Source:* based on data presented in Levy (1983).

Scanning the rank-ordered list, several wars, such as World War II or the Napoleonic Wars, appear to be likely candidates for a most significant war list. Here is the problem. All wars have significance for somebody (especially as long as there are casualties), but not all wars have the same level of significance for everyone. The Korean War (number seven) had great significance for the populations of North and South Korea (and their state-building efforts as well), but the impact of what was termed a *police action* by some of its participants was not as great outside the Korean peninsula.

The Seven Years War was important for determining territorial possession in India and Canada in the mid-eighteenth century, yet this particular issue was not fully resolved until 1815. Stopping the northern expansion of the Ottoman Empire proved immensely important to state building in central and western Europe, but it is doubtful whether much Ottoman expansionary potential survived by the end of the seventeenth century (war number ten). One might also question, at the risk of stirring up a controversy, how widespread and significant the Thirty Years War (war number five) really was outside its principal central European battlegrounds.

Finally, although 48 wars involving great powers took place between 1494 and 1635 (the earliest year in table 1.2), none managed to kill enough soldiers to make the list. Does this mean that wars were somehow less significant before the Thirty Years War than after? Should we therefore expect less war impact in the sixteenth century than in later years? Or is it simply difficult to establish a single battle-death criterion that works equally well for all five centuries?

Similar observations could be made about war lists generated with different criteria (e.g., duration or number of participants). The point remains that the significance of a war is in the eyes of the beholder. In social science terms, this aphorism translates into a theoretical question. Do we have theoretical reason for believing some wars are more significant than others for historical state formation activities? If so, it would then be appropriate to consider operational indicators for the variables isolated by theory as having importance. This practice is the opposite of what sometimes occurs, that is, allowing the operational indicator(s) to establish the nature of the question without due or explicit regard to theory.

We now explore the interaction between the wars and the state formation of the world system's principal powers over roughly the past 500 years. We might assume, as is the norm in realist international relations theory, that all wars, or at least all those involving great powers on both sides, are more or less equal in theoretical importance. This assumption stems from the belief that all wars represent the same phenomenon—the violent clashes of national interest in the anarchic jungle of interstate politics. Yet because some of these major powers were at war for more years than they were at peace, realist theoretical insight is not very helpful in isolating some wars as more important than others. Constants or near constants usually have little or no explanatory power.

The long cycle of world leadership theory (Modelski 1978; 1987b) offers an alternative to the equality of warfare in realist thought. Five wars, identified in table 1.3, are singled out as particularly prominent in the long-cycle rhythm of power concentration and deconcentration. These five wars represent periods of global structural crisis. In the several generation-long periods leading to the outbreak of global war, one state, exploiting its leads in naval power and

**Table 1.3**
**Global Wars**

| Global Wars | Duration |
| --- | --- |
| Italian/Indian Ocean Wars | 1494–1517 |
| Spanish and Dutch Wars | 1580–1608 |
| Wars of Louis XIV | 1688–1713 |
| French Revolutionary/<br>    Napoleonic Wars | 1792–1815 |
| World Wars I and II | 1914–1945 |

economic innovation, emerged from an earlier global war as the system leader. As its relative advantages eroded and competitors began to catch up, the systemic environment became increasingly ripe for a renewed struggle over leadership succession and global policy. Whereas wars between the principal powers were once not that uncommon, global wars—wars that decide who will govern (as opposed to who will rule) the postwar global political system and world economy and wars that usher in the new intervals of capability concentration that make global governance feasible—are not that common. However, they are uncommonly long in duration.

Global wars are deadly and bloody confrontations. Six of the wars listed in table 1.2 are encompassed by the global war schedule. An even more impressive figure is provided by Modelski's (1984) estimate that global wars have been responsible for nearly four-fifths of the last 500 years of great-power battle deaths. Global wars are also clearly long affairs, averaging some 27 years in duration. Given the prize at stake, major power participation is apt to be extensive and unanimous. Who among the most powerful actors can afford to sit on the sidelines while the global system's future policy agenda is decided?

Battle deaths, duration, and participation only hint at the extraordinary significance of these wars. By themselves, or even in combination, they do not define which wars do or do not deserve the global war label. What is definitive about them is their systemic outcome. Leadership succession is not merely contested; it is resolved. Decades of power deconcentration are reversed. At the end of one of these wars, power is again reconcentrated. Since 1494, only the wars listed in table 1.3 have had this reconcentrating impact. This finding has been empirically confirmed by Thompson and Rasler's (1988) analysis of war impacts on a nearly 500-year series of naval power concentration (shown in figure 1.3). The long-cycle theory's designated global wars emerged from the time series examination with positive and statistically significant impacts. Other systemic war candidates, such as the Thirty Years War (1618–48) or the Seven Years War (1755–63) (both found in table 1.2), were associated with negative impacts (indicating continued deconcentration) or impacts that were too weak to merit statistical significance.

Global wars, then, are momentous events for the entire world system. A new system leader emerges with new international responsibilities and overhead burdens. Major rivals have been defeated and, at the very least, suffer serious setbacks to their relative international position. Some states may disappear, and new ones are created. The ground rules for economic transactions across national boundaries are also likely to change.

All of these changes linked to global war generally have domestic impacts as well. Systemic crises become national crises. We also are gradually beginning to appreciate the importance of crisis for explaining domestic policy changes. what might be termed an *oyster shell*, or at least a "punctuated equilibrium,"

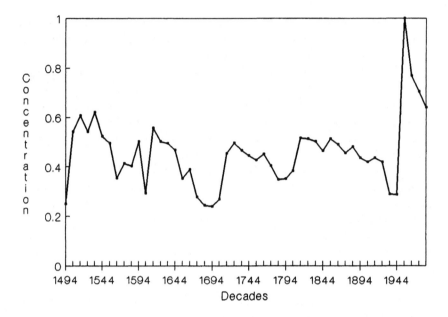

**Figure 1.3.** Concentration in Naval Power, 1494–1983

model (Krasner 1984, 1988; is gaining analytical currency. Gourevitch provides a brief synopsis:

> In the . . . years preceding the crisis, a policy approach and support coalition developed. Then came crisis, challenging both policy and coalition. *Crisis opened the system of relationships, making politics and policy more fluid. Finally a resolution was reached, closing the system for a time, until the next crisis* [emphasis added]. (1986: 21–22)

Gourevitch's emphasis is placed entirely on economic crises, but the imagery applies to global wars as well. National institutions and policies may evolve, drift, or even degenerate gradually over time. Yet incremental evolution and decay are only likely to account for a restricted amount of the variance in policy-institutional change. Real change often depends on the abrupt creation of a crisis setting. Crises open up the oyster shell of policy stasis and equilibrium. Things in general, including structural relationships, coalition alignments, and even a society's tolerance for change, are shaken and become more elastic. Policy decisions that might not otherwise have been made are made, wittingly or unwittingly, in response to the crisis challenge. External crises lower the perceived internal costs of doing or trying to do things differently. In extreme cases, the external threat may be so acute that the domestic implications of meeting the threat simply become irrelevant.

Alternatively, crisis may bring together new political bedfellows, thereby accelerating policy changes that eventually might have come about anyway.

Once the crisis ends, the oyster shell may close, again making abrupt and radical changes most unlikely. It is even possible that all of the changes brought about by the crisis will be reversed or erased as conditions revert, or are forced back, to the precrisis state of affairs. Such an outcome, however, seems unlikely. Some changes will prove difficult if not impossible to undo. Other changes will become accepted as part of the postcrisis norm. All in all, it is most unlikely that the postcrisis equilibrium or state of affairs will return to the precrisis norm. This improbability is especially true of crises on the scale of global war. A minimal expectation, therefore, is a staircaselike pattern of policy change over time. The gradual changes are punctuated by abrupt shocks that literally jolt societies out of their standard operating procedures (SOPs) and structures. Post–global war SOPs and structural relationships are likely to be reestablished, but they will not necessarily be the same ones that prevailed before the war. In a few extreme cases, as Skocpol (1979) argues, the circumstances may even be ripe for revolutionary developments.

What we call an oyster shell model of societal change is definitely an advance on the tendency to compartmentalize and segregate the internal and external etiology of policy change. Compartmentalization may persist to some degree, but some healthy movement toward integration is achieved. The oyster shell approach is also an improvement on the presumption that international events and processes must be functions of domestic decisions and processes, and never the other way around.

Yet, there is a nagging liability with the oyster shell approach. If one's attention is focused primarily on domestic changes, external crises come and go. It is then incumbent on the analyst to assess the damage that has been wrought. If only by default, the adoption of this type of model runs the old risk of continuing to treat the external crisis as a deus ex machina that is somehow alien to the domestic processes, aside from occasional interventions.

What is missing is an explicit appreciation of the roles played by state decision makers not only in reacting to the external crises, but also in bringing them about in the first place. This two-way street is a particularly important facet of the relationships linking global war and the state formation of the system's elite powers. Amending Tilly slightly, our thesis is that global wars made the states of certain powers and these states made global war.

As a consequence, the image of an external shock's opening the national oyster's shell temporarily can be retained only if one does not make too much of the shell's normal impermeability and passivity in receiving external shocks. In global wars, state makers are involved in creating the blows that loosen their state's shells and, less metaphorically, the national resistance to change. To model these reciprocal influences, it is necessary not only to draw double-headed arrows where appropriate, but also to integrate external variables with internal ones. To the extent that states are organizational residues of global wars, the factors that bring about global wars also have important causal consequences for state formation. Yet before we complicate Tilly's model (figure 1.1) with more factors involved in causing one special type of war, we must first elaborate our fourth criticism of the Tilly model. Our objection also has implications for how one maps the relationships between the factors propelling state formation.

### Subordinating Protection to Coalition Making and Generalizing the Model across Time

One principal purpose of Tilly's four activity model (war making, extraction, state making, and protection) is to suggest that Lane was too preoccupied with only one of several state activities. We take this observation one step further and suggest that protection is an activity that is subordinated to an even more central state activity—coalition making. Alliances are made in domestic politics for the same reasons that they are made in world politics: (1) group capabilities can be augmented, and (2) greater control over the behavior of another group can be attempted. State managers seek alliances with various sectors of the state's population to advance the interests of the state managers and the organizational interests of the state. Various sectors of the state's population seek alliances with the state to advance their own group interests. Similarly, members of one state's population may ally with members of another state's population to seek mutual advantages. Who gains protection and how much state protection is provided are functions of the coalitions and accommodations made by and with state managers, whether the managers are kings, bureaucrats, or elected representatives. Protection decisions and, conversely, decisions to repress are thus filtered through coalitional screens. When coalitions realign, expand, or contract, we can expect some alterations in the nature of the protection or repression provided by the state. Different concessions may be offered; various accommodations may be reached.

The second aspect of this criticism is the need to generalize further the meaning of Tilly's conceptualization of state activities. Eliminating or neutralizing external rivals (war making), internal rivals (state making), and the enemies of clients (protection) has a nice symmetry, but such terminology does not keep pace with the changes in activity experienced by the state over time. The basic nature of war making may not have changed very much. State making, however, has gone beyond what initially was minimally necessary to centralize power in the state organization. This statement, of course, assumes that the French state, for instance, was not "made" in the sixteenth or any other century. Rather, the French state continues to be shaped today, continuing a process set in motion by late tenth-century Capetian kings. We prefer to equate state making with state formation or state shaping, processes that presumably continue as long as the state continues to operate as a state.

Enfranchising some segment of a state's population, therefore, is just as much an exercise in state making as is seizing adjacent territory or subordinating robber barons to some semblance of centralized rule. All three may alter the state's structural configuration. All three may make the state something different from what it was before the change in policy. Similarly, as the state's scope of activity expands and as its coalition makeup broadens, new forms of protection follow. State protection against crime, poverty, famine, or disease can be viewed as eliminating or neutralizing the enemies of clients in a very broad sense. Yet the translation is a bit strained. A more generic approach is to equate state protection with applying state resources to improve or preserve the welfare of the state's clients.

The concept of resistance is also apt to be useful. As Tilly observes in what is very much a reciprocal spirit:

> Popular resistance to war making and state making made a difference. When ordinary people resisted vigorously, authorities made concessions; guarantees of rights, representative institutions, courts of appeal. Those concessions, in their turn, constrained the later paths of war making and state making. To be sure, alliances with fragments of the ruling class greatly increased the effects of popular action. (1985: 183)

We envision resistance interacting with state making, extraction, and coalition making. War making-induced extraction efforts have a long history of generating resistance. So too do other forms of expansionary activities (often viewed as encroachments) on the part of the state. The ability of resistance to halt or modify the course of state making depends on a variety of factors, including the numbers of people resisting, who they are, what resources they can claim, and how badly the state makers need their cooperation. Ideally, it should be possible to contrast the interactions of state makers and late sixteenth-century French Protestants, eighteenth-century Scottish Jacobites, or twentieth-century U.S. organized labor in times of war and peace. The need to mobilize resources for war making may lead to increased resistance, but it may also facilitate accommodation and structural change on the part of beleaguered state managers.

### Global Powers and Their Geopolitical-Economic Context

Finally, our second and third criticisms, which argue for avoiding the casting of war making as an exogenous and homogenous set of influences, carry a related implication. Specific wars do not take place in a geopolitical-economic vacuum. This observation applies to a specific type of war, as in the case of global wars, as much as it fits individual wars occurring in a delineated quadrant of space and time. It follows, therefore, that when we can understand the context within which types of wars take place, our ability to identify, monitor, and asses the state-making consequences of these wars will be enhanced.

Put another way, understanding what global wars are about gives us some clear state-making clues to follow. One of the most salient clues has to do with the states on which we should focus. Global wars should exert the most important influences on the principal war participants that are identified in table 1.4. Other states are likely to be affected, but not necessarily to the same extent. Other states may also be just as strongly influenced by war-making activities, but war making of a different, nonglobal kind. We need to proceed cautiously in both our theorizing and our empirical testing, always keeping in mind that we need to specify which types of wars are most likely to affect which types of state actors.

**Table 1.4**
*Global Wars and Their Participants*

| Global War | Global Power Participants |
| --- | --- |
| Italian and Indian Ocean Wars 1494–1516 | Portugal, Spain, France, England |
| Dutch and Spanish Wars 1580–1608 | Spain, Netherlands, England, France |
| Wars of Louis XIV 1688–1713 | Britain, Netherlands, France, Spain |
| French Revolutionary/Napoleonic Wars 1792–1815 | Britain, France, Russia, Netherlands, Spain |
| World Wars I and II 1914–45 | Britain, United States, France, Russia/Soviet Union, Germany, Japan |

*Source:* based on Modelski and Thompson (1988: 16).

Table 1.4 really provides only a loose identification of the cast of global powers. Table 1.5 lists their identities and their years as global powers more specifically. For years, scholars have argued about which states have met selected criteria and when to satisfy the attributes of an international elite status, variously labelled great powers, major powers, and, more recently, super powers. Our list of global powers does not seek to resolve these disputes.[5]

In some cases, there is considerable overlap between the global power identifications and the partial consensuses that have emerged about the other elite groups. Who would quarrel with selecting France and Spain in the sixteenth century, Britain in the eighteenth and nineteenth centuries, or the United States and the Soviet Union in the second half of the twentieth century? In some other cases, the overlap is minimal. Portugal and the Netherlands

*Table 1.5*
*Global Powers*

| Global Powers | Years as Global Powers |
|---|---|
| Portugal | 1494–1580 |
| Spain | 1494–1808 |
| England/Britain | 1494–1945 |
| France | 1494–1945 |
| United Provinces of the Netherlands | 1579–1810 |
| Russia/Soviet Union | 1714– |
| United States | 1816– |
| Germany | 1871–1945 |
| Japan | 1875–1945 |

*Source:* based on Modelski and Thompson (1988: 98).

frequently are discriminated against as unconvincing land powers. Alternatively, Japan and the United States are included somewhat earlier in table 1.5 than is the norm. Several possible candidates are missing altogether: Sweden, Austria-Hungary, Prussia, the Ottoman Empire, Italy.

The inclusions and exclusions are neither arbitrary nor the product of random processes. They reflect a theoretical interest in the global, transoceanic arena that is not coterminous with the more common Eurocentric fixation. The information in table 1.5 also reflects some very specific rules for attaining and losing global power status. States must demonstrate minimal global reach capabilities in the form of battleships, naval expenditures, and genuine oceanic naval activity (as opposed to operating only on a more restricted, regional sea basis).[6] Thus, the emphasis works against the states that did not make, or that were slow in making, the transition to sail-powered navies in and after the sixteenth century. States with navies composed primarily of galley fleets, such as the Ottoman Empire in the sixteenth century, are unlikely to qualify. So too are largely landlocked central European states.

A second set of rules is used for determining how long the global power status is held. Once a state meets the minimal capability-activity criteria, the initiation of its status is pushed back to the end of the preceding global war. Global power status is lost during a global war even if, as sometimes occurred, a state no longer met the minimal capability criteria shortly before the actual outbreak of war. In a few cases, of course, these rules must be qualified by historical circumstances. If a state did not exist (the Netherlands in the early sixteenth and Germany in the early nineteenth centuries), or if it had no global reach capabilities (Japan existed throughout the nineteenth century but did not begin to build a competitive navy before the late 1860s), there is no point in conferring global power status immediately after the preceding global war.

These rules do not make much difference in the chapters that follow. Although we have adopted table 1.5 as a guide, we will not stop suddenly in the middle of analyzing a given global power because we have reached a time after which the state no longer qualifies. Nor will we begin our analyses of, say, France or Spain only in 1494. It is important for the reader to appreciate that we have theoretical reasons for focusing on a specific set of state actors and that our identification of this set follows explicit conventions that are related closely to our theoretical premises. In brief, this is why we largely ignore some favorite examples of major power state making (e.g., Prussia) and favor instead some states that are less fashionable in the study of state-making circles (e.g., Portugal).

A second clue stemming from an appreciation for what global wars are about pertains to what the principal war participants are fighting over and/or which states are most likely to go to war with one another. Certain types of states repetitively clash with reasonably regular outcomes in the sense that one type of state tends to win whereas another type tends to lose. We can anticipate that these differences will be manifested as differences in state-making structures, processes, and outcomes as well.

A great deal more can be said about, and still needs to be done, on the causes of global war (see Modelski 1987a; Modelski and Thompson 1988; Thompson 1988). For our immediate purposes, however, the origins of systemic war can be simplified along the following lines. Global wars represent struggles over whose version of order will prevail in the global political system and world economy. In order to govern, however, a global war must first be won. Global wars are won by coalitions led by the state with the most advanced relative position in global reach capability and economic innovation.

A lead in global reach capabilities historically has meant that the system leader must also be the system's lead maritime power. The most violent opposition to the maritime power's global leadership, in contrast, tends to come from states that are either more regionally oriented than the system leader or whose orientations wobble between regional and global orientations. Competitive fleets may be built but usually in a too little, too late fashion. Global wars break out when a continental challenger's actions or buildup are perceived as threatening in the near future to the system leader's position and the system's operating procedures.

On the other hand, an important motor in the processes leading to global war is the tendency for the system leader's initial, relative economic-technological edge to erode and diffuse. The perpetual jockeying for position among several major contenders and the tendency for some states to be able to catch up with the leader characterize the movement away from a temporary, post–global war concentration of power. As power diffuses, challengers are encouraged all the more not only to continue improving their own relative position, but also to aspire ultimately to systemic leadership.

Yet global wars have not been fought for ever. A global political system worth fighting over first had to emerge. This transoceanic arena only began to take shape around 1500 after the Europeans learned how to sail around Africa to reach the Indian Ocean and Asia. In 1500, national state organizations were still fairly embryonic. Some state organizations, to be sure, were more advanced than others. Portugal and England, for example, were among the first sites of modern state building in Europe. Not coincidentally, they were also among the first states to build and maintain state-owned navies.

The general point is not that global war is the exclusive source of state making, even if we restrict our analysis to the small group of states that have qualified as global powers over the years. It clearly is not. For instance, rulers fought to improve their positions when they could and to protect their positions when necessary long before the Portuguese temporarily monopolized the European spice trade. Local and regional positioning, therefore, is part of the state formation process, especially in the early phases. The English fought to subordinate the Welsh, Scots, and Irish. The rulers of Castile and Aragon felt it necessary to evict the Moors. The French had to expel the English from Normandy. Local and regional war making definitely played a role in this phase of building both states and nations. As we argue in chapters 2 and 3, some elements of this early phase had definite ramifications for later phases as well.

Nevertheless, the emerging development of a global political system and an expanding world economy gradually raised the stakes that were being contested. The costs of competition escalated as well, and a significant component in the ante was the need to develop an efficient state organization to protect and improve the relative positions already gained. The scope and scale of war making—and especially global war making—changed, but it continued to be closely and reciprocally intertwined with state making and resource extraction activities.

In this nexus, geopolitical distinctions had and, we think, continue to have an important role to play. Mann (1986) offers an interesting interpretation of some of these connections, including linkages to coalition making. As military costs began to rise in the sixteenth century, he argues, states were limited to two basic approaches to remaining competitive. They could either learn to mobilize fiscal resources, assuming a sufficiently sizable and stable wealth base, or mobilize manpower, assuming a sufficiently sizable and malleable population base. Because sea powers were leaders in developing wealth in part through trade, which is easier to tax than landed estates, fiscal mobilization was the most likely option for these states to pursue. Even so, taxing trade did not generate enough revenues. Both land and sea powers were forced to assess and levy taxes on property as well. Mann points out, however, that constitutional sea powers and absolutist land powers taxed in fundamentally different ways.

England and Holland relied on taxation of both landed and trading rich with their consent. Absolutist regimes relied on taxation of the landed poor and trading rich, with the consent and repressive help of the landed rich. . . .

In most absolutist regimes, unlike the constitutional ones, the landed nobility were generally exempt from taxation, whereas the peasants, merchants, and urban bourgeoisie were not. Exempting powerful groups from taxation meant that representative assemblies could be avoided—because the main issue of representative government, taxation, did not arise. (Mann 1986: 479)

Mann's argument has an undeniable tautological flavor. Absolutist regimes were able to avoid representative institutions (thereby remaining absolutist) whereas constitutional regimes could not. Nevertheless, the linkages between military organizational-geopolitical orientations, economic structure, tax policies, early types of state-elite coalitions, and governmental institutions seem worth pursuing.

### A More Complicated Model of Global Power State Formation

Figure 1.4 represents a more complicated version of Tilly's abbreviated, four activity model. More elements could be added to the model, but we too are attempting to work with a reasonably manageable map of the global power, state formation process. More arrows are certainly conceivable, but their addition would not necessarily ease communication of precisely how and to what extent these multiple processes are intertwined.

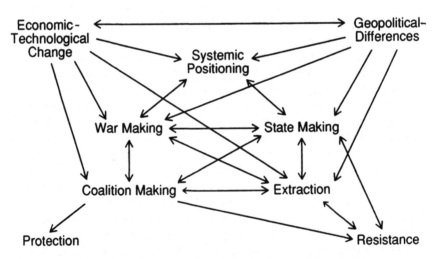

**Figure 1.4.** A More Complicated Version of War Making and State Making

Fundamentally, we have adopted Tilly's four core components (war and state making, extraction, and protection), altered their meanings to some extent, and repositioned two of the four within the state formation map. We have added coalition making, as discussed earlier. We have also added resistance, a concept familiar to Tilly and his approach to the development of the state, as an important ingredient. To these six activities we have added three more model elements (systemic positioning, economic-technological change, and geopolitical-economic differences) to help capture the links between systemic war making and national state making.[7]

A set of variables connected by directed arrows indicates a causal mapping of the principal relationships of interest. Once such a model is specified, the next step usually involves operationalizing and measuring each variable to investigate how well the model maps the relationships. Figure 1.4 is not at this stage. It does not connect variables per se. It connects conceptualizations. Extraction, for instance, encompasses a number of activities. Revenue generation and tax collection are obvious activities that are encompassed. So too are military conscription and public borrowing. If we were to measure extraction by annual revenues, only one of several facets of the extraction concept would be tapped.

War making offers another illustration. One presumption could be that the other activities are somehow transformed by participating in war. We might expect to detect these war interventions by contrasting prewar periods with postwar periods. An interval of warfare becomes the measurement of war making. Yet there are all kinds of war. Some we call interstate wars; others global wars. Some do little damage; others are quite devastating. The point is that intervals of generic warfare do not capture all of these dimensions equally well. If we stretched war making to include preparing for war, moreover, the complexities of capturing the full meaning of this broad conceptualization expand even further.

So, we may conclude safely that relatively broad and vague conceptualizations permit multiple analytical and measurement strategies. Yet the ambiguities invoked by figure 1.4 do not concern us that much. The analysis of war impacts on state-making activities is still in too primitive a mode to worry about very precise specifications. At this stage of inquiry, it suffices that we have an organizing framework that provides some major categorical boxes and suggests which boxes are connected. To move toward greater specification, it is not necessary to explore everything that conceivably fits within the assembled categories. Nor must we pursue every arrow. Even if these pursuits were deemed essential, restrictions on space and time would ensure that a more selective research strategy be devised.

We propose to follow just such a selective research strategy in this analysis. Working our way from the top of figure 1.4 to the bottom, chapters

2 and 3 focus on geopolitics, political economy, and systemic positioning. These two chapters establish the context for the war making of the global powers. In the process, we also consider the utility of a much different approach to studying state making—Stein Rokkan's elaborate state-building framework. Chapters 4, 5, and 6 concentrate on war's impact on extraction activities. Chapter 4 looks at the development of public debt and creative financing procedures. Chapter 5 examines state-spending patterns and revenue collection efforts. Chapter 6 considers the economic wealth base on which borrowing, spending, and taxing are predicated. Moving from extraction to coalition building and resistance and accommodation, chapter 7 investigates the interaction between war and immediate postwar environments, labor union demands, and governmental responses. Summarizing what is learned in this sampling approach to war and state making phenomena is the task in chapter 8.

Accompanying the movement down the figure are gradual shifts in foci on time and global powers. Chapters 2 and 3 emphasize the historical activities of Spain and France, in contrast to the maritime states of Portugal, the United Provinces of the Netherlands, and England. The temporal focus of these two chapters ranges from the eleventh and twelfth centuries to approximately the seventeenth century. Chapter 4 continues this comparative emphasis with the same states, although the primary time frame shifts somewhat forward to the period between the sixteenth and eighteenth centuries. Chapter 5 reviews some of the sparse information that we have on English, French, and Spanish ancien regime spending and revenues. However, the primary focus remains on the nineteenth- and twentieth-century behaviors of Britain, the United States, France, Japan, and Germany. Much the same selection bias appears in chapter 6. Chapter 7, on the other hand, looks only at one global power, the United States, with a temporal focus restricted to the period between 1890 and 1970.

Clearly, this study is not intended to be the last word on the subjects raised. A number of topics remain completely untouched. The historical experiences of some states are slighted, whereas others attract the bulk of the attention. Nor are we equally fair to all of the centuries of activity over which we freely roam. But we are not particularly interested in comprehensive country studies or painstaking descriptive histories. We are concerned with generalizing about the impact of war on the state-making activities of the global powers. We feel this concern ultimately justifies our sampling strategy, even if it does not always excuse the underdevelopment of certain topics.

# 2
# The Geopolitical-Economic Context: Rokkan and the Spanish Case

Chapter 1 argued that war making and global power state making have been and continue to be closely intertwined. Yet all global powers have not participated in the same wars, the same number of wars, or even the same type of wars. Nor are the states that they have created in the process identical in structure or function. Clearly, there is variation in the war-making–state-making connection. For this reason we need to attend to other variables that intervene between war making and state making. Institutions (Strayer 1970; North and Thomas 1973), class cleavages and coalitions (Moore 1966; Anderson 1974), military technology (White 1962; Bean 1973; Finer 1975; McNeill 1982), capitalism (Wallerstein 1974, 1980), public choice (Rogowski 1986; Levi 1988), and agrarian practices (Hechter and Brustein 1980) offer alternative explanatory paths.

Yet what needs explaining? To account for variations in the production of West European grain, for example, crop rotation practices would be of interest. If we are trying to trace why some monarchies became absolutist whereas others evolved into more constitutional inclinations, we presumably would focus on the historical ups and downs in crown-nobility relative power. Alternatively, if we wanted to explain why the global powers emerged first in western Europe and not elsewhere, we would compare developments in China and the Moslem world with those in Europe. Although these questions are certainly interesting, they are not our principal concern in this chapter.

More directly pertinent are the identities of the global powers that consistently opposed one another in the cyclical struggles over the system's governance. Spain and Portugal initially vied with each other and with France, England, and the Netherlands. In the first half of the sixteenth century, Portugal led at sea while Spain triumphed on land. From the end of the sixteenth and into the next century, Spain was defeated by English and Dutch sea power. Whereas the English, Dutch, and French initially fought amongst themselves in the early second half of the seventeenth century, the primary contest at the end of the century pitted the English and Dutch sea powers against the leading land power of France.

Britain and France continued this global power cleavage into the early nineteenth century. Germany replaced France as the principal continental opponent of the leading sea power, Britain, toward the end of the nineteenth century. The contest was not fully resolved, of course, until 1945. By this time, the sea power–land power cleavage matched the United States against the Soviet Union.

Sea powers have fought continental powers in iterative fashion over the past 500 years (Modelski 1987b; Modelski and Thompson 1988; Thompson 1988) because their interests have diverged on how best to organize and manage the global political system and world economy. The rather primitive resolution of whose systemic rules and policies will prevail is one way to capture the essence of global wars. Yet this essence of global wars is not exactly what we wish to explore in this chapter either. Rather, we want to step back a bit from global wars and the conflicts between oceanic and continentally oriented global powers and ask why some states and their state makers developed perspectives and preferences that favored oceanic or continental objectives. In addition, we need to ask whether or not and to what extent the development of these preferences influenced the shape and form of the principal competitors.

To account for the sources of fundamental geopolitical stances, one must explore the convergence of geography, politics, and economics or, as we call it, the geopolitical-economic context of war and state making. Perhaps the best place to begin this exploration is with a consideration of Stein Rokkan's impressive framework for tracing European state building from the end of the Roman Empire to the present. Although Rokkan said little about war making, he made some very insightful observations about the influence of geopolitical-economic variables. In particular, he developed a unique explanation of why European states first emerged on the Atlantic side of the continent. This argument is crucial for appreciating why France, Spain, Portugal, the Netherlands, and England developed as the first global power states.

What is unclear, however, is why it is so easy to make sharp distinctions between two separate classes of western European global powers. England, the Netherlands, and Portugal developed maritime orientations. France and

Spain's primary focus remained landlocked. As a consequence, two different state-making patterns emerged. Rokkan also slighted the role of warfare in historical state making. So, we use a brief review of Rokkan's framework, and some of the problems we encountered in applying it to our questions, as a valuable introduction to the contextual dimension of state making. The limitations of the framework then serve as a springboard for our examination of the geopolitical-economic context of global power state making.

## Rokkan's State-Building Framework

Summarizing Stein Rokkan's arguments on European state building is a formidable and awkward task.[1] The Rokkan approach to model construction was openly eclectic, even imperialistic, and never completed. He co-opted concepts and theories when appropriate, and in each publication the basic model is presented in a slightly different light. As a consequence, Rokkan's arguments took on a Parsonian flavor in one outing only to appear more Wallersteinian in the next exposure. Moreover, Rokkan's explanatory armory of variables continued to expand as did the objects of explanation encompassing the millennium or so since the breakup of the Holy Roman Empire. Ethnic-linguistic mobilization, political centralization, the development of representative institutions, and the emergence of fascism were of equal interest, even if they represented activities identified with different centuries since the early Middle Ages.

Just where one should plunge into the vortex of Rokkan's synthetic model(s) is never obvious. Still, the choice should depend in part on what one wishes to do with Rokkan's observations. For our immediate purposes, it suffices merely to tap into Rokkan's core theoretical position on sixteenth- to nineteenth-century developments in Europe. Figure 2.1 offers what Rokkan referred to as a conceptual map of Europe. By juxtaposing three types of precondition variables (economic, territorial, and cultural), each one associated with different stages or periods, Rokkan situated western European political units according to their basic configuration. His model is extended by adding intervening processes that interact with the preconditions to produce variations in political responses. Table 2.1 presents a quick summary of this multiple-stage modeling effort.

Table 2.1 gives some impression of the overall thrust of Rokkan's explanations. It also reveals Rokkan's strong interest in contemporary mass politics, which, in many respects, is the principal rationale/explicanda for the ambitious explanatory framework. Because we do not share this theoretical interest with the same intensity, our interests focus on the precondition elements, especially those noted in figure 2.1.

### The State-Economy Dimension: West-East Axis

| Territorial Centers | weak | strong | | weak | | strong | stro |
|---|---|---|---|---|---|---|---|
| City Networks | weak | strong | | strong | | weak | wei |
| | Seaward Peripheries | Seaward Empire Nations | City-State Europe | | | Landward Empire Nations | Landw Buff |
| Conditions of consolidation | Distant from City Belt | Close to City Belt | Integrated into Larger System | Consociational Formation | Fragmented until 19th Century | Close to City Belt | Distant from City Belt |
| Protestant State Church | Iceland ← Norway *Denmark* Scotland Wales *England* | | | | Hanse Germany | *Sweden* *Prussia* | Finland |
| Mixed Territories | | | *Netherlands* *Switzerland* | | Rhineland | Bohemia | Bal Territ |
| National Catholic Church | Ireland Brittany | *France* | "Lotharingia" Burgundy Arelatum | | | *Bavaria* | Poland → |
| Counter Reformation | | *Spain* *Portugal* | Belgium → Catalonia | | Italy | *Austria* | Hungary→ |

re 2.1. A Conceptual Map of Sixteenth- to Eighteenth-Century Western Europe

Arrows indicate change in geopolitical position. Territories in italics were sovereign powers in the 1648–1789 period.
: based on Rokkan (1981: 78).

Arguably, the most significant variable in figure 2.1 is geopolitical position. European states are located either within, close to, or distant from an urban trade route connecting Italy and the Mediterranean with the North Sea and Baltic regions. Rokkan viewed this corridor as the heartland of the old Western Empire. Its two chief characteristics were the density of established urban centers and the strength of the Roman Catholic Church, which implies a certain density of ecclesiastical activity as well. These twin sources of density led to a uniform state-building outcome within the Rhine-Danube city belt:

> The very density of established centers within this territory made it difficult to single out any one as superior to all others; there was no geography-given core area for the development of a strong territorial system. . . . By contrast, it proved much easier to develop effective core areas at the edges of the city-studded territories of the old empire; in these regions, centers could be built up under less competition and could achieve command of the resources in peripheral areas too far from the cities in the central trade belt. (Rokkan 1981: 79)

*Table 2.1*
**An Outline of Rokkan's Model of State Formation, Nation Building, and Mass Politics in Europe**

| | Precondition Variables | | |
| --- | --- | --- | --- |
| *Stages* | *Economy* | *Territory* | *Culture* |
| The early Middle Ages | Predominant agrarian structure | Extent of incorporation into German-Roman Empire | Ethnic origins of successful territorial populations |
| The high Middle Ages | Strength/structure of city network | Geopolitical position (vis-a-vis central city belt) | Strength of vernacular literature standard(s) |
| 1500–1700 | Change in geoeconomic position (breakthrough of Atlantic capitalism) | Extent of periphery control (degree of centralization) | Extent of nationalization of territorial culture (success/failure of Reformation) |
| 1648–1789 | | Survival of representative institutions v. absolutist rule | |

| | Intervening Process Variables | | |
| --- | --- | --- | --- |
| Intensified nation building | Character of rural-urban resource combinations | Pressures for centralization/ unification v. movements of liberation/secession | Extent of periphery-center strain |
| Urbanization, industrialization, secularization | Rapidity, localization of industrial growth | Pressures for imperial expansion v. movements for detente, peace | Character of church-state relations |

| | Variations in Political Response Structures | | |
| --- | --- | --- | --- |
| Structuring of alternatives | Sequencing of steps toward universalization of political rights | Frequency/intensity of crises of transition | Sequencing of steps in formation of system of party alternatives |
| Consequent mass alignments | Class/culture conditioning of levels/types of participation | Class/culture conditioning of attitudes to system | Class/culture conditioning of party choices |

*Source:* based on Rokkan (1981: 74–75).

The geopolitics of the European city belt facilitated three waves of state formation. The first wave took place on the northern and western edges of the middle corridor: in France, England, parts of Scandinavia, and the Iberian peninsula. For Rokkan, the operative principle of this first state-building wave was that centralizing forces were able to gain control over peripheral resources. These resources were not only beyond the reach of the central city belts, but also sufficiently extensive in size and resources for the purposes of competitive state making.

As noted in figure 2.1, the western states combined strong political centers with strong commercial cities and networks. These western, seaward states were best situated to take advantage of the shift to what Rokkan termed the new Atlantic–Indian Ocean geoeconomy and the migration of the core of capitalism to northwest Europe. This process was assisted further by the failure of the Habsburgs to create a European empire that would have stretched across the three geopolitical zones.

Bankrupted and stalemated by the French opposition in the mid-sixteenth century (1559), the Habsburg base was terminally divided between the Spanish and Austrian wings by the middle of the next century (1648). Rokkan viewed this territorial split as critical to the future of Europe. Neither Habsburg wing could hope to dominate Europe. To make matters worse, the Habsburg territories were gradually being relegated to a semiperipheral economic status as the entire region underwent a phase of geoeconomic restructuring between 1500 and 1789.

Nevertheless, a second wave of state building did occur on the less favored eastern edge of the central trade corridor: Habsburg Austria, Sweden, and eventually Prussia. These center-building efforts had access to the requisite peripheries, but their city networks, the principal economic variable in figure 2.1, were much weaker than those typically found in the west.

The city belt in the middle of these eastern and western developments was hardly static. The French frontier moved east toward the corridor, absorbing much of Burgundy in the process. External pressures encouraged a city confederation in Switzerland. Habsburg territorial control oscillated in a variety of directions, but not always successfully. A prime example was the failure to retain control over the northern Netherlands and the creation of a second city confederation in that portion of the corridor. Indeed, Rokkan stressed that because the United Provinces of the Netherlands had equal access to the Atlantic and North Sea–Rhine–Italy trade routes, the Dutch were able to use this positional advantage to supplant the earlier economic dynamism of the seaward Portuguese. Yet what was an advantage in the late sixteenth and early seventeenth centuries turned out to be a geopolitical handicap in the later seventeenth century. The Dutch found it increasingly difficult to compete with other core states that enjoyed access to more extensive peripheries.

Several revolutions in the late eighteenth and early nineteenth centuries stimulated a third wave of state building. The French Revolution and Napoleon produced a brief spurt of European empire and a consequent increase in nationalism within the hitherto largely stagnant German and Italian portions of the central European corridor. Roughly simultaneously, the industrial revolution bestowed economic hegemony on the British. The subsequent diffusion of industrial advantages encouraged the development of unification incentives, if only to compete better with the dominant British. In particular, Rokkan interpreted German unification as a defensive alliance between nascent German industrializers and the older Prussian territorial power. The mutual goal was to protect themselves against the economic competition of more advanced economies. They also sought to gain or regain genuinely competitive systemic positions by coalescing military and industrial resources.

The three state-building waves were thus interweaved with two waves of geoeconomic restructuring. In the sixteenth century, the first wave promoted the initially peripheral Atlantic and Atlantic-oriented political economies at the expense of most of the central city belt as well as transzonal attempts at European empire. A second wave operated on the slower moving eastern periphery. In the nineteenth century, the new industrial technologies were at first highly concentrated, creating a new tendency toward peripheralization once again at the expense of the old Rhine corridor among other places. This time, however, the peripheralization wave led to relatively successful attempts to fight back. In the process, a third wave of state building emerged.

Rokkan's emphases on geopolitical position and economic peripheralization may not be wholly original. Nevertheless, it remains extraordinarily useful. Three geographical zones are established.[2] State-making activities are predicted to be less probable (before the nineteenth century) in the middle zone than in the two adjacent and, initially, peripheral zones. The western zone, however, enjoyed the historical edge in state making because the breakthrough of Atlantic capitalism and the development of an Atlantic–Indian Ocean world economy favored states adjacent to the Atlantic. A few centuries later, the development of British hegemony brought about another economic restructuring that, intertwined with the stimulus of Napoleonic empire and warfare, encouraged another round of state building, but this time within the middle city belt zone.

Of course, many things are missing from this brief synopsis. Two model components sorely absent are the role of wars and some principle for explaining why some states in the western zone were so much more successful than others—at both war and state making. To be fair, neither element is entirely missing from Rokkan's framework. Fighting in the sixteenth and seventeenth centuries, we are told, split the Habsburg empire and suppressed the early threat of a forced unification of the three zones. The later Napoleonic combat also had specific consequences for the likelihood of state-building activites.

So, warfare is hardly absent. Yet its theoretical role is very much limited and episodic in effect.

There are also clues about distinctions to be made between western states. Two comparisons have already been recounted regarding the Dutch positional edge over the Portuguese and the larger periphery available to the English vis-a-vis the Dutch. Another concept Rokkan uses (1975: 587) is "geopolitical load," that is, a state's geopolitical position has direct consequences for the state's fiscal needs. An old, even hoary, example is England's limited need for an army because of the national defenses provided by its surrounding waters. France, alternatively, had multiple land borders and, consequently, greater defense needs. Rokkan takes this familiar argument one step further by noting that because France was closer to the central city belt than was England, the French were more likely to develop a strong state apparatus so the territory of the nation-state could be distinctively delimited.

> The military-administrative power of any state can best be gauged through the analysis of its success in controlling interaction across its boundaries, in checking movement of men, commodities and ideas. (Rokkan 1975: 589)

Because the distinctiveness of England (or at least Britain) was largely a product of natural forces and its borders were considerably easier to monitor than were those of France, the development of an absolutist government emphasizing its military-administrative powers was less likely.

Obviously, there is more to the development of absolutism than a state's distance from the Rhine and the consequent ease of monitoring borders. Similarly, the rise and fall of the Dutch was not merely a matter of a fortuitous location that somehow became less fortuitous with the passage of time. At the same time, these observations do offer some insights into state-building processes. The geographical locations of the French and the Dutch were definitely significant factors in their political development. The question at this juncture is how much further we can take the geopolitical-economic context of state making. Without stumbling into the murky realm of either geographical determinism or economism, the geopolitical-economic context of state making in Rokkan's western zone can be exploited to explain why certain western zone states did so much better than some of the other states that were located between the European city belt and the Atlantic. The explicit role of warfare, missing from Rokkan's framework, can also be highlighted in the process.[3]

### Reconsidering Some Aspects of Rokkan's Framework
Five global powers emerged in the European territory west of the Rhine corridor: Portugal, Spain, France, the United Provinces of the Netherlands, and England/Britain.[4] They did not emerge as prominent states at the same

time. Some, such as France and England/Britain, emerged early and remained prominent for centuries. In contrast, Portugal's prominence lasted little more than a century, if that. The staying power of the Netherlands was not much greater. Alternatively, both Spain and France were up, then down, and yet both managed to make repeated comebacks with varying success. One factor that needs explaining is why these states emerged to some level of prominence when they did.

Even more important, however, are the different types of prominence attained by the West European powers. Portugal, the Netherlands, and Britain were Europe's preeminent sea powers and the leading centers of economic dynamism in the sixteenth, seventeenth, and eighteenth to nineteenth centuries, respectively. Preindustrial Spain and France were large, relatively rich organizations based on traditional agrarian economic foundations. Militarily, both France and Spain had sea power in fluctuating degrees over time, but their martial fame was associated most with the size and skill level of their armies. Neither France nor Spain spurned extra-European colonial activities. Even so, their preeminence as major European states was directly predicated on their identities and activities as continental powers.

The range of political-economic opportunities in the world changed according to Rokkan's geoeconomic restructuring. Some states adapted better than did others. As one naval historian summarized the shift:

> In the past, territorial extension founded on military force had been the principal issue of European rivalry. With the seventeenth century, competition on the seas gradually superimposed itself on the traditional pattern of continental relationships. As a consequence of the opening of the Atlantic, there developed a duality in national interests. Expansionist policies concerned with sea routes and colonies were bound eventually to conflict with policies of continental conquest. Thus every state with a frontage on the Atlantic had at least to revise its estimates on the sources of national power. In the new era of trans-Atlantic colonization, overseas trade was to become an essential constituent of a country's prosperity and strength, and the wealth from the huge colonial empire over the horizon would be garnered only by those nations that possessed numerous and well-armed ships. Hence, from overseas trade competition arose the struggle for command of communications, a chronic contest that was to exert a constant and compelling influence upon the external policies of Spain, the Netherlands, France and England. (Graham 1950: 19)

We might suggest that the author of this passage was a century late in timing the beginning of the superimposition of maritime competition on traditional continental attitudes toward expansion. We question later whether the maritime competition was equally "constant and compelling" for Spain, the Netherlands, France, and England. Certainly, it is easy to argue that maritime policies were more constant and compelling for the Dutch and the English than for the continentally preoccupied Spanish and French.

Yet it is this same maritime-continental dualism, long used in geopolitical discourse as a near primordial distinction, that demands explanation. Why did one state follow a continental path whereas another chose the maritime route to success? Unfortunately, Rokkan's figure 2.1 is not very helpful on this score. England, France, Spain, and Portugal (along with Norway and Denmark) are all classified as seaward empire nations with strong territorial centers and city networks. Equally disheartening, the utility of the two distinctions that are made is dubious.

England is labeled Protestant and distant from the central city belt. France, Spain, and Portugal are categorized as Catholic and close to the city belt. Yet in what sense was Portugal, or Spain for that matter, closer to the city belt than was England? If Portugal was misplaced by Rokkan, and we treat it as equally distant from the city belt as England, one might be able to make a case for distance from the city belt predicting greater as opposed to lesser seawardness.[5] Yet both Venice and the United Provinces of the Netherlands were part of the central city belt, and this factor certainly did not preclude their development of sea power and maritime orientations. That leaves only the Protestant-Catholic distinction, which hardly appears promising for differentiating continental versus maritime orientations in the fifteenth and sixteenth centuries.

A more promising line of inquiry involves questioning Rokkan's approach to city networks as an unqualified indicator of economic development. All six of the seaward empire nations are identified as having strong city networks. Yet so are the city belt's city-states: the Netherlands, Switzerland, Italy, and Hanse Germany among others. It is reasonable to categorize the city networks of France and Spain with those of England, Portugal, and the Netherlands? To do so would seem to vitiate some of the significance of the central city belt in Rokkan's framework.

Fox's (1971) distinction between commercial and agricultural towns or societies is particularly useful in this regard. Fox argued that all towns engage in the exchange and distribution of goods to some variable extent. However, we should differentiate between towns that are restricted primarily to local trade or barter and towns that specialize in long-distance trade in expensive commodities.

These long-distance trading towns constituted Fox's commercial category. They also represent the type of towns that predominated in the Rhineland corridor or Rokkan's city belt. To either side of the central corridor linking the Mediterranean and Italy with northern Europe and the Baltic, according to Fox, one is more likely to find towns involved primarily in circulating perishable agricultural commodities on highly localized scales. These agricultural towns provided much of the basic economic infrastructure of the feudal monarchies that emerged in western and eastern Europe.

Table 2.2
Fox's Societal Dichotomy

| Conceptual Distinctions | Societal Types | |
|---|---|---|
| | *Agrarian* | *Commercial* |
| Basic nature of economic system | Many small, relatively limited, autonomous agrarian units | Extended system of relations between independent urban units |
| Economic exchange focus | Immediate environs | Long-distance networks |
| Division of labor tendencies | Emphasis on self-sufficiency | Emphasis on specialization |
| Economic orientation of towns | Usually agricultural market centers | Emphasis on shipping and receiving high value/volume goods to and from distant points |
| Principal transportation medium | Land | Water |
| Characteristic relationship with other like units | Independent | Interdependent |
| Emphasis on territorial control | Strong | Limited |
| Predominant decision-making style | Administrative hierarchy | Consultation and negotiation |
| Characteristic political institutions | Bureaucracy | Representative institutions |
| Military specialization | Army | Navy |
| Principal source of strategic vulnerability | Dependence on maritime supply lines | Existence of land frontier with dominant land power |

*Source:* based on the discussion in Fox (1971).

Fox's agrarian-commercial dichotomy gives rise to a number of comparative statements, some of which are summarized in table 2.2, about structures and behaviors associated with preindustrial societies in which one or the other type of town predominates. Agricultural units are apt to encompass large conglomerations of a number of small, largely self-sufficient economic units. To hold these subunits together, a political system evolves that emphasizes military force, an administrative chain of command, and a marked propensity for concern with territorial control and expansion.

Commercial units, in contrast, are integrated into larger networks of like-minded commercial units. Given the orientation toward an interdependent system of urban trading centers, the interest in territorial jurisdiction is minimal. Where the all-important, long-distance trade is participated in by a number of individuals with wealth, the dominant political emphasis is more likely to favor negotiation and consensus, both within the commercial city and between the various cities in the larger network.

The characteristics of the agricultural units predispose them toward continuing conflict with other agricultural units as well as with the commercial units. The commercial units' characteristics, on the other hand, work toward reducing conflict between similar commercial units; they depend on each other too much for maintaining their prosperity knowingly to destroy one another. The wealth of the commercial units, nevertheless, poses a constant temptation for nearby agricultural societies.

Ideal type dichotomies, such as Fox's comparisons, risk exaggerating the types of abstract characteristics that must ultimately be applied to the real world, where economic systems are more likely to mix agrarian and commercial attributes rather than to fit neatly into a pure category. It is also too easy to quarrel with some of the generalizations that are more difficult to match with historical behavior. The bitter conflicts among the Italian city-states and the trade wars between England and the Netherlands come readily to mind as real-world reminders of the limits to portraying commercial societies as relatively peaceful entities.

Yet the real value of Fox's dichotomies is not found in searching for pure examples of agricultural and commercial states in western Europe. On the contrary, Fox's own purpose for developing his framework was to analyze over time what he termed France's *schizophrenic tendencies*—a sort of national personality disorder manifested in the form of competing agricultural and commercial policy orientations. The principal value of this framework then is to examine each state for the presence of these conflicting tendencies and how they are worked out by state makers. A theoretical payoff is realized to the extent that we can differentiate among western European global powers according to whether agricultural or commercial elements predominated at critical junctures and led to demonstrable behavioral differences.

Given these asserted basic dualisms in economic inclinations and geopolitical orientations, we must also ask what the implications are for state making. For example, is it a coincidence that the two most authoritarian states of the initial five were also the predominately agrarian, land-oriented powers (Spain and France)? Is it a coincidence that the Netherlands and Britain are celebrated as more pluralistic trade-oriented exceptions to the more common European political style of monarchical absolutism?

Whatever the answers, we must also ask what the geopolitical implications have been for the subsequent pattern of warfare and state making. The powers with strong land biases certainly fought one another in and out of Europe. Yet even while Spain and France locked regional horns off and on between 1494 and 1659, a more fundamental and enduring conflict axis was emerging that involved the periodic confrontation of the leading land and sea powers.

Portugal managed to consolidate its late fifteenth-century, geopolitical-economic breakthrough into the Indian Ocean while Spain and France were preoccupied by their wars in Italy. Nearly a hundred years later, Spain absorbed Portugal only to face a Dutch-English maritime coalition. Another hundred years later, Louis XIV encountered the resistance of the same coalition—only this time it was an English-Dutch coalition. Another hundred years were to pass before the Anglo-French, maritime-continental duel was essentially resolved by the outcome of the Napoleonic Wars. Although the 1494–1815 era takes care of our expressed interest in the five original West European powers, the continental-maritime feud pattern persisted into the twentieth century, with Germany adopting the continental role monopolized earlier by the Spanish and then the French. As we contend in chapter 1, these conflicts have been critical for understanding the shape and pace of global power state making.

Thus, to flesh out a portion of Rokkan's framework and also to serve our immediate purposes, we must explain why the West European powers emerged to prominence when they did and what geopolitical orientations were adopted or thrust on them. Moreover, how did these differences in geopolitical orientation lead to the development of a persistent global power conflict axis pitting sea powers against land powers? Underlying these interconnected concerns, of course, is our fundamental interest in global power state making. Therefore, this chapter concentrates on the role(s) of geopolitical-economic factors in shaping the history of global power state making.

Yet the role of warfare also has to be considered. Rokkan argued that the central city belt was much too competitive a region for successful state building to have much of an opportunity before the late nineteenth century. By implication and default, the impression is left that the European zone to the west of the city belt was a somewhat less competitive arena. As such, it was therefore a more likely site for expanding state organizations with strong territorial centers (see figure 2.1) to thrive and prosper.

Although Rokkan clearly meant to emphasize the qualitative dimension of competition *density* in the central zone, any implication that the western zone was a quantitatively less competitive environment must be rejected as historically inaccurate. The nature of the competition was simply different. Pre-nineteenth-century state makers tried to build states in the central zone, and most failed.[6] Some of the western zone state makers also failed. The ones that succeeded were required to engage in literally hundreds of years of intermittent, albeit frequent, warfare at home and abroad—locations that were not well defined. The sources of competition may have been relatively fewer in number, but there is no disguising that competition was dramatically and abundantly present.

The abundant presence of competition is perhaps best illustrated by enumerating part of the historical record of internal and external warfare of the leading states in the western European zone. Table 2.3 lists the summary 1100–1600 record of France, England, and Castile/Spain by century. The numbers are based on the more detailed listings of who fought whom and when reported in tables 2.4 and 3.1. We have not thoroughly exhausted all of the available information on medieval warfare in western Europe. Our listings of internal and external warfare should be viewed as rough approximations.[7] We may have missed some disputes and clashes or misidentified some of the years attached to specific wars; in this period warfare often meant quick raids into enemy territory interspersed by periods of uneasy truces or inactivity. Moreover, the precise distinctions between internal and external warfare are also often blurred in an era when the boundaries of the emerging states were still being formed. Nevertheless, a perusal through the record of West European warfare suggests several interesting generalizations.

Table 2.3
Years of Warfare by Century, 1100 to 1600

| Location/Century | Internal | Years of Warfare External | Total |
|---|---|---|---|
| *France* | | | |
| 12th | 37 | 59 | 67 |
| 13th | 34 | 28 | 51 |
| 14th | 23 | 37 | 47 |
| 15th | 19 | 80 | 77 |
| 16th | 31 | 56 | 74 |
| *England* | | | |
| 12th | 23 | 64 | 82 |
| 13th | 16 | 42 | 48 |
| 14th | 17 | 71 | 72 |
| 15th | 35 | 51 | 76 |
| 16th | 39 | 48 | 71 |
| *Castile/Spain* | | | |
| 12th | 23 | 43 | 58 |
| 13th | 30 | 58 | 71 |
| 14th | 35 | 49 | 72 |
| 15th | 17 | 34 | 47 |
| 16th | 25 | 87 | 92 |

*Note:* years in which both internal and external warfare are ongoing are only counted once. The entries in the total column, therefore, are less than the sum of the internal and external entries for that country.
*Source:* based on the data reported in tables 2.4 and 3.1.

Most clearly, in the formative years of western European state making, these states were at war as often as, and usually more often than, they were at peace. They chose to go to war most often, and not coincidentally, with states that were most proximate. For a period prior to the Hundred Years War (1337–1453), England controlled a substantial portion of the territory that later became known as France. As a consequence, England and France were frequently at war until England was forced to relinquish its continental territories in the late fifteenth century. The French state was thus shaped very much at the expense of the English, just as the ultimate shape of the English state turned out to be, in part, very much a function of French military successes on the European continent. Alternatively put, England had to be forced into accepting boundaries that later proved to be easier to monitor than was France's frontier adjacent to the central city belt.

The English could focus primarily on the French because their other proximate rivals, the Scots, Irish, and Welsh, proved to be fairly weak military threats. They, especially the Scots, were capable of raiding across the borders and allying with the French when mutually convenient, but the Celtic groups remained unlikely threats to conquer and subordinate English territory. Eventually, of course, the subordination process worked in the opposite direction and at the expense of these Celtic populations.

In contrast, the degree of competition in the southeastern end of the western European zone was much more intense, in part because the competitors were less asymmetrically matched. Until the eleventh century, the Iberian peninsula was predominately controlled by various Muslim states that were, in turn, intermittently controlled by Muslim empires centered in Morocco. Limited portions of northern Spain were controlled by Christian forces. For the next several hundred years (through 1492), the principal feature of Iberian conflict was the spasmodic expansion of the Christian north at the expense of the Muslim south. Yet as tables 2.4, 2.5, and 2.6 reveal, the ultimate expansion of the Christian states was relieved fairly often by intra-Christian conflict, both within and between the emerging states. Nor was it unknown for certain Christian states in Spain to ally with Muslim states to defeat the expansion of other Christian states within Spain. The ultimate shape and the basic natures of the states that emerged and survived in the Iberian peninsula were very much conditioned and molded by competition and conflict. Iberian state making and war making from at least the twelfth century on were indistinguishable processes. The nature of the competition was intense, but not so intense, complex, or simply dense that state-building efforts ultimately would be frustrated.

At the same time, we have no reason to assume that the nature and influence of the competitions were the same in each of the western European cases. In particular, we need to look for differences (other than Rokkan's distance from the city belt) that may distinguish England and Portugal from Spain and France, for the influence of territorial location is always a tricky explanatory tool. It is too easy to permit geography to explain more than it should. The best antidote is to examine decision-maker choices and strategies within the context of other given territorial milieux. Before geography can influence behavior it must first be perceived as presenting an obstacle or opportunity. Working out responses to these perceived obstacles and opportunities is often a protracted and not always a fully conscious or premeditated affair. Thus, there is always substantial room for historical contingencies that, in the long run, may count for as much as the more enduring environmental influences on behavior. Even though we may not be able to do much theoretically with these historical contingencies, the exercise of sifting through them will provide an opportunity for considering alternative, more general explanations of the effects of territorial consolidation.

Because we have neither the space nor the inclination to engage in extensive political histories of western European developments, our approach must be selective. We concentrate on the Spanish case in this chapter and the French case in the next chapter as two important and highly similar cases. To the extent that we can make a strong case for their similarities, developing the significance of the geopolitical-economic ways in which France and Spain differ from Portugal, England, and the Netherlands should be a fairly straightforward proposition in chapter 3.

## The Spanish Case

To develop the points that we wish to make, the best place to begin is with the Iberian peninsula and the formative period of the reconquest. The Christian reconquest of Spain was a process characterized by intermittent raids and territorial expansion into the Muslim south, primarily against some twenty intermittently autonomous Muslim city-states in the peninsula (Chejne 1974) and their Almoravid, Almohad, and Marinid overlords in Morocco. It was also marked by a confusing swirl of dynastic succession disputes in the Christian territories, which strongly influenced the number and, ultimately, the geopolitical orientations of the Christian Iberian states. Both of these attributes are reflected in table 2.4, which shows Castilian warfare prior to 1481 restricted almost exclusively to various types of internal conflict and combat with other states in the Iberian peninsula. This last category includes the pre-1350 Moroccan entries, which were always fought on the Spanish side of the Straits of Gibraltar.

The original northwestern kingdom of Asturias gave way to Leon, the ruler of which took the title of emperor to better reflect the political hierarchy

**Table 2.4**
**Castilian/Spanish Warfare, 1100 to 1600**

| Years | Opponent | Years | Opponent |
|---|---|---|---|
| 1109–12 | Aragon | 1333 | Morocco |
| 1111–13 | internal | 1333–38 | internal |
| 1115–17 | internal | 1339–44 | Morocco, Granada |
| 1120 | internal | 1349–50 | Morocco |
| 1122–27 | internal | 1354–56 | internal |
| 1133 | internal | | |
| 1133 | Morocco | 1356–66 | Aragon |
| 1136 | internal | | |
| 1138 | Morocco | | |
| 1139–57 | Morocco | 1365–69 | internal |
| 1140 | Portugal | 1369–70 | Granada |
| 1157–58 | internal | | |
| 1158–64 | Leon | 1370–75 | Aragon |
| 1160 | internal | 1372–73 | Portugal, England |
| 1162 | internal | 1378–79 | Navarre |
| 1164 | internal | 1381–82 | Portugal, England |
| 1166 | internal | 1383–89 | Portugal, England |
| 1168 | Portugal | | |
| 1171–73 | Morocco | 1390–91 | internal |
| 1174 | internal | 1394 | internal |
| 1180 | internal | 1396–97 | Portugal |
| 1183–85 | Morocco | | |
| 1189 | Morocco | | |
| 1195–97 | Morocco, Leon, Navarre | 1405–10 | Granada |
| 1211–14 | Morocco | 1420–22 | internal |
| 1214–17 | internal | | |
| 1217–18 | Leon | | |
| 1224–41 | Morocco | | |
| 1246–52 | Andalusia | 1429 | internal |
| 1252–53 | Portugal | 1431 | Granada |
| 1254–57 | internal | 1438–40 | internal |
| 1260 | Morocco | 1441–42 | internal |
| 1264–65 | Morocco, Granada | 1445 | internal |
| 1264–67 | internal | 1445 | Granada |
| 1270–73 | internal | 1449–50 | Granada |
| 1275–85 | Morocco, Granada | 1452 | internal |
| | | 1455–57 | Granada |
| | | 1461 | internal |
| 1282–84 | internal | 1462 | Granada |
| | | 1465–68 | internal |
| 1287 | internal | 1474–77 | internal |
| 1288–91 | internal | 1475–77 | France, Aragon |
| 1288–91 | Aragon | 1475–79 | Portugal |
| 1291–94 | Morocco | 1481–92 | Granada |
| | | 1495–97 | France |
| 1293 | internal | 1499–1502 | internal |

| Years | Opponent | Years | Opponent |
|---|---|---|---|
| | | 1501–04 | France |
| 1295–97 | Aragon, Portugal | 1505–11 | North Africa |
| | | 1508 | internal |
| | | 1508–09 | France |
| | | 1511–14 | France |
| 1295–1303 | internal | 1512 | Navarre |
| | | 1515 | France |
| 1295–1303 | Granada | 1516–17 | internal |
| 1303–04 | Aragon | 1520–24 | internal |
| 1309 | Morocco | 1521–26 | France |
| 1312–19 | internal | 1521–31 | Ottoman Empire |
| 1321–26 | internal | | |
| 1324–25 | Granada | 1526–29 | France |
| 1331 | Granada | 1532–35 | Ottoman Empire |
| | | 1536–38 | France |
| | | 1537–47 | Ottoman Empire |
| | | 1542–44 | France |
| | | 1548 | internal |
| | | 1551–56 | Ottoman Empire |
| | | 1552–56 | France |
| | | 1556–59 | France |
| | | 1559–64 | Ottoman Empire |
| | | 1568–78 | internal |
| | | 1569–80 | Ottoman Empire |
| | | 1579–81 | Portugal |
| | | 1579–1608 | Netherlands |
| | | 1585–1604 | England |
| | | 1589–98 | France |
| | | 1591–92 | internal |

*Sources:* Merriman (1918); Sorokin (1937); Chejne (1974); O'Callaghan (1975); Oliveira Marques (1976); Dupuy and Dupuy (1977); Hillgarth (1978); Lomax (1978); Levy (1983); Kohn (1987).

of a territorial unit divided into increasingly independent subunits. Actually, it would be inaccurate to speak of trends toward increasing autonomy before the twelfth century. Movement toward and away from greater centralization fluctuated depending on the dynastic personalities involved, their health, the number and gender of their offspring, and their perspectives on territorial inheritance principles.

By roughly the midtwelfth century, however, the Leonese empire had evolved into a tripartite allocation of territorial control. Portugal had emerged in the west. Aragon, soon to be united with Catalonia (1137), had developed in the east. Castile had become the predominant Christian state in the center. We do not imply that this tripartite division remained frozen in time or that it was always accepted by the three states involved. The division was contested on occasion, but it managed to survive for several hundred years—more than enough time to affect Iberian geopolitics even after the three states were united in the late sixteenth century.

An important principle in the logic of the reconquest was that each Christian state was expected to expand to its immediate south. Expansion to the southwest or southeast was considered a violation of a Christian neighbor's sphere of influence and, if attempted, usually led to war between those Christian states, with one or more of them briefly in league with the presumed Muslim foe. As a consequence, the Christian states remained pretty much within their own zones of expansion.

One result of this conflict management principle was the early withdrawal of both the eastern and western wings, Aragon-Catalonia and Portugal, from the expansionary drive south. The reason is that both states reached points roughly in the midthirteenth century at which further southern expansion meant one of two things. An end of coastline to conquer signified that to reach the next area of expansion, namely the shores of northwest Africa, would require a maritime effort. The Iberian alternative entailed a lateral shift in direction that would quickly meet strong Castilian resistance.

Accordingly, Portugal and Aragon more or less abandoned to Castile the drive to reconquer the Iberian peninsula. Their own expansionary energies shifted elsewhere. The Portuguese eventually assumed the lead in Atlantic exploration, partly to continue the Iberian expansion into northwest Africa. They found that they could circumvent the Moroccan empire's control of Sudanese gold by sailing down the northwest African coastline in the early fifteenth century. As a consequence, the pre-1500 record of Portuguese warfare, summarized in table 2.5, differs from the records of Castile and Aragon; the Portuguese-Moroccan wars continued after 1350, but they were fought on Moroccan soil as part of the Portuguese movement into Africa.

The Aragonese-Catalan thrust turned primarily eastward to develop a Mediterranean maritime empire stretching eventually as far as Athens. The Aragonese war record, recapitulated in table 2.6, thus resembles the Castilian series (see table 2.4) only in the twelfth century. In the first third of the thirteenth century, the king of Aragon-Catalonia was confronted with a strategic dilemma of sorts. His Aragonese subjects were pressing for a continuation of the southern drive into Muslim Valencia. His Catalan subjects preferred an attack on the Muslim kingdom, located in the adjacent Balearic Islands, that was interfering with the security of Catalan trade. Although the campaign against Valencia was only delayed, selecting the Balearic option began an extensive drive into the Mediterranean that elevated Aragon-Catalonia to the position of premiere western Mediterranean sea power in the fourteenth century.[8]

**Table 2.5**
**Portuguese Warfare, 1100 to 1500**

| Years | Opponent |
| --- | --- |
| 1140 | Castile |
| 1147 | Morocco |
| 1160–68 | Morocco |
| 1168 | Morocco, Leon |
| 1169–73 | Morocco |
| 1178 | Morocco |
| 1184 | Morocco |
| 1189–91 | Morocco |
| 1197 | Morocco |
| 1212 | Morocco |
| 1217 | Morocco |
| 1225–38 | Morocco |
| 1249 | Morocco |
| 1252–53 | Castile |
| 1281 | internal |
| 1287 | internal |
| 1295–97 | Castile |
| 1299 | internal |
| 1321–24 | internal |
| 1326 | internal |
| 1336–38 | Castile |
| 1340 | Morocco, Granada |
| 1355 | internal |
| 1369–71 | Castile |
| 1372–73 | Castile |
| 1381–82 | Castile |
| 1383–85 | internal |
| 1383–89 | Castile, France |
| 1396–97 | Castile |
| 1415–18 | Morocco |
| 1437 | Morocco |
| 1438–41 | internal |
| 1449 | internal |
| 1458 | Morocco |
| 1460 | Morocco |
| 1463–64 | Morocco |
| 1471 | Morocco |
| 1475–79 | Castile |
| 1481–83 | internal |

*Sources:* Oliveira Marques (1976); Dupuy and Dupuy
(1977); Hillgarth (1978); Lomax (1978); and
Kohn (1987).

**Table 2.6**
*Aragonese Warfare, 1100 to 1500*

| Years | Opponent | Years | Opponent |
|---|---|---|---|
| 1101–03 | Zaragoza | 1309 | Sardinia |
| 1105–07 | Zaragoza | 1315 | Tlemcen |
| 1107–34 | Morocco | 1323–26 | Sardinia, Genoa, Pisa |
| 1109–12 | Castile | 1330–36 | Genoa, Pisa |
| 1118 | Zaragoza | 1334–48 | internal |
| 1120 | Morocco | 1339–44 | Morocco |
| 1125 | Granada | 1343 | Majorca |
| 1143 | internal | 1343–49 | Genoa |
| 1146–49 | Morocco | 1344–48 | internal |
| 1148–49 | internal | 1347–55 | Genoa |
| 1151 | internal | 1349–50 | Morocco |
| 1152–54 | Muslims | 1353 | internal |
| 1157 | Muslims | 1356–66 | Castile |
| 1158–59 | internal | 1358 | Sardinia |
| 1186–94 | internal | 1370–75 | Castile |
| 1196–97 | Leon | 1378 | internal |
| 1204 | internal | 1381 | internal |
| 1212 | Morocco | 1382 | Milan |
| 1219–27 | internal | 1386 | internal |
| 1229–35 | Balearics | 1388 | internal |
| 1232–53 | Valencia | 1392–98 | internal |
| 1252–53 | internal | 1398–1403 | Tunis |
| 1259–62 | internal | 1408–13 | internal |
| 1265–66 | Murcia | 1420 | Genoa |
| 1272–80 | internal | 1420 | internal |
| 1282–1302 | Naples | 1423 | internal |
| 1284–85 | internal | 1435 | Genoa |
| 1285–95 | France | 1435–43 | internal |
| 1285–98 | Balearics | 1450–54 | internal |
| 1288–91 | Castile | 1450–58 | Genoa |
| 1292–94 | Morocco | 1461–72 | internal |
| 1295–97 | Castile | 1462–74 | France |
| 1303–04 | Castile, Granada | 1475–76 | Castile |

*Sources:* Merriman (1918), Sorokin (1937), Shneidman (1970), Chejne (1974), O'Callaghan (1975), Oliveira Marques (1976), Dupuy and Dupuy (1977), Hillgarth (1978), Lomax (1978), Bisson (1986), and Kohn (1987).

According to Shneidman (1970), ironically the Mediterranean impetus came only after the Aragonese-Catalan scheme to construct a land empire stretching from Aragon through southern France to northern Italy had been thwarted by the French (the fighting known as the Albigensian Crusade). Caught between two formidable land powers, Castile and France, Aragon-Catalonia began increasingly to specialize in sea power and maritime trade centered around Barcelona. Rivalries over trade with North Africa and the control of various islands in the western Mediterranean, especially Sicily, brought the expanding Aragonese empire into conflict with the French, Pisans, and Genoese. Their opposition, nevertheless, did not stop the development of the farflung Mediterranean empire stretching from Aragon through Naples and Sardinia to Athens. This thirteenth- to fourteenth-century development probably is most responsible for first linking Iberian geopolitics to Italian-continental commitments.

Thus, we have the early development of three Iberian states with very different geopolitical orientations and expansionary thrusts. The state with the long Mediterranean coastline turned toward that sea. The state with the long Atlantic coastline ultimately became the first European sea power in the Atlantic. The state in between continued the fight on land for nearly another two and one-half centuries. Apparently, we have a simple explanation for why some states become sea powers and others remain landlocked in their strategic thinking. Yet things are not always what they seem.

Castile had a more than respectable maritime tradition. Initially focused on the northern Cantabrian-Basque coasts, Castilian sailors had engaged in whaling and fishing and in transporting wool and other commodities to and from Flanders, France, England, and Castile. After Seville was reconquered in the thirteenth century, it soon assumed the identity of a Genoese Atlantic outpost. In the south, Castilian naval operations became concerned with preventing further Moroccan invasions into the peninsula. In the north, the Castilian galley navy became a factor in the Anglo-French Hundred Years War, attacking the English coast and providing much of France's naval protection in this period (Ramsey 1973: 85–86).

Nor did things remain the way they were in the thirteenth and fourteenth centuries. By the end of the fifteenth century, Isabella and Ferdinand had brought about a merger of Castile and Aragon-Catalonia. Between 1481 and 1492, Granada, the last Muslim territory on the Iberian peninsula, was finally conquered. The year 1492 also marked Columbus's first discoveries across the Atlantic in the name of Castile, primarily because the Portuguese knew that Columbus's arguments and measurements were incorrect and therefore rejected his earlier overtures.

In the last decade of the fifteenth century, a newly ascendant Spain faced several strategic options. It could rest on its *reconquista* laurels and attempt no further territorial expansion. It might have completed the unification of the peninsula by attempting to conquer Portugal. A third option involved continuing the war with the Muslims on African soil. Another option involved reviving and defending the Aragonese-Catalan commercial empire in the Mediterranean against European and Ottoman encroachments. Alternatively, the even older Catalan claims, as part of the old Carolingian empire, to portions of southern France might have been revived. Last, the Atlantic discoveries were awaiting exploitation.

The first option does not seem to have received any consideration. A number of authors have described the Castilian-Aragonese state as a war machine designed for territorial expansion. Lomax is representative when he asserts that the reconquest transformed late medieval Castile into

> essentially a society organized for war, a dynamic military machine which would function well so long as it had more lands to conquer. It might be disconcerted by military defeats, but it could survive them. What threw it into complete confusion was the end of the attempt at conquest, and when the kings stopped leading their armies against Granada they implicitly invited their barons to find a new role which could only be that of fighting each other. (Lomax 1978: 177)

Recognition of this principle, according to Lomax, prompted Ferdinand and Isabella to resolve their main domestic problems with extensive intraelite strife by reigniting the war machine in 1481. Once reignited by resuming the attack on Granada, after being idle in the fourteenth century, it would have been extremely difficult simply to transform the state machine into some other entity. To allow it to idle again might have meant a major threat to the tenure of the crown incumbents.

The second Portuguese option was postponed for another century. The remaining three options were all pursued more or less simultaneously. Of course, not everyone agrees with this assessment. Merriman (1918: 75–76, 279) argued that the Mediterranean option was pursued first due to geohistorical influences and contingencies.

> The coincidence that Castile was partially shut off from access to the sea by the declaration of the independence of Portugal, at almost precisely the same moment that Aragon acquired it by union with Catalonia, produced results of lasting importance. It explains why Spain's first imperial ventures were made to the eastward, in the Mediterranean Sea, rather than to the westward in the Atlantic. (Merriman 1918: 279)

Technically, Merriman is probably correct in the sense that Ferdinand of Aragon seemed inclined to move in an eastward direction as soon as Castile's first priority (the conquest of Granada) was accomplished. Troops dispatched in 1480 to deter an Ottoman invasion of Italy conceivably represented an early expression of this inclination. Yet it was the fateful decision to block French expansion into Italy in 1495 and the beginning of the long European duel between France and Spain that Merriman had in mind. This Aragonese geohistorical inclination was responsible for laying the foundation for Spain's increasing involvement in European continental politics after 1495. This same involvement also contributed to the downfall of Spain as a global power.

Our point is not the same as Merriman's argument that things might have been different if Portugal had not developed as an independent state from the twelfth century on. The fact that Spain in 1494 represented the union of the central and eastern successors of the old Leonese empire, as opposed to some other combination, did not dictate the Spanish plunge into the European cockpit of Italy. The long Aragonese-Catalonian involvement in Sicily, Sardinia, and Naples from the thirteenth century on did, however, make the Italian commitment in the fifteenth century much more probable.

We have no quarrel with this assertion. Rather, our point is that the Spanish decision makers had to choose whether and in which direction to continue their expansion. Their strategic error was not so much one of choosing an Aragonese solution over a Castilian one. The real error was attempting to pursue the Aragonese preference (blocking the French expansion in Italy), the Castilian preference (continuing the reconquest in North Africa), *and* the Portuguese preference (exploiting the possibilities associated with Atlantic oceanic power). Overcommitment and overextension were facilitated and even encouraged by geohistorical developments, but they were not determined by the peculiarities of Iberian geography. Decision makers still had to make choices. The ultimate problem was that there were too many options from which to choose, and in the long run, Spanish decision makers unwisely attempted to do more than was possible.

By 1580, Spain had become, as Stradling (1981:30) comments, an "empire of empires."[9] Within the preceding century, Castile had expanded its late fifteenth-century absorption of Aragon-Catalonia, its Mediterranean empire and Muslim Granada to include inherited, former Burgundian territories to the northeast and east of France, the Aztec and Incan empires of the New World, and the Philippine archipelago. Finally, Portugal, with its own extensive imperial system stretching from Brazil to Macao, was absorbed as well.

Not all of this impressive collection of real estate had been acquired by force. Those former Burgundian territories centered in the Netherlands, for instance, were inherited through Charles, the great grandson of Charles the Bold of Burgundy and the grandson of Maximilian of Habsburg, emperor of the Holy Roman Empire. Charles had succeeded Ferdinand as ruler of Castile and Aragon in 1516, only to be elected Holy Roman Emperor in 1519. Thereafter, the European commitments of Spain and its conflict with France were greatly intensified. Yet the increasing involvement of Spanish resources in Europe was, as we have seen, not entirely novel. Nor did it exclude imperial involvement in other spheres, as demonstrated by the long duel with the Ottoman Empire over control of the Mediterranean—another nondeparture from the pre-Habsburg record. However gained, the imperial commitments of the sixteenth century ensured the continuing role of warfare in sixteenth- and seventeenth-century Spanish state making.

Even more fundamental, the Castilian-Spanish enterprise was based on a rather shaky and fragile economic foundation. There was no single Spanish economy. The various regions that had once been separate kingdoms were only minimally interconnected, if at all. Within each region, various economic systems functioned somewhat independently. Hamilton (1934) and Mackay (1981), for instance, find it difficult to discuss general economic trends, such as prices, in fifteenth-century Castile because there was so much variation across the Castilian economy.

Ringrose (1983), echoing parts of Fox's thesis, makes a strong case for a coastal-interior dualism in Spanish political economy—a dualism that prevailed at least from the sixteenth century and continued into the nineteenth century. The principal commercial cities of Seville, Cadiz, and Barcelona were coastal centers exposed to and integrated into the maritime trade of the Mediterranean and Atlantic. Yet even within this commercial fringe, the level of cohesion and connection was not that great, especially in the sixteenth century. A depressed, Mediterranean-directed Barcelona was not linked closely to an Atlantic-oriented Seville. Nor was this lack of linkage discouraged by governmental policies that maintained the Castilian monopoly of New World trade, organized around Seville, into the eighteenth century.

Ringrose's own emphasis is placed on the coastal-interior division and the difficulties of moving goods in and out of the interior:

> The government in Madrid was perennially faced with accommodating two distinct patterns of economic life within a single political structure. The coastal districts could rely on the maritime trade network for food when domestic supplies failed. Thus they could accept the risk of specialization in export crops and manufacturing, with correspondingly more efficient use of resources. During the difficult seventeenth century these areas escaped demographic crisis, and many coastal zones experienced growing output, population, and commercial activity. On the other hand, the interior was hampered by a precarious climate, poor soil, and isolation from distant supplies when local crops failed. The only product that could bear the cost of transport to the sea and still be profitable was wool. Thus the interior could not risk economic specialization and had to commit its resources to basic food crops as insurance against bad harvests. Constantly threatened by food shortages, the interior was severely limited in its ability to find more efficient ways of organizing production. (Ringrose 1983: 5)

For all the economic limitations of the Spanish interior, and especially the Castilian interior, political dominance rested with the interior interests as long as the wool industry prospered. The heavy dependence on wool, however, meant that the underdeveloped Castilian economy was committed to the export of a raw material and, therefore, subject to the usual vicissitudes of international market fluctuations.

That it had become the chief European wool producer by 1300 (Vicens Vives 1969: 242), thanks in part to English production problems related to its continental entanglements in France, was an important influence in shaping the Castilian political economy. Vicens Vives (1969: 241–42) points out that the dominance of wool exports tended to restrict economic growth to one sector of economic life and restricted it furthermore only to those areas in which the sheep were actually resident (the Basque north and the Andalusian south). This extreme emphasis on an agrarian-herding economy discouraged the development of an urban middle class (and its political influence) as well as such competing industries as textiles. It also served to protect the socioeconomic position of the nobility who controlled the sheep.

This same traditional nobility was able to defeat local efforts to persuade the crown to restrict wool exports substantially in order to encourage its domestic consumption by fledgling textile producers (Hillgarth 1978, vol. 2: 495). This political-economic outcome sharply contrasts with the English experience where exports were reduced to promote textile production:

> Castile chose the opposite course; thus it conquered the Italian wool market but missed all chances to become a great producer and exporter of cloth. (Lopez 1987: 396)

Equally dependent on the sheep were the Castilian-Spanish monarchs who relied heavily on the taxes generated by wool production. In the second half of the sixteenth century, wool sales began to decline, the amount of available pasture diminished (due to governmental auctions by a monarchy in need of money), and the total size of the Castilian flock was reduced. To make matters worse, in 1563 the Mesta, the association of sheep owners, extracted a royal promise that its taxes would not be increased in the future. Although a large payment was necessary in 1563 to make the deal, Lovett (1986: 242) indicates that the Mesta's tax immunities lasted until 1684.

The revenues of the Spanish empire, inadequate though they often may have been, came primarily from Castilian sources. The other incorporated kingdoms retained separate treasuries and more or less sought to cover their own operating costs. Wool exports and the exploitation of the American territories made Castile the richest component of the empire. Dominguez Ortiz (1971: 29) adds that the political centrality and relative submissiveness of Castile made it more convenient to "turn the [tax] screws harder there than anywhere else." Or, as amplified by another historian:

> The [Castilian] representative institution, the cortes, although far from subservient, could not shelter behind the formidable breastwork of rights which rendered the neighbouring Kingdoms virtually impregnable to royal demands. (Lovett 1986: 230)

As it turned out, the tax screws could not be turned tighter forever.

As noted earlier, wool sales began to decline as early as the second half of the sixteenth century. Disease, rising prices, harvest failures, substantial depopulation, general economic stagnation on an unusual scale, heavy imperial taxes to pay for warfare that never seemed to end, and the decline in the royal revenues from American gold and silver operated in seemingly overwhelming conjunction to undermine the Castilian core of the seventeenth-century Spanish imperial undertaking.

We recognize that the causes of the decline of Spain in the seventeenth century are still disputed (Phillips 1987). Nevertheless, figure 2.2 depicts part of the problem by contrasting the average annual inflow of one source of revenue, the royal treasure share, with the average annual outflow of one form of imperial expenditure, the military costs for the fighting in the Netherlands sector.[10] As Parker (1979a: 40–43) argues at some length, we need to be careful about linking these two particular flows too closely. Kamen (1980: 135) also suggests that the seventeenth-century decline in American treasure may be misleading due to dishonest official recordkeeping and increasing defense costs in New Spain. Nor was American silver the most important single source of royal revenues. Elliott (1970: 85–87) points out that the Habsburg silver mines in Europe outproduced the American mines by a factor of four between 1521

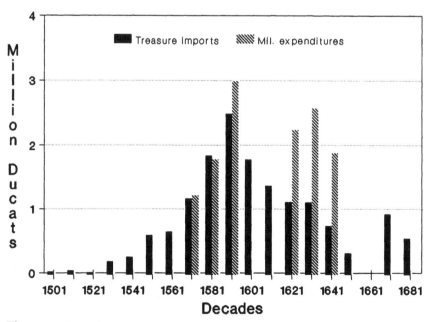

**Figure 2.2.** Annual Average Royal Treasure Imports and Military Expenditures in the Netherlands

and 1544. Only in the second half of the sixteenth century did American silver become a significant source of royal income—rising from 11 percent of total revenues in 1554 to as much as 20 to 25 percent in the 1590s.

Yet these proportions are also misleading for, as Elliott (1970) also argues, American silver constituted the chief inducement for underwriting royal borrowing. The royal credit line, crucial in a period characterized by heavy deficit spending primarily due to war expenditures, was thus closely linked to the royal share of treasure inflows.

In this sense, what figure 2.2 best illustrates is the basic dilemma of persisting imperial-continental military commitments that decision makers find difficult to walk away from despite declining resources.

In the eighteenth century, Spain was able to recover some of the global power status that had largely evaporated toward the end of the previous century. It was never able, nonetheless, to regain the lofty politico-military position attained in the sixteenth century. One reason is that its politico-military position had rested on a weak and vulnerable economic base that depended on the export of a single cash crop and the exploitation of American minerals. It proved extremely difficult to sustain a leading global power position with what we now refer to as a classically dependent economy.

Another partial reason for decline can be traced to Spain's continental orientation. Contrary to popular impressions, Spanish sea power, other than the traditional galley forces, emerged relatively late. Only in the 1570s did a Spanish oceanic navy capability begin to develop, largely in response to the need to protect the New World treasure fleets from European attacks. Despite the boost provided by the co-optation of the Portuguese fleet in the next decade, the Spanish were never able to apply their sea power in a way that might be expected to defeat their Dutch and English maritime opposition in the late sixteenth century. As a consequence, Spain could not suppress the Dutch revolt, and less directly, it could not hold on to the Portuguese empire that broke away in the 1640s.

### Conclusion

In sum, Castile-Spain was an organization designed for, and accustomed to, territorial conquest. Only through war could a centralized state be created in the middle of the Iberian peninsula. And only a highly centralized state could cope with frequent warfare and territorial expansion. However, the centralized state that was forcibly created rested on an extremely weak economic foundation. Although capable of generating substantial resources for a time, dependence on a single export commodity limited the possibilities for commercial development in the domestic economy. It also exposed the

Spanish economy to the customary international demand and price fluctuations. A pronounced coastal-interior economic dualism and the low level of economic integration further restricted the likelihood of transforming the agrarian-herding nature of the Spanish political economy.

The likelihood of commercially oriented elites rising to other than intermittent political influence in this context remained equally remote. Instead, once the home base was consolidated in the late fifteenth century, Spain continued to expand its territorial holdings in several directions. Its economic empire was primarily characterized, not surprisingly, by crude extractive techniques at the expense of concentrating on developing an extensive commercial network. Consequently, much of the wealth generated by these activities ended up in non-Spanish hands.

This chapter's selective focus on the Spanish geopolitical-economic context highlights what appear to be distinctive factors accounting for the nature of Spanish war and state making. The obvious question that arises is whether these factors, involving a militarized territorial consolidation process, geography, and structural liabilities in the domestic political economy, are unique to Spain or common to France as well? If they are unique to Spain, we have made no theoretical headway. If, on the other hand, France proves to possess similar attributes, we can be more confident in asserting that these contextual factors constitute some fundamental roots of geopolitical orientations as well as global power war and state making. An examination of the French case may also reveal some additional factors overlooked or not fully appreciated in the Spanish case. Finally, if we can also demonstrate the absence of the highlighted Spanish-French attributes in Portugal, the Netherlands, and England, our argument can be strengthened even more by the available empirical evidence. These comparative questions are addressed in the next chapter after an initial review of the French case.

# 3
# The Geopolitical-Economic Context: France and the Maritime Powers

Underlying our search for geopolitical-economic roots is the assumption that political actors operate in what Abrams (1982: 3) once called a two-sided world. Political actors construct the world in which they operate. They are also constrained by that world. Hence, political actors are free to make choices, but their choices are shaped by the structures and history they and their predecessors have made.

The interactive shaping of choices is also a sequential process.

> Once an historical choice is made, it both precludes and facilitates alternative future choices. Political change follows a branching model. Once a particular fork is chosen, it is very difficult to get back on a rejected path. (Krasner 1984: 225)

The trick for the analyst, then, is to ascertain, first, what choices were made from among which contextually shaped possibilities; and second, how did previous choices and contexts channel subsequent behavior along certain structured paths—in this instance, toward or away from maritime-commercial, geopolitical-economic orientations.

In the previous chapter, we suggested that Spain's behavior in the sixteenth and seventeenth centuries was in part a function of its location, several hundred years of territorial consolidation in the Iberian peninsula, and certain structural weaknesses in the composition of its political economy. How much can a focus on these attributes tell us about French behavior in the same era?

### The French Case

A perceptive British naval historian (Graham 1950) once observed that France should have been in a very strong position to take advantage of the opening of the Atlantic-based political economy. It possessed excellent harbors on both the Mediterranean and Atlantic coasts. For all practical purposes, the French economy was self-sufficient, wealthy, and able to recover fairly quickly from serious setbacks. Moreover, maritime inclinations were as natural to France as they were to England. Why, then, did England specialize in sea power whereas France did not?

Graham's answer first noted that some of the French advantages proved to be disadvantages as well. The excellent harbors were not collection points for the main continental trade routes. The bicoastal situation, too, proved to be double-edged whenever the French navy sought to concentrate its Mediterranean and Atlantic fleets. This maneuver was usually a strategic prerequisite for meeting the English/British navy near the English Channel on something resembling equal quantitative terms.

Even more critical than the location of harbors and the number of coastlines, the

> essential differences lay in the attitudes of kings and governments; but these, in turn, were largely prescribed by the facts of geography. In the building and maintenance of fleets, British governments were to show greater constancy than did the French, simply because, thanks to the English Channel, there were no continuous and exhausting conflicts of interest. Because of long interior frontiers, France was repeatedly drawn deep into Europe. The age-old rivalry of Bourbon and Hapsburg drew like a magnet on the arms of France, and made French sea power a thing of intermittent enthusiasms. For three centuries France was to be torn between continental and maritime ambitions, and the periods of maritime ardour were never long enough to compensate for the prolonged intervals of indifference and neglect. (Graham 1950: 40)

Emphasizing decision-maker attitudes and exhausting conflicts of interest is a welcome correction to the more traditional stress on the overdetermining influences of geographical features. Yet it is fair to ask whether Graham goes far enough for, as indicated in the cited paragraph, the presumed sources of the attitudes and conflicts of interest are the somewhat static, long land frontiers of France and the dynastic animosities of the Bourbons and Habsburgs. It may be true that both dynastic warfare and the influence of land frontiers are similar to the reason some people climb mountains—because they are there—or, in the specific case of dynasties, because they are proximate and in each other's way. Yet before the conflicting dynasties became proximate along those long land frontiers, the frontiers first had to be created. The manner of creation and the specific territory, people, and resources encompassed by the creation of those French boundaries also tell us about subsequent French state making, strategic orientations, and Graham's exhausting conflicts of interest.

In the year 987, the first Capetian king was elected to succeed the Carolingian dynasty in the area that was to become France. As hinted at by the election mechanism, the king of France in the late tenth century was less than omnipotent. The Capetian royal domain was also severely restricted to a small area in the vicinity of Paris/Ile de France. Limited in resources of every kind, French kings might reign but they could hardly be expected to rule. To alter this situation, it was necessary to subordinate the numerous feudal magnates and principal power rivals to the authority of the king and thus gain direct control over their territorial resource bases. Hence, expansion of the royal domain and what we now call state centralization were processes that went hand in hand. The techniques to accomplish the improvement of the crown's position varied. Strategic marriages, legal manipulation, inheritance windfalls, and, of course, internal warfare all played useful roles.

The centralization process in France was slow and not without setbacks. Several hundred years were required before the extent of the French kings' territorial control began to resemble the shape of contemporary France. A great deal of the combat tied up with this consolidation process, and a partial explanation for its length, was due to the close ties between England and France during this period. The twelfth-century Plantagenet English kings, due to the outcome of the Norman Conquest, were also the feudal lords of several western French provinces located between Normandy and Aquitaine. The many wars of the Middle Ages between France and England (listed in table 3.1), as a consequence, combined the usual interstate rivalries with those of domestic French feudal rivalries, resistance to royal expansion and taxes, and an ongoing contest between dynasties (Capetian versus Plantagenet and later Valois versus Lancastrian) over control of the French crown.[1]

The second half of the fifteenth century proved to be a major turning point for the shape of royal territorial consolidation. The duchies of Gascony in the southeast and Normandy in the northwest were regained by the middle of the century. The English were expelled roughly at the same time. In the last quarter of the century, informal and formal control over Burgundy, Anjou, Provence, Guyenne, Brittany, and Orleans was achieved. It is not coincidental that France's first modern invasion of Italy in 1494 came at roughly the same time that most of France had finally been subordinated to royal authority.

Yet it has been pointed out by a number of observers that however successful the French political and territorial consolidation, albeit still incomplete as late as the early seventeenth century, economic consolidation was much more difficult to accomplish.[2] For this reason, reference is often made to the multiple French "economic personalities" (Fox 1971; Milward and

**Table 3.1**
**English and French Warfare, 1100 to 1600**

| England | | France | |
|---|---|---|---|
| Years | Opponent | Years | Opponent |
| 1101–02 | internal | 1101–03 | internal |
|  |  | 1106 | internal |
|  |  | 1109 | internal |
| 1109–13 | France | 1109–13 | England |
|  |  | 1111–17 | internal |
| 1116–19 | France | 1116–19 | England |
|  |  | 1120 | internal |
| 1123–35 | France | 1123–35 | England |
|  |  | 1124 | Holy Roman Empire |
| 1136 | internal | 1130 | internal |
| 1136–38 | Scotland | 1132 | internal |
| 1138–54 | internal | 1137 | internal |
| 1149 | Scotland | 1139–40 | internal |
| 1155 | internal | 1142 | internal |
| 1158 | Wales | 1153 | internal |
| 1159–89 | France | 1159–89 | England |
| 1163 | Wales | 1164 | internal |
| 1165 | Wales |  |  |
| 1169–72 | Ireland | 1173–75 | internal |
| 1173–74 | internal | 1177–78 | internal |
| 1174 | Scotland | 1180–86 | internal |
| 1194–1200 | France | 1194–1200 | England |
| 1202–04 | France | 1202–04 | England |
|  |  | 1203 | internal |
|  |  | 1207–31 | internal |
| 1213–17 | France | 1213–17 | England |
| 1214–16 | Scotland |  |  |
| 1215–17 | internal |  |  |
| 1219–23 | Wales |  |  |
| 1222 | internal |  |  |
| 1223–25 | France | 1223–25 | England |
| 1224 | Wales |  |  |
| 1228–31 | Wales |  |  |
| 1233–34 | Wales | 1233–34 | internal |
|  |  | 1238 | internal |
| 1241 | Wales | 1241 | internal |
| 1242–43 | France | 1242–43 | England |
|  |  | 1244 | internal |
| 1245 | France | 1245 | England |
|  |  | 1251 | internal |
| 1257 | Wales | 1253–55 | Flanders |
| 1259 | France | 1259 | England |
| 1263–67 | internal |  |  |
|  |  | 1280–81 | internal |

*Table 3.1—continued*

| England | | France | |
|---------|----------|--------|----------|
| Years | Opponent | Years | Opponent |
| 1272–77 | Wales | 1284–85 | Aragon |
| 1282–84 | Wales | 1285 | Castile |
| 1284 | internal | | |
| 1287 | internal | | |
| 1294–95 | internal | | |
| 1294–98 | France | 1294–98 | England, Flanders |
| 1297–99 | internal | | |
| 1297–1328 | Scotland | | |
| | | | |
| 1300 | internal | | |
| 1300–03 | France | 1300–03 | England, Flanders |
| 1306 | internal | 1305 | internal |
| | | 1314 | internal |
| 1315–16 | internal | 1314–15 | Flanders |
| 1320–22 | internal | | |
| 1324–27 | France | 1324–27 | England |
| 1326–27 | internal | 1326 | internal |
| 1330 | internal | | |
| 1332–33 | Scotland | 1328 | Flanders |
| | | 1334 | internal |
| 1337–40 | France | 1337–40 | England |
| | | 1341–43 | internal |
| 1346 | Scotland | | |
| 1346–47 | France | 1346–47 | England |
| 1355–60 | France | 1355–60 | England |
| | | 1357–58 | internal |
| | | 1360–68 | internal |
| 1366–69 | Castile | | |
| 1368–75 | France | 1368–89 | England |
| 1376–89 | France, Scotland | | |
| 1380–81 | internal | 1378–82 | internal |
| 1386 | Castile | 1382 | Flanders |
| 1387–88 | internal | | |
| 1391 | internal | | |
| 1394 | Ireland | 1396 | Ottoman Empire |
| 1397 | Ireland | | |
| 1398–99 | internal | | |
| | | | |
| 1400–09 | internal | | |
| 1402–03 | Scotland | | |
| 1402–06 | France | 1402–06 | England |
| 1414–15 | internal | 1411–14 | internal |
| 1415–44 | France, Genoa | 1415–44 | England |
| | | 1418 | internal |

**Table 3.1—continued**

| England | | France | |
|---|---|---|---|
| *Years* | *Opponent* | *Years* | *Opponent* |
| | | 1438 | internal |
| | | 1440 | internal |
| | | 1443–44 | internal |
| | | 1444 | Switzerland |
| 1449–53 | France | 1449–53 | England |
| | | 1455 | internal |
| 1450 | internal | 1464–65 | Burgundy |
| | | 1465–67 | internal |
| 1455–64 | internal | 1467–77 | Burgundy |
| | | 1471–72 | internal |
| 1467–71 | internal | 1472–75 | Aragon |
| 1475 | France | 1475 | England |
| 1480 | Scotland | 1477–82 | Austria |
| | | 1485–88 | internal |
| 1482–84 | Scotland | 1486–89 | Austria |
| 1483–85 | internal | | |
| 1488–92 | France | 1488–92 | England |
| 1489 | internal | | |
| 1495 | internal | | |
| 1496 | Scotland | 1492–93 | Austria |
| 1497 | internal | 1494–97 | Spain, Austria |
| 1499 | internal | 1499–1500 | |
| | | 1501–04 | Spain |
| | | 1508–09 | Spain, Austria |
| 1511–14 | France | 1511–15 | Spain, Austria, |
| 1513–15 | Scotland | | England |
| 1517 | internal | 1515–16 | Spain, Austria |
| 1521–26 | France | 1521–26 | Spain, England |
| 1522–23 | Scotland | | |
| | | 1526–29 | Spain, England |
| 1532–34 | Scotland | 1536–38 | Spain |
| 1534–37 | internal | 1539 | internal |
| 1540 | internal | 1542 | internal |
| 1542–50 | Scotland | 1542–44 | Spain |
| 1544–46 | France | 1544–46 | England |
| 1549 | internal | 1548 | internal |
| 1549–50 | France | 1549–50 | England |
| 1553–54 | internal | 1552–56 | Spain |
| 1556–60 | France | 1556–59 | Spain, England |
| 1557 | internal | 1559–60 | England |
| 1561–67 | internal | 1562–63 | internal |
| 1562–64 | France | 1562–64 | England |
| 1569–75 | internal | 1567–70 | internal |
| 1576–83 | internal | 1572–77 | internal |

*Table 3.1—continued*

| England | | France | |
|---|---|---|---|
| Years | Opponent | Years | Opponent |
| | | 1579–80 | internal |
| | | 1585–98 | internal |
| 1585–1604 | Spain | 1589–98 | Spain |
| 1594–1600 | internal | | |

*Sources:* Sorokin (1937), Dupuy and Dupuy (1977), Levy (1983), and Kohn (1987).

Saul 1973; Wallerstein 1974; DeVries 1976; Clark 1981; Parker 1983; Braudel 1984). A southern coast geared to Mediterranean trade, an eastern fringe oriented toward the Rhineland, and a north and west attracted to the emerging Atlantic economy—all tethered to a large, traditional, underdeveloped, and highly localized agrarian heartland.

These problems of fragmentation and multiple economic vectors were compounded by the limited contacts that existed between coastal towns and between the commerce-oriented towns and their own immediate hinterlands. Clark (1981: 17) links these liabilities by suggesting that the primary economic hinterlands for the major coastal and river cities were located not inland but overseas in other states and colonies. Uneven growth potentials and growth rates across regions and between the subsistence-oriented heartland and the more urban fringes of the French state helped matters little.

Two further geopolitical-economic disadvantages, stressed by Braudel (1984), deserve mention. One is the sheer size of the French state. As Archer Jones comments about the Hundred Years War,

> In a war with so large a country as France, the English strategy basically had relied on raids to extract political concessions. The alternative, persisting strategy to occupy the country, would have taken years of sieges. French pursuit of and attacks on raiding armies had led to the great English victories of Crecy and Poitiers, but these, though inflicting heavy casualties on the French, had not taken any castles or walled towns nor prevented the French from assembling new armies. The thousands of square miles and the millions of people of France swallowed up English armies of 10,000 and even 20,000 men. The English had an inadequate ratio of force to French space and population and had no solution to the defensive strength of fortifications. (1987: 168)

A very large territory can be difficult to conquer. It is even more difficult to mobilize and to govern, particularly when the territory is heterogenous and underdeveloped. Moreover, as in the Spanish case, there was no obvious central location that could combine political leadership with economic and cultural dynamism at the national level and lead in connecting the French economy to the outside world. Instead, a landlocked political center in Paris competed with, and attempted to subordinate, an industrializing Lyons or a trading La Rochelle, to name two prominent examples.

The centrifugal tendencies of the gross and heterogenous French political economy, an entity that probably should not be spoken of in a singular sense, made political authoritarianism/absolutism much more likely. But it also meant that France was much less likely to constitute the dynamic center of the emerging world economy. The geopolitical-economic odds were against that happening. These odds also were stacked against the ascendancy of an elite or the development of a society geared to take advantage of the opportunities associated with the developing Atlantic economy.

Braudel summarized the French problem as he saw it in a fairly compatible if somewhat tautological fashion.

> France was thus carved up, by these key towns on her coastal or continental margins, into dependent zones, corridors or sections, which communicated through urban mediators with the all-controlling European economy. And it is in this perspective that the dialogue between "trading France" and "territorial France" can best be grasped. If the trading community, despite all these advantages, did not succeed in taking over territorial France it was because the latter was an awesomely dense mass, which did not lend itself easily to mobilization; but it was also because France did not occupy in the international order a position comparable to that of Amsterdam or London, and thus lacked the vigour characteristic of a front-rank economy that would have been required to stimulate and develop regional economies which did not always spontaneously thirst after expansion. (Braudel 1984: 351–52)

Geography and political economy worked against France in a variety of ways. Another element also is important in the development of French orientations toward state making and strategy. Chapter 1 established the abstract groundwork for the reciprocal and spiralling connections between war making and state expansion. France provides a superb and telling empirical example.

The main exception to the medieval expectation that kings would depend on their own estates for the expenses associated with managing the kingdom was war. As demonstrated in table 3.1, France was essentially created through several hundred years of warfare, primarily but not exclusively with the English. In a period of military emergency, the French king would seek special monetary subsidies and military levies from his nominal feudal vassals and subjects. The feudal levies gradually gave way first to mercenaries when it was realized that they were more reliable for subordinating other parts of the French kingdom. They also possessed greater war-making skills. Yet mercenaries had to be paid more or less regularly. What amounted to a gradual commercialization of the military sector thus put greater pressure on the crown's ability to extract the resources necessary to pay its troops.

Even more money, and money that was available on a continuous basis, was needed when a standing army was created (1445) to suppress the excesses of unemployed mercenaries during the pauses within the Hundred Years War (1337–1453). Nevertheless, the basic tax structure of the ancien regime had already emerged a century before 1445. Parker (1983: 9) estimates that by the beginning of the sixteenth century, taxes that had been levied temporarily in wartime had become permanent to the extent that royal estate revenues had been reduced to about 10 percent of the total revenue base. That figure was reduced even further later in the same century (4 percent in 1576).[3]

The issue of spiralling demands for increased revenues is discussed in chapters 4 and 5. What needs attention at this juncture is one of the principal reasons for increasing spending and taxes, namely, the growth in the size of the armed forces. Table 3.2 provides some information on the expansion of West European armies. In both Spain and France, army sizes literally mushroomed between the fifteenth and seventeenth centuries. Whereas the Spanish reached their high-water mark in the Thirty Years War, the size of the French army levelled off in the eighteenth century, only to expand in the Napoleonic Wars and then again in World War I.

Nor, of course, were the French alone in this process. One simple reason for growing armies was that the armies of other states were swelling—a competitive process that has continued into the twentieth century. Still, the French were important leaders in this development. They increased the commercialization of warfare by using mercenaries in the fourteenth century. In the fifteenth century they were forced to develop the gendarmerie, the first standing army in western Europe since the Roman Empire, to police the mercenaries in years when they were less indispensable.

Other dimensions of the escalation in military expenses were the introduction of artillery and the increasing reliance on firepower (including musketeers) on the battlefield. According to Parker (1988: 9), the catalyst for major changes in military firepower was the 1494 French invasion of Italy. During the first global war, it became evident that cities were no longer as invulnerable as hitherto thought. Artillery made it possible to breach walls once considered unbreachable. An immediate consequence of this development, of course, was an increase in the costs of defensive fortifications, as walls were made even thicker where possible. This response led to the development of more and larger artillery pieces.

The French are usually given the credit they deserve for these innovations in military organization. The point we wish to stress, however, is much less commonly made. The first major impetus to growth in the size of the French army stemmed from the need to expand the extent of the initial royal domain. Relying once again on David Parker's data (1983: 7), the core of the French

**Table 3.2**
**West European Army Sizes**

| Year | Castile/ Spain | France | England | United Provinces | Prussia/ Germany |
|---|---|---|---|---|---|
| 1200 | | | 25,000 | | |
| 1214 | | 50,000 | | | |
| 1327 | | 35,000 | | | |
| 1346 | | 60,000 | 32,000 | | |
| 1367 | 37,500 | | | | |
| 1415 | | 30,000 | 12,000 | | |
| 1475 | 20,000 | 40,000 | 25,000 | | |
| 1487 | 56,000 | | | | |
| 1491–94 | 60,000 | 28,000 | | | |
| 1555 | 150,000 | 50,000 | 20,000 | | |
| 1595 | 200,000 | 80,000 | 30,000 | 20,000 | |
| 1635 | 300,000 | 150,000 | | 50,000 | |
| 1655 | 100,000 | 100,000 | 70,000 | | 4,000 |
| 1675 | 70,000 | 120,000 | | 110,000 | |
| 1690 | | 400,000 | 70,000 | 73,000 | 30,000 |
| 1705 | 50,000 | 400,000 | 87,000 | 100,000 | |
| 1710 | 30,000 | 350,000 | 75,000 | 130,000 | |
| 1756–63 | 98,000 | 330,000 | 200,000 | 40,000 | 162,000 |
| 1778 | | 170,000 | | | |
| 1789 | | 180,000 | 40,000 | | |
| 1812–14 | | 600,000 | 250,000 | | 300,000 |
| 1816 | | 132,000 | 225,000 | | 130,000 |
| 1830 | | 259,000 | 140,000 | | 130,000 |
| 1860 | | 608,000 | 347,000 | | 201,000 |
| 1870 | | 454,000 | 345,000 | | 1,200,000 |
| 1880 | | 544,000 | 248,000 | | 430,000 |
| 1900 | | 715,000 | 624,000 | | 524,000 |
| 1914 | | 1,000,000 | 650,000 | | 3,400,000 |
| 1929 | | 666,000 | 443,000 | | 115,000 |
| 1937 | | 825,000 | 645,000 | | 766,000 |
| 1944 | | | 4,500,000 | | 9,125,000 |

*Sources:* Ropp (1962), Bean (1973), Finer (1975), Parker (1979a: 96, 1979b: 205, 214), Contamine (1984), Hale (1985), Jones (1987), Kennedy (1987: 56, 99, 154).

king's army at the beginning of the thirteenth century amounted to some 436 knights. If the king was fortunate and his summons heeded, this small number could be increased to as many as 12,000 men, counting feudal levies and peasant infantry. By the end of the Hundred Years War, as shown in table 3.2, this number had more than quadrupled to some 50,000. The initial expansion of the French army was thus tied into the process of state centralization and expansion, and it continued to be tied into this state-making process.

The expansion of the state was a critical factor in fueling the growth of the French army. It could be argued in some respects that the state expanded because the number of army personnel grew. Yet it is much easier to defend the assertion that the army grew because the expanding state needed more troops to hold on to acquired territory and to obtain more. Some amount of state expansion also made army growth more feasible. Contamine (1984), for instance, suggests that large armies could be assembled in the Middle Ages. But nascent states, such as France, simply lacked the financial and administrative means to keep large forces in the field for more than a few weeks at a time. Hence, French state building, army expansion, and rising governmental expenses are inextricably intertwined. The interconnections established between the eleventh and fifteenth centuries continued in subsequent centuries, when the expansion of France continued beyond the boundaries we customarily think of as delineating France.

Indeed, a case can be made for the momentum of expansion itself being a prime force in this unfolding sequence of war and state making. In both the Spanish and French cases, it could be said with some exaggeration that the national boundaries had been forcibly aligned with the state boundaries toward the end of the fifteenth century. Spain controlled the non-Portuguese part of the Iberian peninsula by 1492. A map of the French royal domain at approximately the same time would finally begin to resemble the shape of contemporary France. Both conditions were the culmination of roughly 500 years of subordinating and evicting the local opposition. Is it likely that the momentum of this state-making process could have been stopped by satiated state makers (assuming that we could identify satiated state makers)? Whether there were any satiated state makers is, of course, doubtful. The point remains that the safest expectation is that the process of territorially expanding the state would continue until or unless the resistance became too great.

Because France and Spain came to blows in Italy almost immediately after filling out what we think of as their retrospectively conventional nation-state shapes, there is a tendency to disconnect the many years of internal state centralization and expansion that preceded 1494–95 from the external Italian wars that followed. Yet, in some respects, the Italian wars were merely a continuation of the Iberian *reconquista* and French royal centralization processes. Both sides were asserting dynastic claims. Both sides had a medieval history of clashing over the control of Italian territory. So, even though some things began to change in Europe after 1494, it would be a mistake to assume that all things had begun to change.

The pre-1500 state-making activities of Spain and France were like rolling stones developing momentum, organizational capabilities, and military firepower. There is little risk of determinism in suggesting that these rolling stones were highly likely to collide somewhere—if not in Italy, then over control of Navarre, Catalonia, or even southern France. The probability was high because successful expansion tends to continue until blocked by a stronger force.[4] The European expansion of Spain and France had not been blocked successfully before 1494–95.

Without becoming bogged down in imagining the many twists and turns that French and Spanish boundaries might have taken, the theoretical point remains that global power warfare at the end of the fifteenth and the beginning of the sixteenth century can be viewed as a direct extension of global power state-making activities. An expansionary momentum had been generated that was very difficult to divert, even with the discovery of a new world. The alternative to continued territorial expansion was not particularly attractive to state makers. A centrifugal pattern of internal warfare had been established in both Spain and France when the expansionary momentum was either relaxed or rebuffed. Succession disputes competed with separatist tendencies that were a consequence of the patchwork and forced amalgamation that the states of Spain and France represented.

The expansion of military forces made their continued employment more important as well. Describing the French situation after 1559, McNeill observes,

> The fact that employment in Italy had come to an end for French fighting men also had something to do with the repeated outbreaks of domestic disorder, since unemployed and restless soldiers could be counted on to respond eagerly to any occasion for the exercise of their profession. (1982: 124)

It is not necessary to accept the unqualified equation of external threat and internal cohesion to appreciate the movement back and forth between bouts of internal and external warfare in the formative history of Spain and France (see tables 2.4 and 3.1). Internal and external warfare could certainly overlap. External foes looked for and frequently found internal allies, and vice versa. Still, this pattern overlapped with the second, alternating pattern. A lull in the late medieval expansionary drive invited and encouraged internal discontent on the part of underemployed and dissatisfied nobles. Intensive bouts of internal warfare, of course, may have encouraged external attacks, but the toll of such bouts on available resources made it more difficult to take on new external opponents eagerly until after some period of recuperation.

Similarly, as long as an intensive bout of external warfare was going reasonably well or at least continued to possess good prospects, the potential for a rewarding division of the spoils of war helped to discourage elite discontent. As a consequence, the momentum of territorial expansion was conducive for leadership tenure and, therefore, a force that needed to be cultivated continually by prudent rulers, especially French and Spanish kings.

After several hundred years of it, territorial expansion had become a way of political-economic life.

One more geopolitical-economic feature deserves some mention at this point, even though the general topic is raised again in chapter 6. The European central corridor's commercial wealth was an attractive and seductive prize for the predominately agrarian, politico-military states in western Europe. At later points, the Atlantic-oriented sea powers successively supplanted the Italian city-states led by Venice, the southern end of the city belt, as the dynamic center of the Eurocentric world economy; therefore, they became attractive and seductive prizes in their own right. Is it possible to link the strategies of global powers, such as Spain and France, to this fundamental geopolitical-economic split between states that were centers of economic dynamism and states that were not? The answer is yes, for we have been doing it throughout this chapter. But one more step can be taken.

A curious pattern developed in the system's early global wars that links geopolitical-economic position to the onset of these systemic wars. As usual, Braudel's evocative imagery captures part of this pattern nicely.

> At the same time, these states [west European monarchies] had before their eyes the successes of the merchant states better placed than they at the crossroads of trade; they were aware of what amounted to their inferior position, so that their chief preoccupation was to join the superior category at all costs, to move into the centre. One method was to copy the model and to appropriate the recipe for success—England's idee fixe in her competition with Holland. Another was to create and mobilize the resources and revenues required for foreign wars and for conspicuous luxury which was after all one way of governing. It seems to be the case that every state anywhere near the centre of a world economy became more quarrelsome, going out to make conquests as if the proximity excited its bile. (Braudel 1984: 53)

Later in the same rich volume, Braudel provides a strong hint of the rest of the pattern we have in mind. Discussing whether French leaders were aware that the "headquarters of the European world-economy" was moving to and from such places as Venice, Antwerp, and Amsterdam but always remaining outside French borders, Braudel noted that

> [France] tried—unsuccessfully—to gain a foothold in Italy in 1494; but in any case, between 1494 and 1559, the magic circle of Italy forfeited its leadership of the European world-economy. The attempt was repeated, again without success, a century later in the Netherlands. But it is more than likely that even if the Dutch wars had ended in 1672 with a French victory—which was certainly a possibility—the centre of the European world-economy would have been transferred straight from Amsterdam to London—not to Paris. It was firmly established in London when the French armies eventually occupied the United Provinces in 1795. (1984: 324)

To Braudel's list we can add Spain's interest in Italy in the 1490s and its later conquest of Portugal in 1580. The catch-up pattern that emerges is one of repeated attempts on the part of the western continental land powers to seize the centers of economic and trading activity. They did so, in part, to compensate for their own lack of a genuine competitive capability and, in part, to "move to the top of the table" (to borrow another Braudelian phrase).

Their attempts to capture the center of the world economy in the traditional way, that is, by force and territorial expansion, were doomed not only in terms of style—the successful economic centers were successful partly because they avoided territorial expansion at least in Europe—but also because the timing of the attempted seizures was always out of synch with economic realities. These Spanish and French efforts to obtain a quick economic fix were invariably too late to accomplish the intended goal. By the time their troops arrived, the economic dynamism of the target had been dissipated or was in the process of moving on to a new active zone—a process, one might add, that was only hastened by the attacks of the continental powers.

This pattern of political-economic tardiness provides some explanation as to why France and Spain fought in Italy in the late fifteenth and early sixteenth centuries. It also tells us something about why Spain waited until the late sixteenth century to complete its dominance of the Iberian peninsula. The French moved against the Dutch in the last third of the seventeenth century, and to a much lesser extent, the eventual French subordination of the Dutch in the late eighteenth century also fit the pattern.

Other things were occurring at the same time, and this pattern is by no means the best single explanation of pre-Napoleonic global warfare; it is a piece of the puzzle. Even so, this catch-up pattern does seem to fit the iterative record of global warfare quite well between 1494 and the 1790s. The bad timing also says something about why France and Spain ultimately lost to the maritime powers.

However, the pattern of attempts to seize the system's economic center and thereby to catch up quickly was not a perpetual one. Although it could always reemerge in the future, Napoleon's aptly named Continental System, which attempted to close Europe to British economic competition, marked a tactical shift to a new, dominant, global power pattern of playing catch up with the system's economic leader.[5] As a response to the increased significance of industrialization and the commanding industrial edge of the system leader after the Napoleonic Wars, a new, more sophisticated politico-economic strategy emerged. The principal line of attack (and defense) became one of organizing a region, typically by force and intimidation, around a challenger vying to catch up with the system's established economic leader and its allies. Excluding the leader's goods from the region would help to protect and enhance the competitive position of the challenger within the region and, by eliminating an important market, weaken the established leader at the same time. The strategy was really one of erecting protectionist barriers on a regional as opposed to the more conventional national scale.

France attempted to do this at the beginning of the nineteenth century. The creation of the German state in the mid-nineteenth century owes a great deal to this type of strategic thinking. Around the same time period, Japan was forced out of a relatively successful isolationist stance by pressure from the British and Americans. In self-defense, a long period of catch up ensued that, eventually, was to lead to the idea of a Greater Co-Prosperity Sphere in East Asia. Earlier in the twentieth century, Soviet decision makers had determined that the only way to catch up with the other global powers was to remove themselves as much as possible from the capitalist world economy. One global war later, the Soviets were in a position to remove a good portion of the East European region from the capitalist system as well. Not coincidentally, much of this same territory had figured prominently in pre–World War II German plans to organize its own regional economic bloc for *lebensraum* and, of course, to improve its own competitive position.[6]

Hence, the global power catch-up pattern has changed with time. But catching up continues to be an important motivation for national policies and strategies. As a consequence, the global power process of catching up plays an important explanatory role in accounting for the specific nature and timing of state-making and war-making activities.

## Why Spain and France Were Different from Portugal, England, and the Netherlands

Many attributes and characteristics could be used to differentiate the west European major powers. How one chooses among the available factors depends, in part, on what one is trying to explain. Our selective analysis of the Spanish (chapter 2) and French cases has highlighted several factors that we consider important in explaining key geopolitical-economic and related state-making differences among the five global powers. Figure 3.1 summarizes these factors and their many interconnections.

At the core of our model are the interrelated factors of size and the structural heterogeneity of states built piece by piece. Large territorial size and a quilted assemblage of multiple, poorly integrated subunits (provinces, counties, cities, duchies, states, kingdoms) are the roots of Spanish and French behavior from the sixteenth through the eighteenth century. Given the heterogeneity of the areas in question, the only sure way to avoid the mosaic problem was to remain small. However, in an age of ambitious state-making entrepreneurs and imperial expansion, staying small and retaining some

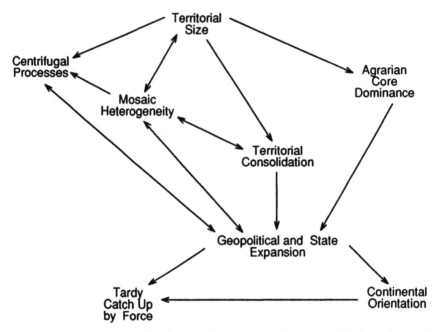

**Figure 3.1.** The Geopolitical Economy of Preindustrial Continental Orientations and State Making

semblance of autonomy proved to be difficult goals to achieve in Europe's western zone. Ironically, this emphasis on escalating size was the reverse of what was taking place in the central city belt stretching from the Netherlands to northern Italy.

A large size and a mosaic structure implied the increased probability and strength of centrifugal political processes. Elites in malintegrated subunits perceived various incentives to break away from the unwelcome policies of the larger political system in which they were peripherally embedded. Burdensome taxes to finance distant and unappealing imperial wars were one major grievance. Insufficient protection when some of the consequences of those imperial wars came closer to home was another. Defeat and frustration in the imperial undertakings also encouraged challenges over who should rule. So too, perversely, did the absence of imperial undertakings.

Gross size also implied, as it turned out, an increased probability that the economic foundation of the state would be characterized by a bulky agrarian core that was likely to use traditional methods, that represented a large number of localized and poorly articulated economic subunits, and that proved extremely difficult to mobilize or to tax. Long-distance commerce and industry were peripheral to this interior mass geographically and politically. More commercially oriented elites might have opportunities to reverse these priorities but only for brief periods. More typical are the multiple economic personalities attributable to both Spain and France, with coastal and interior forces pulling against one another and different points of the compass pushing along entirely different market trajectories.

The centrifugal threat, the dominance of a traditional agrarian infra-structure, and the mosaic territorial structure with its accompanying multiple frontier possibilities combined to provide the need for coercive territorial consolidation. The nature of this process, in turn, geared the triumphant state to further expansion, as long as the resistance was not too strong. Geographical expansion in the late fifteenth century meant continuing a momentum that had been building over the preceding three to four centuries.

The administrative expansion of the state was difficult to avoid. To carry out territorial consolidation successfully, kings needed larger and more permanent armies than before. These armies had to be paid. More tax collectors were needed to extract the necessary resources from the population. Tilly's classic formulation neatly summarizes this process.

> The formation of standing armies provided the largest single incentive to extraction and the largest single means of state coercion over the long run of European state-making. Recurrently we find a chain of causation running from (1) change or expansion in land armies to (2) new efforts to extract resources from the subject population to (3) the development of new bureaucracies and administrative innovations to (4) resistance from the subject population to (5) renewed coercion to (6) durable increases in the bulk and extractiveness of the state. (1975: 73)

In the process, Spain and France developed their strong continental inclinations. State makers in both countries were aware and appreciative of the advantages associated with the development of maritime commerce and naval power. Repeated efforts were made to improve Spanish and French capabilities for exercising sea power. Short-term improvements were achieved. Spain assembled huge fleets for the attempted attacks on England in the 1580s and 1590s. The French, under Cardinal Richelieu, created the beginnings of a competitive navy literally overnight and nearly from scratch. Richelieu's navy was allowed to deteriorate. Yet less than half a century later, Colbert had recreated the French navy and built it into the largest navy of the European global powers.

The problem was that these efforts were always intermittent, never sustained. The commerce–sea power advocates could never hold the levers of power long enough to bring about a permanent change in attitudes. Nor could they overcome the long-standing propensities for pursuing continental commitments. The limitations of the resource bases involved—and these were similar though not exactly the same for Spain and France—made it impossible to pursue continental and maritime interests simultaneously for very long. Some of the financial implications of these resource limitations are discussed in the next chapter.

For present purposes, however, the links between finite resource bases and choices to be made between continental and maritime pursuits are what Graham meant by his geopolitical reference to conflicts of interest. Forced to choose between emphasizing sea or land power at any given moment, it was only too easy for those states with multiple continental commitments to favor putting the lion's share of resources into their land forces. This propensity had been acquired in the era of territorial consolidation. It was a habit reinforced by political economies that tended to peripheralize maritime-commercial economic activities. This choice was also where their consequent comparative military advantage seemed to lie after years of the territorial consolidation process. Finally, once created, navies and ports are easier to abandon, or at least neglect, than are large armies and multiple land frontiers. If there really was a choice to be made, the geopolitical-economic odds were against Spain's and France's acquiring full-fledged maritime-commercial orientations.

## The Maritime Powers

The case so far has been made almost exclusively in reference to Spain and France. Is our argument so powerful and appealing that we can ignore examining the global powers with contrasting orientations? No matter how compelling readers may find the argument, it can never be anything more than an interpretation. We can never prove conclusively that some states developed maritime orientations and others did not because of factors $X$, $Y$, or $Z$. We can only try to make our argument as persuasive as possible. For some readers, understandably, this means that we should spend as much time on the Portuguese, English, and Dutch as we have spent on the Spanish and French. Yet consideration of space and the emphases of this study suggest a different tactic.

We do not need to demonstrate that Portugal, the Netherlands, and Britain were commercially minded sea powers; the statement is hardly controversial. In succession and for finite intervals of time, these three states were the system's leaders in commerce and sea power between the sixteenth and nineteenth centuries (see Modelski and Thompson 1988). However, if we contend that the geopolitical-economic roots of the problem concern territorial size, the territorial consolidation process, and the nature and position of the economic base, then we must at least show how or to what extent these factors were different in the Portuguese, Dutch, and English cases from the Spanish and French cases.

The more conventional approach to discussing the development of the maritime powers would emphasize their possession of the attributes regarded as crucial for sea power. In his discussion of the elements underlying the development of sea power, for example, Mahan (1890: 25–89) included the ease of access to the sea, the length of coastline, the quality of harbors, and the size of the population involved in sea-related activities. Yet all five of the global powers discussed in this and the preceding chapter possessed Atlantic coastlines, good harbors, fishermen and ship builders, and access to the sea. Although one could argue about who had more or better harbors or ship builders, the presence of these types of attributes in all five cases has encouraged us to pursue less orthodox explanations for the divergence between continental and maritime orientations.[7]

Table 3.3 demonstrates the disparities in population among the five initial global powers. In both population and area, the home bases of Spain and France dwarfed those of Portugal, the Netherlands, and Britain. Based on these conventional attributes of power alone, it would be extremely difficult to predict that the two continental giants ultimately would lose to the three smaller states. Yet smallness proved to be an important advantage in the preindustrial era.

**Table 3.3**
**Population in Western Europe**

| State | 1400 | 1500 | 1600 | 1700 | 1800 | 1900 |
|---|---|---|---|---|---|---|
| England/Wales | 2.50 | 3.75 | 4.25 | 5.75 | 9.25 | 33.00 |
| British Isles | 3.50 | 5.00 | 6.25 | 9.25 | 16.00 | 42.00 |
| Spain | 5.50 | 6.50 | 8.50 | 8.00 | 11.50 | 18.50 |
| Portugal | 0.90 | 1.25 | 2.00 | 2.00 | 2.75 | 5.00 |
| France | 11.00 | 15.00 | 20.50 | 22.00 | 29.00 | 41.00 |
| Netherlands | 0.60 | 0.90 | 1.50 | 2.00 | 3.25 | 7.00 |

*Source:* based on information in McEvedy and Jones (1978).

One advantage of smallness is that the lack of economic cohesion—the multiple economies and economic personalities so characteristic of Spain and France—is less probable when the territorial size of the economy is relatively modest. A lack of economic cohesion and integration is not ruled out; it is simply less likely when interior distances are limited. Cohesion was further benefitted in each of the three cases by the availability and development of interior waterways to better connect the national economy. Portugal had the navigable rivers that Castile lacked. The Dutch built their canals and dikes and enjoyed excellent access to the main rivers of the European middle corridor. The English possessed a 700-mile interior network of navigable water routes that was complemented by the external coastal route.

It might also be argued that small size facilitates—even though it certainly does not guarantee—the development of dominant economic centers. In each of the three maritime powers, one city (Lisbon, Amsterdam, London) dominated in economic and cultural activity, population size, access to the sea and quantity of port traffic, and its proximity to the center of government. Lisbon and London were also longtime nodes in the maritime network linking Italy and the Mediterranean to northern Europe. Amsterdam supplanted the central role once played by Antwerp in this western transportation system that had been revived in the late thirteenth century as an alternative to the land routes between Italy and Flanders. Thus, even though the general economies of Portugal and England were inherently agrarian in nature, there was also extensive experience in the long-distance trade networks of Europe—an activity in which the Dutch port cities had long specialized.

If trade was not as central initially to the Portuguese and English economies as it became in the Netherlands area, at least it was not a peripheral activity. Diffie may be exaggerating the Portuguese case somewhat, but his basic point seems valid.

> Seldom in history has a landed nobility been so closely associated with the marketing of the produce of its holdings. Seldom have kings been so concerned with commerce and processing of the country's crops. (1960: 61)

One reason for this development, beyond Portuguese impoverishment, was that the best markets for its products (cork, wine, olives, fish) were not in nearby Castile but in northern Europe. Davis (1973: 3) notes that Portugal's location made it northern Europe's closest supplier of Mediterranean produce. By the mid-fourteenth century, export-oriented cultivation had taken over land once used to grow basic foodstuffs, to the extent that corn had to be imported regularly from Morocco.

Along somewhat similar lines, the marketing of English wool had long been concentrated on Bruges and later Antwerp as the leading centers of textile manufacturing and trade entrepots. However, the nature of English trade dependency was substantially altered by developments in war financing and domestic politics during the Hundred Years War. As the principal export, the wool crop was an extremely attractive source of money for English kings seeking quick financing for military emergencies and expeditions. In this respect, the English crown differed little from the heads of Castile/Spain. Wool exports were taxed directly, but the crop and the taxes anticipated from it, or some proportion of it, could also be used as collateral for loans or as a commodity that the crown might acquire and sell abroad, unlike the Spanish custom, to directly enhance the royal treasury.[8]

In the early fourteenth century, Edward III defaulted on Italian loans linked to future wool taxes. Faced with severe liquidity problems, the Italian financiers were forced to withdraw from the English market. They were replaced in the 1340s as a source of war loans by an informal group of English wool traders and financiers who were granted a near monopoly over English wool exports. A second royal default eliminated this group as well, but they were replaced in turn by the English Company of the Staple. Over the decade of the 1350s, this institutionalized group expanded its Parliamentary-granted control over wool exports to approximate a near monopoly. It also became the main source for crown war loans.

The early increase in English control over their own wool trade, and the political significance of wool merchants to the royal crown

> was thus a product of political and fiscal causes. It was not a manifestation of English trade 'come of age,' still less a stage in the economic growth of English trade and economy. It was brought about by successive acts of royal policy and as a result of a bargain between the King and merchants. (Postan 1987: 293)

It was also very much a product of war and the difficulties associated with war financing. Discussing the greater political strength of English trading interests, as opposed to their counterparts in France, Wallerstein (1974: 182–83) suggests that trade policies were much more open in France in the late Middle Ages and that, by the sixteenth century, France had acquired fewer "powers of economic direction" than had England. Fourteenth-century developments in the wool trade provide one illustration. Another indicator of England's economic direction and bias toward trading interests were the early protectionist restrictions placed on the English activities of Italian and Hanseatic merchants in the mid-sixteenth century.

Another way in which smallness was an asset had to do with the natures of the territorial consolidation processes experienced by the three maritime states. As one of Rokkan's two defensive confederations of adjacent towns, the United Provinces of the Netherlands virtually skipped the process of territorial consolidation, as experienced in Spain and France, en route to becoming a global power. Its initial and principal territorial problem was holding on to what little European territory it had against Spanish and then French threats and attacks.

Portugal's consolidation process, on the other hand, was more traditional and, not too surprisingly, shared some of the characteristics of the Castilian model. But it was circumscribed by the Atlantic on one side and usually stronger Castile on the other. As described earlier, it was also completed fairly quickly, that is, in roughly a century of more or less continuous expansion southward against Muslim opposition. Equally important, the process of territorial consolidation, although fairly piecemeal in approach, managed to avoid the patchwork or mosaic characteristics of the French and Spanish processes.

The nonmosaic nature of the consolidation process was due basically to an expansion of Christian northern Portugal into Muslim southern Portugal. Many members of the Muslim elite fled to Iberian territory that remained Muslim and, in the process, removed one potential source of internal threat. The Portuguese crown, one of the two principal land owners in the north (the other being the Church), also maintained substantial control over the newly conquered southern territories. Urban centers were kept under crown ownership; rural estates were granted as forms of royal patronage, not so much to individual nobles but primarily to military brotherhoods (Oliveira Marques 1976). Centrally located Lisbon soon became the principal governmental site for a country characterized initially by a pronounced north-south division.

By avoiding the problem of territorial heterogeneity, Portugal also managed to minimize the standing army problem. In some respects, however, Portugal was fortunate in being able to obtain external military assistance on opportune occasions—whether it was Crusader assistance in capturing Lisbon in the twelfth century or the English armies used against Castile in the fourteenth century.

Of the three maritime states, England experienced the most traditional territorial consolidation process. Although it was a fairly conventional process of forcibly centralizing and subordinating various subunits and local rivals to a single center, two features of the English process made it unique among the global powers.

First, the territorial consolidation of the England we know today was accomplished long before the not-coincidentally brief (seven-month) Norman Conquest of 1066. The Saxon kings had completed much of the consolidation process by the middle of the tenth century. Finer (1975: 113) advances the specific date of 985—nearly a century before the arrival of the Normans. When the Normans did arrive, as Strayer points out, they were careful not to reverse what earlier efforts had already achieved.

> Moreover, a long series of conquests had prevented the rise of strong provincial rulers or the development of deeply entrenched provincial institutions. Danish invasions wiped out all the old Anglo-Saxon dynasties except the House of Wessex. The slow reconquest of central and northern England by the Kings of Wessex in its turn wiped out the Danish ruling families. Each regime preserved its own customs but there was no king of Kent, of Mercia, or of the Danelaw to build enduring institutions on the basis of these differing customs.... And when as a result of the second Danish conquest of the eleventh century, certain great families began to take root in some shires, they were soon uprooted by William

the Conqueror. . . . And most of his followers received not compact territorial units, but widely scattered grants of manors and rights of government. By 1100 it was clear that no earl or baron had a sufficient concentration of land or power to create an autonomous provincial administration. If England was going to have permanent institutions they would be royal institutions. (1970: 36–37)

Thus, what we now know as England was consolidated comparatively early. Yet, half of France was once English territory, and much of the French territorial consolidation process involved English resistance. Should the Anglo-French wars of the late Middle Ages count as part of the English consolidation process as well? The answer, a qualified yes, leads to the second special feature of the English territorial consolidation record.

The English wars fought almost entirely in France were just that—wars fought in France. Troops had to be raised, fed, transported, and paid. Taxes had to be increased. Still, the number of troops was not that great (see table 3.2), and, when unemployed, they did not cause problems in England necessitating a standing army to police their excesses. For the most part, they were quickly disbanded in peacetime.

Most significantly, the English had lost almost all of their French territory by 1453. During the next 50 years, the English also lost their most proximate allies in France, Burgundy, and Brittany, as the French territorial consolidation process neared completion. The growing size of continental armies and the resources available to France and Spain further discouraged a return to the European mainland. As Wernham (1966: 13) suggests, the English were forced by developments into accepting their island status: "Lack of men and lack of money, and the growth of two great military powers in western Europe, thus forced the Tudors into policies more insular and more defensive than those of their . . . predecessors."

Wernham's "more insular and more defensive" orientation took time to develop. Nor were these attitudes eagerly embraced. At least a century past the 1453 benchmark was needed before English rulers finally began to accept their reduced territorial size and a location physically separated from the European continent. In the interim, the English were saved from the problem Braudel termed the "dangers of gigantism" by the intimidating strengths of Spain and France, their mutual preoccupation with each other, and the relative poverty of England. English decision makers thus were encouraged by geopolitical-economic circumstances into accepting begrudgingly their relatively unique (by European standards) island status.

### The Issue of Domestic Political Conflict

These changes in external attitudes were paralleled and reinforced by structural changes in England's internal sociopolitical arrangements that have been the subject of so much study and controversy. Lachman's (1987) analysis is particularly helpful in this regard. Although Lachman ignores the realm of external geopolitics for the most part, he describes the unfolding of domestic developments from the thirteenth through the mid-seventeenth century in a way that is compatible with our contextual emphases.

Lachman's primary interest concerns the perennial question of why England made the transition from feudalism to capitalism so much earlier than its continental rivals. His answer, although too complicated to repeat in full, centers on the outcomes of several centuries of English elite conflict. Lachman first focuses on a tripartite national elite and a more complex local elite, all analyzed in terms of their control of land. At the national level, Henry VIII needed to expand his resource base so that he would be less financially dependent on Parliamentary grants and more able to wage war in Europe. To achieve these goals, he subordinated one of the three national elite components, the clergy, by breaking with the Pope and seizing clerical landholdings in the 1530s. Yet the pressure of war expenses in the 1540s (two million pounds with only one million in income according to Goldstone 1988: 117), the need to suppress potential rivals at home, and the virtual absence of a royal bureaucracy to administer the seized holdings contributed to a state-making process that departed significantly from continental patterns.

War expenses consumed a sizable proportion of the newly expanded royal resource base, as Anderson (1974: 124–25) stresses. The noble magnates, the second component in the national elite (the crown was the third element), were successfully subordinated to royal authority in the sixteenth century through force, intimidation, and, most important, the court-centered dispensation of royal patronage, but more of the crown's wealth base was consumed. London merchants, representing the principal source of locally available capital, forced the king to sell even more of the former clerical property instead of providing loans to cover the extraordinary expenses of war making in the early seventeenth century. These outflows discouraged the expansion of a state bureaucracy and increased royal dependence for administration on the local gentry, from whose ranks local officials were appointed.

> The English crown had alienated most of its lands, its rights to landed income, and its ability to regulate land use in order to eliminate or incorporate all potential national rivals. The system of court patronage, while making it impossible for claimants to the throne to build the coalitions needed to challenge a sitting monarch, exhausted crown revenues and assets, retarding the bureaucratic development central to absolutist power. Because the crown could not tap agrarian resources directly, landlords were able to collectively veto, by withholding resources [through Parliament and in terms of local tax assessment

and collection efforts], royal initiatives on the international and national levels. (Lachman 1987: 99)

As Lachman contends, the English outcome constitutes a major qualification on the argument that the need for resources to pay for escalating military expenditures led to bureaucratic growth, the expansion of the state, and royal absolutism. In the English case, however one evaluates the increase in military capability for external war, the process of acquiring the capability did not enhance the domestic political position of English royalty. Instead, royalty became more dependent on national and local elites who directly controlled the resources needed for state operations in the external arena. One primary manifestation of this royal dependency was the gradual institutionalization of Parliament as a mediating instrument for the political extraction of resources.

Our geopolitical-economic model, displayed earlier in figure 3.2, does not incorporate a specific elite conflict dynamic, such as the English one developed by Lachman, because there is substantial national variation in these dynamics. The English process clearly departed from the Spanish and French patterns. Nor was it the same as the Portuguese and Dutch patterns.

The balance of power between the Portuguese nobility and the crown fluctuated throughout the pre-1580 period in which we are interested. The flux in power relationships continued in spite of the 1383–85 revolution that pitted the landed nobility against a broad coalition of forces supported by the urban middle class and lower-ranking aristocrats. The broader coalition won and inaugurated a new dynasty that, a generation later, produced Henry the Navigator. The revolution also created a new landed nobility that replaced the losers of the civil war. Most commentators on Portuguese developments during this period attribute some portion of the expansionary impulses of the fifteenth century to the demands of a nobility created, to some extent, only a few years before but still subject to the conventional aristocratic needs for money and glory.

In the Dutch case, a monarchy was established only after the sixteenth- to seventeenth-century period on which this chapter focuses. A centralizing process was both aided and discouraged by the loose union established by the seven northern Netherlands provinces in 1579. The United Provinces were clearly dominated by the strongest of the seven, Amsterdam. But because Amsterdam's commercial interests would not be best served by surrendering central political authority to a Prince of Orange, a principal axis of internal political conflict developed involving the defense of provincial autonomy (and the hegemony of Amsterdam) versus the centralizing attempts of the aristocratic *Stadtholder* (see Rowen 1988). As a matter of course, the unusually decentralized nature of the United Provinces marks it as something of a political maverick among the early global powers.

### The Influence of Context

This variation in the maritime powers' domestic political structures and processes serves to make our point about the influence of context. The struggles between crown and gentry in England, crown and nobility in Portugal, and merchant oligarchs and the House of Orange in the United Provinces did not lead directly to the ascension of maritime-commercial orientations in these states. The contribution of these political conflicts was primarily indirect and both positive and negative in effect. In the end, the Portuguese attempted to mix maritime commerce in the Indian Ocean with old-fashioned territorial expansion in Morocco and lost their autonomy in the process. In the Dutch case, the development of a strong maritime-commercial orientation preceded the political battles over whether and how to centralize the government of the United Provinces.

The outcome of elite conflict in England prior to the mid-seventeenth century produced a comparatively weak monarchy that was handicapped in what goals it might pursue in Europe or at home. It was even overthrown for a number of years due to the civil wars of the 1640s. In time, the international aspect of the royal handicaps proved to be an asset for the development of a maritime-commercial orientation. English foreign policy was subjected to important domestic restraints in an era (roughly 1450–1650) when it could ill afford to be too persistent in its continuing interest in continental involvements. The domestic constraints meant fewer governmental bureaucrats and regulations, less in the way of taxes than might have been the case, and a very small standing army.

These factors did not produce a predominant maritime-commercial orientation, any more than did England's small size or the absence of a recent militarized territorial consolidation history. Rather, they were background factors conducive to the gradual transition (see Wilson 1965) from an initially agrarian economy, with too great a dependence on wool exports, to the world's leading maritime-commercial power and its first industrial power.

> It was England's good fortune, therefore, that it could rarely be governed according to the whim of the crown supported by a narrow group of nobles and officials propped up by an army . . . the crown . . . had to tread carefully or it would encounter dangers. This made for weak government when the crown and its leading subjects could not reconcile their differences . . . but it provided very long periods of government that was stable and to some degree attuned to the prevalent opinion of the well-to-do, particularly on economic and social

questions that did not involve matters of high principle. . . . Finally, the financial check held back the crown from costly expenditure in wartime. . . .

English government was cheap in peacetime, and even in war, down to the 1690s. . . . England was fortunate, therefore, in its form of government; the vaunted efficiencies of absolutism passed it by, to its advantage in these centuries and in the longer run. On the whole, its people were able to pursue their occupations without political interruptions; and this was perhaps the most basic of the advantages England had on its economic development over the sixteenth and seventeenth centuries. (Davis 1973: 210–11)

Geopolitical-economic context did not determine outcomes. Certain features of the geopolitical-economic environment, however, did facilitate the occurrence of some outcomes, just as they discouraged the occurrence of others. Size, the strengths and weaknesses of the home economic base, and the nature of the territorial consolidation process made certain state-making practices, such as expanded and expanding bureaucracies, tax burdens, armies, and, in general, states, more or less likely in a system characterized by the frequent recourse to external and internal warfare.

Precisely how these processes were played out within each state by the elite actors who had to interpret their environmental contexts and respond to their positive and negative cues was highly contingent on local circumstances. The specific processes of elite conflict and coalition building, therefore, are difficult to model in the generic sense, and for the most part (chapter 7 is a partial exception), we leave their modeling to other analysts—specialists and generalists alike—at least for now. To pursue this particular avenue in the present study would detract from our longer-standing and, in some respects, more modest interest in assessing some of the impacts of war on certain global power state-making processes, such as resource extraction and expenditure (chapters 4 through 6).

However, one way to summarize our interpretation of how these contextual factors interacted to influence war and state making differentially in Europe's western zone is to suggest that two types of global power states emerged in the sixteenth and seventeenth centuries. Spain and France represented one type; Portugal, the United Provinces of the Netherlands, and England the other.

The Spanish and French states emerged, we have argued, partially as a consequence of where they were located. A related factor was the great need for long-term coerciveness in pulling and keeping together heterogenous political subunits within the large-sized territories that resulted. Also critical were the inherent weaknesses of the consequently malintegrated political economies that provided the wherewithal to operate in the international arena. Yet because they became the type of state that they did, Spain and France proved to be militarily powerful on land, much less powerful at sea, and not very competitive in the world economy. The French and Spanish type of state was not a conducive setting for cultivating maritime-commercial instincts, activities, and strategies. To compensate, they tried to catch up with the more dynamic centers of economic activity by brute force but were invariably too late to achieve what they sought.

We have also suggested that the form assumed by the maritime powers was due at least in part to their ability to avoid many factors that shaped Spain and France. They possessed different locational advantages. They shared the absence of a recent or lengthy phase of coercive territorial consolidation. Moreover, their small size, locational advantages, and comparatively weak states (at the domestic level, at least) interacted, minimally, to permit and, more maximally, to encourage the rise of a maritime-commercial outlook as the predominant orientation of the state's elite and decision makers.

As a consequence, the maritime powers were not always militarily powerful on land. The Dutch proved something of a seventeenth-century exception. Their land frontiers may have left them little choice, but they were also in a position to pay their troops regularly enough to be able to drill them in relatively new tactical formations.

> The armies of the United Provinces were exceptional for the very simple reason that they were regularly supplied and paid. If one could pay one's troops throughout the year, instead of hiring and firing them as occasion demanded, one could discipline them, train them, drill them, turn them in short into *professionals*. But this required ample and continuous supplies of money. Money in the necessary quantities could come only from trade. (Howard 1976: 37)

The maritime powers were quite strong at sea. Each in historical turn exercised the most powerful oceanic capability in the world system. The predominance of maritime-commercial elites and attitudes greatly enhanced the probability that these states would become the world economy's center of economic activity, again each in its turn and with successively greater influence over the functioning of the world economy. That they were not strong states in the continental tradition facilitated these outcomes. At the same time, the Dutch and the English ended up defeating the states usually credited with great strength by being able to mobilize and apply their resources more effectively. We are thus left wondering which states genuinely deserve the appellation of strong state.

### The Other Global Powers

Finally, let us continue this line of inquiry to encompass the more recent successors to the first five global powers discussed in the last two chapters. Can we apply our geopolitical-economic model to Germany, Japan, the United States, and the Soviet Union? The answer is mixed.

Some elements of the model certainly seem to fit. The territorial holdings of Brandenburg-Prussia were not initially adjacent to one another. The extraordinary emphasis placed on the development of the Prussian army had its roots in this geopolitical factor and the consequent need for force to hold the territories together. Much later, force and war were considered necessary to unify the German state in the nineteenth century.

The Soviet Union's immense size was not foreordained. Rather, it stemmed from centuries of imperial expansion, beginning with the small Muscovy core, in a process similar to the Castilian and French experiences. Kochan and Abraham (1983:29) specifically note that the size of the thirteenth-century Muscovite Principality resembled the extent of Capetian territory at the beginning of the French centralization process. The same authors compare Ivan III (1462–1505) and France's Louis XI as creators of centralized states and note that sixteenth-century Russia and Spain "overcame feudal disunity and Islamic opponents at more or less the same time" (Kochan and Abraham 1983: 50–51).

Nor does it seem coincidental that the strong nature of the Russian/Soviet state developed in an expanding, poorly integrated, predominately agrarian economic setting in which commercial-maritime interests tended to be peripheral most of the time—Peter the Great notwithstanding. Both Kochan and Abraham (1983:50–51) and Wesson (1986:15) trace some of the distinctive and enduring elements of Russian politics to the nature of rapid expansion in the fifteenth and sixteenth centuries.

Pintner is even more directly relevant to our current emphases. Two of his generalizations stand out, particularly:

> The basic problem that has confronted all Russian rulers, at least until the late 1930s, has been how to maintain a large military establishment with the meager surplus above subsistence that could be produced by the poor and scattered peasantry. (1978: 362)

Recent attempts at restructuring reforms (*perestroika*) suggest that the "basic problem" did not quite disappear in the late 1930s.

Pintner's second observation is even more fundamental.

> The present situation in the USSR conforms to what has been the typical pattern throughout most of Russian history . . . the desire of the state to play the role of a major power in the world leads it to mobilize a very large portion of the national income for state purposes, and to do this a thorough-going system of bureaucratic penetration keeps control of the population. (1978: 380)

Combining Pintner's two generalizations, a less than desirable systemic position, the drive to catch up, and the relative absence of economic surplus have led to an unusually intensive type of state making. Although the results may be extreme, the general process leading to the nature of the Russian/Soviet state is not distinctively different from that of the other global powers.[9]

Japan also underwent an intensive bout of coercive centralization in the late sixteenth century and immediately thereafter attempted to expand into the Asian mainland. According to our argument, this is what England might have done in Europe if the Tudors had had to do what the kings of Wessex had accomplished centuries earlier. We would have to add the stipulation that the eleventh-century Normans would have had to suffer the same fate as the thirteenth-century Mongols, who failed in their efforts to reach the island of Japan. Presumably, if this scenario had come to pass, the English invasion of Europe would have been rebuffed, just as the Japanese were in Korea at the end of the sixteenth century. Whether the English would also have retreated to their island and been able to isolate themselves to the same extent as the Japanese were able to do for 250 years seems highly unlikely.

However, White (1988) raises an interesting issue related to this uniquely successful isolation. State growth took place in Tokugawa Japan (1600–1868) in the absence of war. That growth did not conform to the European style oriented to supporting a large military force with extensive extractive powers. Instead, the Tokugawa regime developed its increasingly centralized coercive and regulatory powers primarily to maintain domestic order. White concludes from this development:

> Indeed, perhaps the case of Japan indicates the overemphasis of war as a cause of state growth. Tokugawa Japan fought no wars and thus needed no massive standing army, a less penetrating administrative structure, a less extractive revenue agency, and less complete subordination of subnational actors, but still saw the emergence of an "absolute" state. (1988: 14)

Two aspects of this conclusion are worth emphasizing. First, as White implies, the absence of war did have some impact on the structure of the state that emerged in Japan. It may have had "absolute" characteristics in terms of its attempts to centralize and monopolize the state's coercive powers, which is what White has in mind when he uses the term. Still, he implies that it was not as intensive as the form of absolutism that developed in the more competitive environment of western Europe.

Second, White probably is correct in arguing that the significance of war to state building in general is exaggerated. Quite a few states have been created, and most of them are found outside of western Europe. Quite likely, a fair number owe much less to the impact of war than do the European global powers on which we have been concentrating. However, Tokugawa Japan was not a global power. By the time it had become one (after 1868), though, it was quickly re-acquainted with external warfare and the consequent impacts on state making.

McNeill (1982: 187) highlights another facet of this consideration of comparative geopolitical economy, war, and the relative uniqueness of Japan. In contrast to the almost instinctive urge to focus on the obvious links between sea power and island-dwelling populations, he emphasizes instead the number of islands in the Japanese chain. When a proximate group of islands are controlled by politico-military rivals, as was the case in Japan before the imposition of the Pax Tokugawa, "continental patterns of mobilization in which command plays a more prominent part and the market remains subordinate" are more likely to prevail. The impact of this root factor on explanations of why pre-1945 Japan pursued a fairly traditional strategy of territorial, continentally oriented expansion remains debatable. The implications, nonetheless, are most intriguing.

Another global power often considered to have developed under unique circumstances is the United States. The territorial consolidation of the large United States was certainly coercive. Yet the relatively weak resistance did not bring about a large standing army or a strong state. The multiple economic personalities of the American economy persist to this day, but the 1861–65 Civil War sealed the political-economic triumph of the northeastern commercial-maritime interests.[10] Roughly half a century later, the United States began to emerge as the next successor in the line of system leaders initiated more than 400 years earlier. So, we are not convinced that the U.S. case, if explored in more depth, would pose major problems for extending our model either.

Arguably, there are continuities we could exploit to continue the story into the contemporary period. There also are important discontinuities that would complicate our initial effort to account for a fundamental divergence in global power war and state making in the sixteenth and seventeenth centuries. Time is one of these intervening variables. The scattered territories of Brandenburg-Prussia did not lead immediately to the imperial German challenge of the late nineteenth and early twentieth centuries. Among other things, a Napoleonic shock via global war first had to intervene to galvanize the German states into a nineteenth-century restructuring (see Gillis 1978). Even though there are continuities, the trials and tribulations of fifteenth- and sixteenth-century Muscovy are considerably removed in some respects from the post-1917 environment of the Soviet Union.

Another intervening factor of great significance is the development and diffusion of industrial power. This development amounted to a third overlap in the sense of the phrase used by Graham and cited in chapter 2. Territorial power was first overlapped as an important politico-military consideration by commercial-maritime power. Both were later overlapped by industrial power. The name of the interstate competition game did not change much, but it did become more complicated. To compete and catch up with an industrializing

Britain after 1815, it was necessary to copy the same economic techniques. Before the 1815 divide, Spain and France (and Russia) may not actually have had any more freedom in choosing how to compete and catch up, but they at least thought and acted as if they did. After 1815, the impulse to catch up with the advanced industrialization of the system leader became overridingly predominant.

A third intervening consideration is that small size no longer appears to be as advantageous as it once was. The emergence of the two continental-sized states in Eurasia and North America has escalated the minimal territorial size and resource base needed to compete at the highest levels of systemic confrontation. The more recent development of nuclear weapons simply adds another nasty wrinkle with which we would have to deal in pursuing the continuities and discontinuities of the geopolitical-economic roots of global power war and state making.

## Conclusion

We have chosen to avoid these topics for now. Chapters 2 and 3 have served a minimal purpose in establishing the significance of distinguishing two fundamental types of global powers in pursuing the connection between war and state making. If we have provided a new, albeit hardly novel, and persuasive account of why this divergence came about when it did, so much the better. The following chapters track some of the consequences of this fundamental and persisting divergence in global power state orientations.

# 4
# *The Innovation of Public Debt*

In this chapter, we advance two generalizations. First, the earlier winners in the struggle for world leadership owed a significant proportion of their success to their ability to obtain credit inexpensively, to sustain relatively large debts, and generally to leverage the initially limited base of their wealth to meet their staggering military expenses. Conversely, the defeat or demise of the earlier losers, despite their possession of relatively extensive resource bases, can be traced partly to their failure to generate or maintain a sufficiently competitive financial capability. Second, the success of the winners of world power is double-edged. Winning leads to successively higher levels of permanent debt burdens, which stimulate attempts to reduce governmental operating expenses (as in retrenchment or austerity policies) after the conclusion of a global struggle for succession.

Winners are able to establish the rules of the global political system and the world economy by virtue of their victory and relative capability. But their ongoing and recently acquired financial burdens, as well as the type of geopolitical-economic system they represent, have required that this be done as inexpensively as possible. The result is a tendency toward world political leadership and management "on the cheap" in the immediate postwar era, just when the newly emerged world power occupies its strongest relative position in the global hierarchy.

## Public Debts in the Sixteenth through the Eighteenth Century

If war was an overriding concern of global power states in the sixteenth century, equally pressing problems were the challenges of generating and extracting sufficient resources to pay for the wars. When Louis XII asked what it would take to assure success in his plans to conquer Milan, the response was, "Most gracious King, three things are necessary: money, more money and still more money" (quoted in Ardant 1975: 164). The global powers were usually capable of covering most of their peacetime operating costs, but any extraordinary expense tended to provoke financial crises of varying seriousness. War expenses, while almost regular enough to be considered ordinary, naturally constituted the principal source of extraordinary costs. Table 4.1 provides some examples of war expenses.

*Table 4.1*
*A Sampling of War Expenses in the Sixteenth Century*

| Years | Wars | Average War Costs | Annual Revenues | War Costs as Percentage of Revenues |
|-------|------|-------------------|-----------------|--------------------------------------|
| 1482–92 | Spain vs. Granada | 80.000 | 150.000 | 0.533 |
| 1515 | France vs. Milan | 1.800 | 4.900 | 0.367 |
| 1523 | France (Italian mobilization and Scottish exped.) | 2.000 | 5.150 | 0.389 |
| 1544 | France vs. England and Charles V | 6.000 | 9.000 | 0.667 |
|  | England vs. France | 0.650 | 0.250 | 2.600 |
| 1554 | France vs. Charles V | 13.275 | 11.000 | 1.207 |
| 1585 | England in the Netherlands | 0.126 | 0.250 | 0.504 |
| 1590s | Spain in the Netherlands | 9.000 | 22.200 | 0.405 |
| 1600 | England in Ireland | 0.320 | 0.374 | 0.856 |

*Note:* War costs and revenues are stated in different currencies: for France, million livres tournois; for England, million pounds sterling; for Spain, million maravedis in the 1480s and million florins in the 1590s.
*Source:* based on information in Hale (1985: 233).

In examining table 4.1, keep in mind that the information is merely representative. The data for any given year do not necessarily encompass all military costs of the year for any global power. In the 1590s, for example, Spain was also fighting in France and sending armadas to England. The main point is that a particular military campaign or military theater could easily generate annual costs equal to one-third and frequently more of a state's total income. These expenses had to be covered in some way.

Although a number of different techniques were used, two basic financing styles emerged. The style practised by the continentally oriented global powers failed to generate enough money to cover Spanish and French military expenses. The style developed by two of the maritime-commercial powers, and ultimately adopted by the rest of the field, did manage to generate sufficient sums of money that enabled these relatively small states to compete successfully with the continental giants. Accordingly, how the early global powers financed their military expenses provides us with another way of differentiating the global power winners from the losers. In the process of tracing these financial paths, we also learn more about the differential effects of war-induced resource extraction on, and one of the more enduring sources of state expansion for, global power state making.

### Spain and France

The wars of the sixteenth, seventeenth, and eighteenth centuries grew increasingly more expensive. To remain competitive, the leaders of all states were forced to spend more money than they had access to through normal or even emergency taxation procedures. Nevertheless, the contrast between the early victors (the Netherlands and Britain) and the early unsuccessful challengers (Spain and France) is not one of states that gained access to credit and states that did not. However, one primary difference between the winners and the losers· is that the winners were able to obtain continued access to relatively inexpensive credit whereas the losers failed to establish efficient credit procedures or to maintain uninterrupted access to credit, despite their advantages in terms of relative wealth. For example, late sixteenth-century Spain is said to have had annual revenues ten times greater than those available to England's Queen Elizabeth (Davis 1973: 68). Late seventeenth-century France is reckoned to have had five times the annual revenues and two to three times the natural wealth of England (Dickson and Sperling 1970: 285), quite possibly throughout the eighteenth century (O'Brien and Keyder 1978: 57–60).[1] Yet in both cases, the states with greater overall economic capacity were defeated by the states with superior credit and financial capabilities.

The rulers of Spain and France were not strangers to the necessity of loans, especially during periods of wartime and crisis.[2] However, their approaches to creating debt were characterized by largely ad hoc practices that nevertheless became increasingly predictable from the end of the fifteenth to the end of the eighteenth century. When deficits either occurred or were anticipated, loans were sought. In the Spanish case, two types of debts emerged, *juros* and *asientos*. *Juros* represented funded debts. Annual interest payments would be derived from future specified revenue sources, as in pledging repayment for a loan via some percentage of the sales tax. *Asientos* were unfunded debts that tended to involve high interest rates. In the first half of the sixteenth century, the interest rates on these *asientos* from foreign bankers ranged between 17 and 49 percent (see table 4.2). In comparison, *juros* tended to pay in the vicinity of 5 to 7 percent interest.

Table 4.2
Spanish Royal Debt Information, 1504–1713

| Year | Comments |
| --- | --- |
| 1504 | .299 million ducats in funded debt (*juros*) |
| 1516 | .349 million ducats in funded debt |
| 1516–35 | 28 million ducats borrowed |
| 1520–32 | 17.6% average interest rates on foreign loans to Spanish crown |
| 1522 | 36% of ordinary revenues allocated to interest payments |
| 1533–42 | 21.3% average interest rates on foreign loans to Spanish crown |
| 1538 | Funded debt charges consume 61.4% of royal income; an additional 1.12 million ducats are needed for charges on the floating debt |
| 1543 | 65% of ordinary revenues allocated to interest payments |
| 1543–51 | 27.8% average interest rates on foreign loans to Spanish crown |
| 1546 | Most royal income pledged through 1550; insufficient money available to pay interest charges and no new loans feasible; all Indies treasure confiscated, encouraging greater fraud in future Indies trade declarations |
| 1552–56 | 48.8% average interest rates on foreign loans to Spanish crown |
| 1554 | Revenues are said to be pledged in advance through 1560 |
| 1556 | 68% of ordinary revenues allocated to interest payments |
| 1557–60 | 36 million ducats in funded debt; 1.6 million ducats in annual interest payments; interest payments in arrears; bankruptcy declared, leading to forced reduction in prevailing rate of interest and consolidation of floating debt to *juros* earning 5–7% interest |
| 1559 | Peace with France necessitated by lack of money |
| 1574 | 74 million ducats in funded debt |
| 1575 | Bankruptcy declared; most charges on royal revenue made since 1560 suspended; negotiations result in major reduction of interest rates; governmental credit suffers major setback; Antwerp sacked by Spanish mutineers in 1576, contributing to the decline of Antwerp as the leading economic center in Europe and further uniting Dutch provinces' opposition to Spain |
| 1590s | 4–6 million ducats in annual interest payments |
| 1596 | Bankruptcy declared; interest payments suspended when it proved impossible to obtain new loans |
| 1598 | 85 million ducats in funded debt; separate peace is made with France |
| 1599 | Ordinary and extraordinary revenues pledged through 1600; coinage debasement begun in response to governmental need for money |
| 1607 | 8 million ducats in *juro* interest payments; 22.7 million ducats in floating loans outstanding; revenues anticipated to 1611; bankruptcy declared; monetary problems contribute to truce with Netherlands in 1608 |
| 1623 | 112 million ducats in funded debt |
| 1627 | Bankruptcy declared |
| 1632–37 | 30 million ducats raised in floating loans |

*Table 4.2—continued*

| Year | Comments |
|------|----------|
| 1647 | 13 million ducats needed for military campaign; 60% drop in silver receipts and inability of the government to raise more than 3 million from bankers lead to declaration of bankruptcy |
| 1650 | Revenue anticipated through 1655 |
| 1652 | Bankruptcy declared |
| 1656 | Bankruptcy declared |
| 1662 | Bankruptcy declared; floating debt system undermined making it increasingly difficult to raise large loans |
| 1665 | 9 million ducats in interest payments |
| 1667 | 221.6 million ducats in funded debt |
| 1677 | Half the value of *juros* (fixed debt) annulled and remaining obligations taxed (5% on pre-1635 *juros* and 15% on post-1635 *juros*) |
| 1685–87 | *Juro* value annulled further (in 50–75% range); interest payments restricted to 4% |
| 1701 | *Juro* annual liability equals 9.2 million ducats |
| 1703–04 | *Juro* interest payments consume 39% revenues |
| 1713 | *Juro* annual liability equals 9.9 million ducats |

*Sources:* Davies (1937), Elliott (1963), Vicens Vives (1969), Kamen (1969, 1983), Dominguez Ortiz (1971), Parker (1979c), Lynch (1984), and Stradling (1981).

The fragementary information summarized in table 4.2 indicates what happened to Spanish royal credit over the years. As the magnitude of the various types of debt accumulated, the size of the interest payments rose. At the same time, unpledged revenues became more and more scarce, thereby constraining the ability to repay previous loans. At repeated intervals, the Spanish crown discovered that it had no unpledged income or that no one was willing to lend additional funds. A form of bankruptcy was declared on such occasions (in 1557, 1575, 1596, 1607, 1627, 1647, 1652, 1656, and 1662). Interest payments would be suspended and negotiations would begin (sometimes lasting several years) with creditors to alter the terms of the outstanding loans. The rates of interest would be reduced. *Asientos* might be turned into the less expensive *juros*. Old sources of loans might be forced out of the market, but new sources could be expected to replace them until the next bankruptcy. Only gradually did Spain lose its credit worthiness or, more accurately, its ability to generate new loans.

On repeated occasions, however, financial exhaustion forced Spain to seek a cessation of its military activities. The years 1559 and 1607 are two of the more prominent examples. Parker (1979c: 73) notes that future taxes could usually be mortgaged only two or three years in advance, regardless of the promised interest rates. In 1607, Spain's future revenues were claimed through 1611, and because of a serious currency debasement, very little could be anticipated in the way of increased tax revenues. Hence, Spain—no longer able to fight now and pay later—had little choice but to accept a Dutch-proposed armistice that paved the way for the Netherlands' systemic leadership in the seventeenth century. The Dutch ascendancy was also aided by the 1575 bankruptcy that contributed to the demise of Antwerp as the European economic center.

Eventually, Spanish financial credit evaporated in conjunction with its increasing inability to repay loans (due to the size of its debt and the seventeenth-century economic decline discussed in chapter 2). Vicens Vives manages to combine two useful metaphors—toboggans and vicious circles—to summarize the decay and collapse of the Spanish financial system.

> After the bankruptcies of 1557 and 1575 the road ahead was all too clear. These unfortunate precedents and the ever-growing difficulties of the Crown combined to place it on a sort of toboggan, in which every new suspension of payments . . . only brought it closer to the indescribable chaos of the late 17th century. Thus foreign aid became more and more necessary. And so the vicious circle was complete; the larger the State's debts became, the harder it was to meet them; and, conversely, as collection became more difficult, higher and higher guarantees were demanded. (1969: 384)

Although the French case paralleled the Spanish case, it did not duplicate it. French kings also reduced unilaterally the amount of money they owed or the size of the interest rate on repeated occasions (1596, 1604, 1643, 1661, 1664, 1715, and 1770), as noted in table 4.3. Because France's economy was richer than Spain's, the French were able to engage in mortgaging future revenues longer and on a larger scale, but in the process, French monarchs experienced many of the same problems that were well known in Madrid.

> Francois I began his reign (1515–47) with a legacy of debt and by 1523 was facing a serious crisis which he ultimately resolved by selling offices and borrowing heavily from Lyons bankers. Henri II (1547–59) inherited this system of borrowing and ended his reign in a grand financial crash. Unable to depend thereafter upon the ruined and disappointed merchant bankers, Catherine de Medici and her three reigning sons (1559–89) were chronically short of funds, and that shortage was one reason why they called three meetings of the Estates General (1560, 1576, 1588) and two Assemblies of Notables (1560, 1583) in thirty years. Of the Bourbon Kings who ruled for the two hundred years from 1589 to 1789, all except the first of them, Henri IV (1589–1610), struggled unsuccessfully to make ends meet and all financed their governments by emergency measures. . . . Deep financial trouble was normal throughout the life of the French monarchy. It was the times of relief, not the continual difficulties, which were abnormal. (Bosher 1970: 3–4)

At the beginning of the sixteenth century, French kings had debt obligations that originated several hundred years before, but these obligations

*Table 4.3*
*Growth of the French Public Debt, 1522–1944*

| Year | Debt size (in livres tournois or francs) | Comments |
|---|---|---|
| 1552 | | 200 thousand borrowed from Parisian merchants at 12.5% —inaugurated *rentes sur l'Hotel de Ville* bond series |
| 1536–37 | | 300 thousand borrowed from Parisian merchants |
| 1543 | | 225 thousand borrowed from Parisian merchants at 8.33% |
| 1547–59 | | 4.5 million borrowed at Paris alone |
| 1560 | 42 million | |
| 1576 | 100 million | |
| 1595 | 300 million | |
| 1596 | | Interest payments suspended, some debts repudiated |
| 1604 | | Some debts annulled or reduced, interest rates decreased unilaterally |
| 1615 on | | Delays in interest payments, political influence increasingly helpful in obtaining interest payment |
| 1642 | 600 million | |
| 1643 | | Debt principal forcibly reduced to 250 million, interest rates scaled down |
| 1661 | | Debt principal and interest forcibly reduced |
| 1664 | | Debt principal and interest forcibly reduced |
| 1678 | 157 million | |
| 1684 | 227 million | |
| 1697 | 427 million | |
| 1707 | | Inability to increase taxes or obtain new loans; issuing of paper money and substantial currency depreciation |
| 1714 | 3.00 billion | |
| 1715 | | Debt principal forcibly reduced to 1.7 billion |
| 1763 | 2.36 billion | |
| 1768 | 2.48 billion | |
| 1770 | | Debt interest forcibly reduced |
| 1783 | 3.31 billion | |
| 1786 | 3.96 billion | |
| 1789 | 4.21 billion | High service charges and large unfunded debt lead to the convening of the Estates General and ultimately to the overthrow of the monarchy |
| 1799 | 926 million | After debt repudiation and redemption in confiscated land and inflated currency |
| 1814 | 1.27 billion | |
| 1815 | 2.56 billion | |
| 1823 | 2.64 billion | |
| 1830 | 4.43 billion | |
| 1848 | 5.95 billion | |
| 1856 | 8.15 billion | |
| 1873 | 21.70 billion | |
| 1883 | 27.40 billion | |
| 1903 | 30.80 billion | |

*Table 4.3—continued*

| Year | Debt size (in livres tournois or francs) | Comments |
|------|------------------------------------------|----------|
| 1913 | 33.64 billion | |
| 1918 | 154.39 billion | |
| 1924 | 315.90 billion | |
| 1934 | 319.38 billion | |
| 1938 | 412.58 billion | |
| 1944 | 1800.00 billion | |

*Note:* Some caution in the interpretation of this series is warranted due to several changes in the French currency unit and its value over the 1522–1944 period.
*Source:* extracted from the discussion in Hamilton (1947).

were not considered large in scale. Royal debts only began to escalate after the global war invasion of Italy and onset of the wars with Spain. The 1522–59 figures listed in table 4.3 pertain only to loans raised in Paris and not other cities. The royal debt rose to 42 million livres tournois by 1560, more than doubled by 1576, and tripled again by the end of the sixteenth century. In contrast, French royal revenues (1514, 7.7 million; 1547, 14 million; 1574, 21 million; 1581, 32 million; 1610, 32.6 million; 1643, 79 million; 1661, 84 million, according to Dent 1973: 9) had also increased, but only by a factor of four between 1574 and 1661. The 1642 royal debt was more than 14 times as large as the debt reported in 1560.

French "bankruptcies" occurred about as frequently (1596, 1604, 1643, 1661, 1664, 1715, and 1770) as the Spanish ones did. French financial problems were compounded further, however, by the practices of tax farming and venal office holders. Tax collection and much of state financing essentially became private enterprises. Businessmen would pay a fee for the right to extract specific revenues. Any extractions above and beyond the agreed on fee or rent were regarded as profit to be kept by the tax farmers. Venality refers to the somewhat related practice of selling public offices, usually but not always pertaining to financial affairs. The owners of these offices, not surprisingly, merged their public bureaucratic function with private entrepreneurship. The administrativ outcomes of these practices, which were also the rule in borrowing money for the state, included gross extractive inefficiency, little ability to monitor accurately or to assess the state's financial status, and a fair amount of institutionalized corruption. Equally important, as Tilly (1986: 61) and many others point out, a sizable proportion of the collected taxes simply never became available to the state "because they went into the pockets of tax farmers, creditors, and sticky fingered officials instead."

Dent summarizes the French ancien regime financial problem:

For all the apparently effortless increases of French taxation, the French fiscal system staggered from one crisis to another, barely performing the complicated feat of standing upright under two centuries of buffeting. Though the amount of money that was supposed to accrue annually to the Crown might double again and again, the monarchy was able only at the very best of times, and for short and infrequent periods, to break even. It had to run faster and faster to stay at best balanced on a knife-edge between bankruptcy and solvency. (1973: 9–10)

The procedures for creating royal debts and the necessity for accumulating debt were only part of the French financial problem. As in the Spanish case, the procedures only worked well enough to keep the state barely afloat fiscally, with occasional lapses into bankruptcy, credit failures, and financial exhaustion. Great strains were placed on a relatively limited, ineffective, and inegalitarian tax system. Domestic political unrest, resistance, and rebellion were the partial consequences. Unlike the Spanish experience, though, one financial crisis was instrumental in bringing about the late eighteenth-century collapse of the French monarchy and the French Revolution. By 1789, the size of the royal debt was substantial but, as it turned out, not quite as large as that of its neighbor and principal rival, Britain. One critical difference was that the French state was paying 6 percent or higher interest rates and some 318 million livres per year in service charges. British interest rates and service charges were about half those with which the French were struggling to cope (see Bosher 1970: 24).

On several occasions between 1555 and 1720, both Spain and France made attempts to modernize their public credit operations. Every time, the short-lived innovations were overwhelmed by rising war expenditures and the reversion to traditional credit procedures. Even so, H. Van der Wee (1977: 391) gives credit to the state bankruptcies as a collective "first important step in the systematic development of a consolidated funded national debt," with respect to the tendency for bankruptcy declarations to lead to negotiations for the conversion of short-term to long-term loans. Overall, however, the Spanish and French financial approach to meeting the rapidly increasing expenses of competition in the emerging global political system yielded diminishing returns, temporary insolvency, and, ultimately, failure and defeat.

### Portugal

There is no need to argue that Portugal's term as a world power or system leader was fully comparable with those of its successors. From an evolutionary perspective, the Portuguese era is perhaps best viewed as a transitional period in which the locus of activity moved away from the Mediterranean toward the new Atlantic and northwestern European center. Each successive systemic leader enjoyed access to a broader resource base than its predecessors, thereby increasing the potential scope and influence of leadership. Each successive system leader was also in a position to learn from its predecessors and to borrow their most successful techniques.

In these respects, the first system leader operated from a distinct disadvantage. Its resource base was fragile. Its state-making models were more apt to be the nearby, expanding powers of Spain and France. As a consequence, Portuguese debt problems and practices were similar to those of the continentally oriented powers.

Portugal's claim to global power status rested, to a considerable extent, on its attempts to establish a maritime empire in the Indian Ocean, even though its imperial efforts were never as profitable as they might have been. As early as 1508, the Portuguese crown had arranged to sell the entire royal monopoly of Asian pepper to an Italo-Flemish syndicate based in Antwerp. By 1520, the rising expenses associated with Portugal's involvement in Morocco and India, in addition to the expenditures of the royal family, forced the Portuguese to request advance payments from the syndicate to pay for the following year's expedition to India. The pepper syndicate quickly became a perpetual deficit banker to the Portuguese crown (Diffie and Winius 1977: 414). After 23 years (1543), the debt owed to the pepper syndicate amounted to about 2.2 million cruzados, and Portugal had ceased paying its annual interest charges. This indicator of financial problems was followed in 1549 by the Portuguese crown's unilateral decision to reduce the size of its debt payments and to sever its relationship with the Antwerp syndicate.

Even though Portuguese records are unusually scarce, the second half of the sixteenth century appears to have been a general period of increasing financial difficulty. By 1557, the Portuguese debt had reached approximately 3.9 million cruzados—a 77 percent increase from the 1543 figure. The government declared bankruptcy in 1560 and lowered interest rates unilaterally in 1563. And, as noted by Oliveira Marques (1976: 279), whereas government bonds had been issued on an average of 1 per 7 years between 1500 and 1554, between 1555 and 1580 the average was 1 per 2.6 years.

Another clear manifestation of these financial difficulties was the near-constant attempt to keep the normal operating expenses of the empire to a minimum. As a consequence, the Portuguese naval presence in Asian waters was usually too limited for the effective policing or adequate defense of the empire's numerous outposts. Moreover, the relatively easy absorption of Portugal by Spain in 1580 took place shortly after the Moroccan intervention (1578) had led to the capture of a substantial number of highly placed Portuguese. The ransoms that were subsequently paid are said to have consumed "nearly all the remaining cash in Portugal" (Diffie and Winius 1977: 428, n. 5). Thus, the long cycle's first system leader failed to develop an efficient system of public credit. In many respects, its sixteenth-century approach to public debt resembles the practices of Spanish and French rulers more closely than it does those of its immediate successors to world power.

### The United Provinces of the Netherlands

Towns in medieval northwestern Europe, which were regarded as better credit risks than were monarchs, developed the fund-raising practice of selling municipal annuities. The newly independent Dutch provinces, which were closely linked in the economic and political sense to some of these towns, simply transferred the municipal procedures to the state level. However, one amusing irony of global power development is that these procedures were only available because, initially, they had been forced on the provinces during the first half of the sixteenth century by officials in the reign of Charles V (Tracy 1985: 213–14). Thus, an early Habsburg need for money to fight imperial wars led to the loss of one of its most productive sectors in more ways than one.

Although in theory these annuities were redeemable, they tended to constitute perpetual investments in governments. Despite, or perhaps in part due to, their small population and land area, the Dutch provinces gradually were able to expand the initially local investor pools into something resembling a national pool. By greatly improving the efficiency of the credit service operations and by avoiding default and debt repudiation after the sixteenth century, the United Provinces were able to expand their credit under conditions of high investor confidence and, therefore, at relatively low interest.[3] As attitudes toward credit and loan practices became more liberal, interest rates throughout Europe declined dramatically.

The Dutch appear to have played a trend-setting or leadership role in reducing the cost of public money lending. For instance, Dutch interest rates declined from between 20 and 30 percent in 1500 to between 9 and 12 percent in 1550, and to 3 percent or less during the seventeenth century (North and Thomas 1973: 143). The Provinces also benefitted, in terms of lower costs, by becoming the financial center of the world economy. The decentralized nature of the Dutch Republic's credit operation proved equally advantageous. Because each province was responsible for its own debt operations, Dutch investors (and presumably the Dutch debt managers as well) had only a poor understanding of the magnitude of the collective public debt.[4]

Partially due to this lack of information and largely because of the high costs of the wars of 1667–1713, Riley (1980: 5) contends that, even though the Dutch were financial pioneers in rationalizing the process of government credit inflation, the United Provinces became the first nation-state to approach an exhaustion of its credit resources. There is, then, a close relationship between the primary maritime province of Holland's 160 percent increase in provincial debt between 1652 and 1713, the allocation of 70 percent or more of its revenues for interest payments, and the approximate 37 percent absolute decline in the size of the Dutch war fleet. (The province of Holland was primarily responsible for the provision of the fleet.) During the same period, the Dutch share of global naval capabilities dropped from 41 percent in 1652 to less than 29 percent in 1713 (see Modelski and Thompson 1988: 117–19).

### Britain

Prior to the late seventeenth century, English royal finance-debt problems resembled those of France and Spain, with two exceptions. The scale of operation was much smaller, and the English Parliament was a more important political actor than were the legislatures in France and Castile. However, neither exception was a constant.

Parliament's involvement in state finances had increased during the Hundred Years War period, but the fifteenth- and sixteenth-century improvement in the English crown's wealth base, primarily via the seizure of monasterial land, constituted a threat to the long-nourished royal dependence on legislative war-making subsidies. As noted in chapter 3, the sixteenth century was a painful period for war-making state makers. Inflation was rampant, a situation particularly noticeable in war costs.

Russell (1973) suggests that the sixteenth-century cost hikes proved particularly difficult for English monarchs—even more so than for France and Spain. For one thing, Parliament represented a significant obstacle to increasing royal income, especially for unpopular wars. Also, royal revenues were tied closely to land rents that did not increase with inflation, thanks to inertia and the divided loyalties of local administrations. The same could be said for land taxes and assessments. Another factor was the English crown's relatively greater insecurity (compared to Spanish monarchs, for instance), especially after Elizabeth I, and the related decline in the size of the royal estates due to attempts to enlist and reward royal supporters. Crown lands were also sold to pay for war costs.

For these reasons and others discussed in chapter 3, royal income only doubled between 1510 and 1604, while prices escalated by a factor of five. Elizabeth's successor, James I, inherited a debt of 400,000 pounds, which he managed to double during the next 14 years. Royal income and expenditure also increased, with revenues in the 1630s rising to more than three times what peacetime spending had been in the Elizabethan era. But these increases were not enough to save the royal financial system or the monarchy when put to the test. In 1640, Charles I needed to raise an additional one million pounds to deal with an ongoing Scottish war. Parliament balked; members argued that the crown had access to sufficient revenues and that the economy could not afford the additional financial burden. There was also considerable incentive to use this opportunity to intensify the crown's financial dependence on Parliament.

Charles's vulnerability was increased even further because he was unable to borrow any money at this critical juncture. No source was prepared to lend any. As early as 1615, lenders had begun to refuse further credit to the monarchy, and by 1620, the City of London had demanded that remaining crown lands be put up as loan collateral in place of the more usual, anticipated customs duties (Goldstone 1988: 118). In the ensuing two decades, a variety of often rather desperate techniques were used to augment ordinary revenues. They accomplished little more than further antagonizing tax payers and briefly postponing financial collapse.

> Crown finances of the late 1630s made up a fragile and tottering structure. The expedients of Ship Money, monopolies, and sale of honors, combined with heavy indebtedness, kept the monarchy afloat, but only so long as there was peace. Crown debt had exceeded a million pounds by the 1630s, and only constant extensions, rescheduling of debt, and the assignment of future revenues enabled the government to continue interest and current borrowing. Late in the decade half the Crown's ordinary revenue was hypothecated to cover current debt obligations. The Crown was now living on credit to cover its peacetime costs; any extraordinary expense meant instant financial disaster. (Goldstone 1988: 119)

This familiar description certainly facilitated the outbreak of civil war and the downfall of the Stuarts. Yet in the two and one-half centuries following the conclusion of civil war, Britain was able to defeat the French challenges for the systemic leadership position in two periods of global war (1688–1713 and 1792–1815), despite the fact that the French possessed superiority in terms of population, land area, natural wealth, and tax revenues. A significant factor in these contests, as well as in the less conclusive mid-century conflicts (the Austrian Succession, Seven Years, and American Revolutionary Wars), was the successful creation of a system of public borrowing based on the Dutch model and initiated in the early phase of the late seventeenth-century Anglo-French struggle.

P. G. M. Dickson (1967: 9–12) has presented a detailed analysis of the development of the British national debt, which credits this institutional innovation (in the British context) with the following effects:

1  In the context of an economically underdeveloped country characterized by an equally underdeveloped bureaucracy and a relatively limited tax base, revenues secured through debt instruments "enabled Great Britain to supply a decisive margin of ships and men" to the Anglo-French conflict.
2  The adoption of an institutionalized public borrowing system in the 1690s, as opposed to ad hoc royal loans, made possible the development of the

City of London as the world's financial and investment center by the middle of the eighteenth century.

3   Victory in the intermediate wars of 1739–63 preserved and extended the North American and West Indian markets, thereby creating a decisive increase in the demand for exports.

4   The combination of the increase in demand for exports and the availability of extensive capital services greatly facilitated Britain's late eighteenth-century lead on industrialization.

5   The creation of a successful public borrowing system buttressed the development of a stable and efficient government in addition to facilitating the development of Parliament as a national focus for major political interests.

In sum, Dickson presents a persuasive argument for the creation of a national debt as vital to the success of Great Britain after 1700. He may overstate the implications of British credit exploitation, but probably not by much. Mathias and O'Brien (1976: 623), for example, estimate that the British government borrowed at least 75 percent of the extra finances needed to prosecute the wars of 1702–13, 1739–48, 1756–63, and 1775–83 and 42 percent of the expenses for the wars of 1793–1815.[5] These estimates are even more impressive than the numbers provided by Dickson and recounted in table 4.4.

**Table 4.4**
*The Role of Loans in British Wartime Expenditure, 1688–1815*

| War Years | Expenditure | Revenues | Amount Raised by Loans | Loans as Percentage of Expenditure |
|-----------|-------------|----------|------------------------|-----------------------------------|
| 1688–1713 | 143.0 | 97.0 | 46.0 | 32.2 |
| 1739–48 | 95.6 | 65.9 | 29.7 | 31.1 |
| 1756–63 | 160.6 | 100.6 | 60.0 | 37.4 |
| 1776–83 | 236.5 | 141.9 | 94.6 | 40.0 |
| 1793–1815 | 1657.9 | 1217.6 | 440.3 | 26.6 |
| Totals | 2293.6 | 1623.0 | 670.6 | 29.2 (Average) |

*Source:* based on Dickson (1967: 10).

Whatever the exact scale of British eighteenth-century dependence on war-induced borrowing, a subject discussed in the second half of this chapter, other factors are also substantially important to the emergence of Britain as the eighteenth- and nineteenth-century system leader. The fact remains that Britain was able to amass and sustain enormous debts, without sacrificing economic and political stability, in the process of expanding and defending its global role. At the very least, the British national debt played an essential facilitative function in the initial eighteenth-century rise and the early nineteenth-century reemergence of British leadership.

In sum, the United Provinces of the Netherlands and Britain neither invented the concept of public debt nor possessed a monopoly on the ability to convert private assets into public resources through borrowing.[6] From the late sixteenth through the eighteenth century, however, the Dutch and then the British were able to develop and exploit their innovative and institutionalized access to short- and long-term credit to defeat ostensibly wealthier opponents who had proved poor credit risks. In this sense, leadership in the development of financial capabilities and modern public finance systems was, in some respects, initially more important than economic wealth per se.

On the other hand, public credit alone does not explain the prenineteenth-century successes of the Dutch and the British. Their uninterrupted access to loans at relatively low interest rates to meet wartime military costs is an important factor, but only one of several. Nor do we suggest that economic growth or the growth advantages accruing to trade-oriented economies have no bearing on the continued access to public credit and investor confidence. On the contrary, our argument implies that the commercial-maritime powers were more likely than their continentally oriented rivals to adopt efficient and stable credit practices. They were also more likely to be able to develop long-term borrowing procedures.[7]

Even so, both the Dutch and the British were ultimately forced to retreat, however reluctantly, from their respective leadership roles, partly because of the size of their debts but, more fundamentally, because they had lost their status as the world system's lead economy. The interaction of enormous debts and the loss of economic leadership meant that they could no longer afford the high overhead cost of world power. Although not defeated in global warfare, the financially exhausted world powers of the second and fourth long cycles were superseded by allies who could better afford the world leadership role. Britain had replaced the Dutch just as, substantially later, the United States replaced the British.

## War and the Persistence of Debt Burdens

The generalization that war tends to increase the size of national debts is hardly controversial. However, three more specific generalizations are possible:

1   Global wars, as opposed to interstate wars, are the most important sources of public debt for system leaders.
2   The increase in the burden of public debt created by global wars is relatively permanent for system leaders.

3 The magnitude of a state's public debt in the context of a maritime-commercial political system imposes restraints on its exercise of world power, even when it is enjoying its strongest relative capability position.

The significance and permanence of the impact of global war on the public debt can be readily demonstrated by examining the nature of historical fluctuations in real public debt. Figures 4.1 and 4.2 provide the simplest demonstration by charting the real national debt of Britain (1691–1985) and of the United States (1792–1985). The data on public debts were taken from Mitchell (1962); Mitchell and Jones (1971); United Kingdom, Central Statistical Office (various years); U.S. Department of Commerce (1975); and U.S. Office of the President (various years). The same sources, as well as Mitchell (1981), were used to develop corrective price series expressed in constant 1913 values.[8]

Little imagination is required to visualize the step-like impact of global wars on the British and American national debts. In the British case, the concluding global war of the second long cycle (1688–1713) and the interstate wars of the eighteenth century create a gradual and rough ramp-like increase in the public debt; this is follows by a major-step increase with the French Revolutionary-Napoleonic global wars at the end of the third long cycle. The post-1815 debt remains relatively stationary until World War II and the end

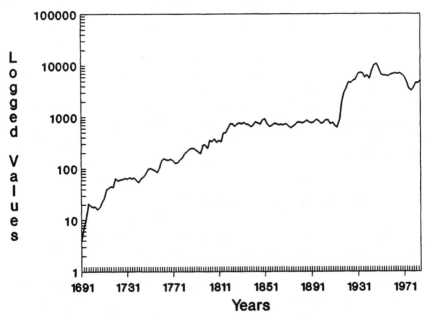

*Figure 4.1.* British Public Debt, 1691–1985 (logged million 1913 pounds)

of the British role as a world power. Only then is there a significant decline in real public debt.

This relatively recent deviation from the historical pattern is easily accounted for in terms of (1) the nature of American assistance during and after World War II (as in the substitution of lend-lease programs for traditional wartime loans), and (2) the dramatic postwar inflation that has increased at a rate faster than the public debt, thereby reducing debt levels expressed in constant 1913 values.

The charting of the United States resembles a staircase even more clearly, with the American Civil War providing the first major step and World Wars I and II the second and third steps. Despite post–World War II inflationary increases similar to those encountered by Great Britain, the U.S. experience differs from the British in the post-1945 step down in real public debt. Whereas Britain's real debt appears to be returning to the level of World War I, the American values suggest fluctuations around a new equilibrium considerably higher than the short-lived level attained between World War I and the Great Depression of the 1930s. Because the United States achieved world-power status only after 1945, it is not difficult to contend that post-1945 U.S. debt fluctuations are more similar to post-1815 (and, to a lesser extent, post-1713) British debt fluctuations than they are to the direction of change manifested in contemporary British debt burdens. This is to be expected: the mantle of

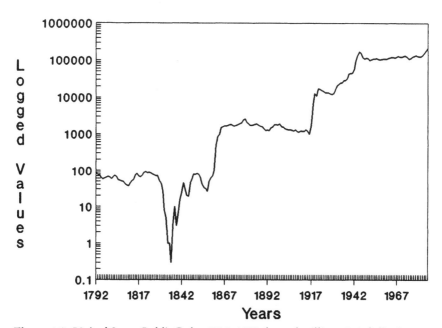

***Figure 4.2.*** United States Public Debt, 1792–1985 (logged million 1913 dollars)

systemic leadership—"passed on" by Britain to the United States—is hardly cost free.

The graphic evidence in figures 4.1 and 4.2 is corroborated by the decidedly conservative calculations of the increases in debt attributable to global and nonglobal wars. The estimates reported in table 4.5 are conservative because they have been created by simply calculating the net change in debt size between the first and the last year of a war. However, increases in the debt principal continue long after the end of the war. To the extent that war-induced debt levels are relatively permanent, the full costs of war (especially in the case of global wars) are virtually perpetual. Readers will note that our calculations do not match those advanced by Dickson (1967) and Mathias and O'Brien (1976), further underlining the conservative nature of our current test.

*Table 4.5*
*A Conservative Estimate of War Impacts on Real National Debt*

| Periods of Global War | Periods of Interstate War | Increase in Debt Size | Percentage Increase |
|---|---|---|---|
| | BRITAIN | | |
| 1691–1697 | | 17.0 | 414.6 |
| 1702–1713 | | 20.9 | 115.5 |
| | 1718–1720 | 23.3 | 51.7 |
| | 1727–1728 | –0.4 | 0.0 |
| | 1739–1748 | 28.1 | 47.3 |
| | 1756–1763 | 57.8 | 63.3 |
| | 1778–1783 | 67.0 | 46.6 |
| 1793–1815 | | 271.2 | 129.5 |
| | 1854–1856 | 33.0 | 5.0 |
| 1914–1918 | | 1,923.2 | 310.1 |
| 1939–1945 | | 3,755.0 | 58.1 |
| | UNITED STATES | | |
| | 1898 | 129.1 | 7.2 |
| 1917–1918 | | 4,853.9 | 274.0 |
| 1941–1945 | | 125,118.4 | 272.0 |
| | 1950–1953 | –3,706.8 | –3.3 |
| | 1965–1973 | 4,643.6 | 3.9 |

*Note:* Calculations of change are made between the first and last year of warfare. Increases of debt size are expressed in terms of constant 1913 million British pounds (for Britain) and 1913 million U.S. dollars (for the United States).

The calculations in table 4.5 demonstrate that each successive period of global war has a successively greater absolute impact on the size of the national debt. If one contrasts the debt increases associated with periods of global and nonglobal wars, moreover, little comparison is possible with respect to the scales of the increases found in the columns for each type of war. Global wars clearly have had a much more significant impact on the levels of public debt than have interstate wars. This, too, is hardly surprising in view of the different states involved and the degree of intensity and mobilization associated with global versus nonglobal warfare.

### Modeling Debt

Fortunately, it is possible to conduct tests of the first two generalizations that are considerably more sophisticated and systematic than are the sometimes misleading techniques of visual scrutiny and percentage comparison. G. E. P. Box and G. C. Tiao (1975) have developed a set of statistical procedures for assessing the impact of discrete events on behavioral processes. Formulated from a set of stochastic, univariate, Box-Jenkins time-series models constructed to remove autocorrelation in a series of observations, the procedures also build on the Campbell and Stanley (1966) quasi-experimental time series design. In general, the impact assessment model can be expressed as:

$$Y_t = f(I_t) + N_t$$

In this equation, $f(I_t)$ constitutes a functional relationship between the intervention and the affected series $(Y_t)$. $N_t$ represents an ARIMA model noise component that describes the stochastic behavior of the time series around the $Y = f(I_t)$ relationship. The basic strategy of the Box-Tiao impact assessment models involves first identifying the parameters of the noise component (ARIMA structure) of the time series. After the ARIMA parameters have been identified, an intervention component is selected, based on a priori expectations about the nature of the impact (i.e., whether it is abrupt/gradual or permanent/temporary), and added to the noise component. The parameters of the full model (both noise and intervention components) are then estimated.

Discussing these matters in further detail would interrupt the flow of our analysis of global power debt. We believe it is possible to follow the broad nature of the more technical analyses without fully appreciating the underlying statistical theory. However, some understanding of the modeling procedures is important in evaluating the approaches we take and the results that are achieved. Moreover, we use these impact assessment models in chapters 5, 6, and 7. Therefore, a brief discussion of the Box-Tiao procedures appears in the appendix at the end of this chapter.

We have described the impact of global wars on debt levels as staircase-like, which implies abrupt, permanent interventions. The functional form of such an intervention is $f(I_t) = \omega_o I_t$, where the omega parameter $(\omega_o)$ represents an estimate of the difference between the pre- and postintervention levels, and $I$ equals 1 during wartime and 0 otherwise.

For Britain, global wars include the War of the League of Augsburg and the War of the Spanish Succession (1689–97; 1701–13), the French Revolutionary and Napoleonic Wars (1793–1815), World War I (1914–18), and World War II (1939–45). Because some of the 1689–97 fighting preceded the creation of a national debt, however, we exclude this period from the Box-Tiao analysis. The United States participated only in the last two global wars (1917–18 and 1941–45). Our hypothesis that global wars are the most important source of increases in the public debt leads to the expectation that global wars will have a greater impact than nonglobal or interstate wars. Thus, periods of interstate war (for Britain, 1718–20, 1727–28, 1739–48, 1778–83, and 1854–56; for the United States, 1898, 1950–53, and 1965–73) are treated as constituting a second intervention category.

### Debt Increases and Their Persistence

Estimation of the appropriate intervention and noise parameters produced the results reported in table 4.6. Basically, the British and American debt histories yielded similar results—statistically significant parameters for

**Table 4.6**
*Impacts of Global and Interstate Wars on British and U.S. National Debt*

|  | Intervention Component $\omega_o$ | Noise Component $\phi_1$ | Noise Component $\theta_0$ | Noise Component $\theta_1$ | Overall Goodness-of-Fit RMSE | Overall Goodness-of-Fit Q |
|---|---|---|---|---|---|---|
| *Britain (1691–1975)* | | | | | | |
| Global Wars | .09* | .39* | | | .009 | 23.5 |
| | (.03) | (.06) | | | | |
| Interstate Wars | .04 | | | | | |
| | (.03) | | | | | |
| Interstate Wars | .06* | | .03* | | .005 | 24.3 |
| (1691–1792) | (.01) | | (.007) | | | |
| *United States (1866–1980)* | | | | | | |
| Global Wars | .15* | | | –.36* | .004 | 33.0 |
| | (.03) | | | (.05) | | |
| Interstate Wars | .01 | | | | | |
| | (.03) | | | | | |

*Note:* Two of the three series have been transformed by a constant value (10 for the British 1691–1792 series; 15,000 for the American series), and all three have been logged to achieve variance stationarity. Standard errors are reported in parentheses below the parameter coefficients.

\* denotes statistical significance at the .05 level.

*Noise component identifications:*
   (1)   Britain (1691–1975)—first order, first differenced autoregressive process ($\phi_1$);
   (2)   Britain (1691–1792)—white noise with a significant trend parameter ($\theta_0$);
   (3)   United States (1866–1980)—first order, first differenced moving average process ($\theta_1$).

the global wars and insignificant parameters for the interstate wars. In both cases, the effect of global war on public debt levels is abrupt and permanent, as hypothesized.

Although different magnitudes of impact were hypothesized for the two classes of war, we did not fully anticipate the statistical insignificance of interstate wars. From figures 4.1 and 4.2 and table 4.5, it is apparent that most of the interstate wars are associated with some appreciable change in debt levels. In comparison to the global wars occurring at roughly the same time period, however, their impacts tend to be relatively unimportant. The problem appears to be one of historical context. If we consider several hundred years of global wars, the impact of interstate wars is fairly minor. But if we alter the historical context and ask whether interstate wars had a significant impact before the French Revolutionary and Napoleonic Wars, the second British series (Interstate Wars, 1691–1792) answers the question affirmatively. By eighteenth-century standards, eighteenth-century British interstate wars did have a significant impact on the national debt. Their significance pales only when a longer time span is encompassed.

Similarly, different global wars do not influence the real public debt series in precisely the same way. Table 4.7 treats each global war as a separate intervention. In the case of the United States, the impacts of the two twentieth-century world wars are roughly comparable. In the British series, however, the early impact of the Spanish Succession phase of the first global war in our intervention set is too weak for statistical significance, and the other three wars exert somewhat different degrees and types of influence. The impact of World War I, for instance, is nearly twice that (in logged terms) of the 1793–1815 wars with France. The impact of World War II, a period during which the status of world power passed from Great Britain to the United States, required the fitting of an abrupt, temporary model (as opposed to the abrupt, permanent interventions found to fit the other cases of global wars). This departure from the norm reflects, in large part and as previously noted, the historically unusual increases in postwar inflation. Even so, the large delta ($\delta$) parameter, an indicator of the impact's rate of decay, signifies a fairly slow return to preintervention levels.

In general, the application of the more systematic Box-Tiao models tends to corroborate what has been observed by visual inspection of longitudinal debt fluctuations and by simple (albeit conservative) calculations of the evident impact of war. Wars, and global wars in particular, constitute the principal and most dramatic sources of increases in the public debts of the world system's leading states. For world powers, these increases in the debt burden are permanent in the absolute sense.

Yet, absolute public debt levels can be quite misleading, whether expressed in constant or current values. Ongoing policy debates in the

*Table 4.7*
*Impacts of Global Wars on British and U.S. National Debt*

| | Intervention Component | | Noise Component | | Overall Goodness-of-Fit | |
|---|---|---|---|---|---|---|
| | $\omega_0$ | $\delta$ | $\phi$ | $\theta_1$ | RMSE | Q |
| *Britain (1691–1975)* | | | | | | |
| Spanish Succession | .01 | | .40* | | .008 | 24.5 |
| (1701–13) | (.04) | | (.06) | | | |
| French Revolutionary/ | .15* | | | | | |
| Napoleonic Wars (1793–1815) | (.06) | | | | | |
| World War I | .28* | | | | | |
| (1914–18) | (.06) | | | | | |
| World War II | .15* | .94* | | | | |
| (1939–45) | (.06) | (.13) | | | | |
| | | | | | | |
| *United States (1866–1980)* | | | | | | |
| World War I | .21* | | | −.55* | .003 | 30.5 |
| (1917–18) | (.05) | | | (.08) | | |
| World War II | .14* | | | | | |
| (1941–45) | (.03) | | | | | |

*Note:* The American series has been transformed by a constant value (15,000), and both series have been logged to achieve variance stationarity. Standard errors are reported in parentheses below the parameter coefficients.

    * denotes statistical significance at the .05 level.

*Noise component identification:*
    (1)  Britain (1691–1975)—first order, first differenced autoregressive process ($\phi_1$);
    (2)  United States (1866–1980)—first order, first differenced moving average process ($\theta_1$).

American political arena, not unlike similar controversies in late eighteenth-century Britain, illustrate this potential problem. We do not suggest that global war debts have an inevitable rachet-like effect on system leaders, leading to impending financial doom. In fact, the picture is quite different if one considers the national economic capacity for sustaining high levels of public debt. World powers that remain at the center of the world economy, leading in productivity, growth, and innovation, have a strong opportunity to ameliorate the relative debt level (public debt as a proportion of gross national product) by expanding their economic resource base faster than they create new debt obligations.

    Figure 4.3 illustrates this process as experienced by Great Britain and the United States since the late eighteenth century.[9] During periods of global warfare, the public debt level grows more quickly than does the economy. Between global wars (excluding 1919–39), the reverse tends to apply. Increases in relative debt, therefore, tend to be considerably less permanent than are increases in absolute debt levels, but only as long as significant rates of economic growth are maintained. Both Britain and the United States, for example, were unable to return to pre–World War I relative debt levels in the interwar years. Major downward adjustments in relative debt levels had to await the end of World War II and, in the British case, a substantially reduced role in global politics. In the U.S. case, however, the apparent leveling off, in the 1970s, of the decline in the relative debt suggests that even relative public debt increases are not necessarily temporary.[10]

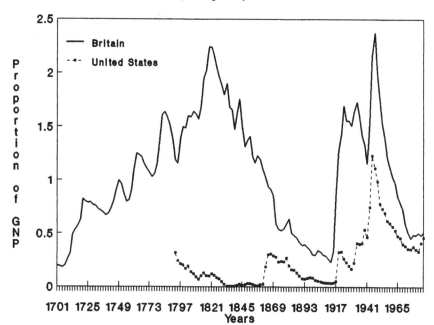

**Figure 4.3.** Debt as a Proportion of GNP, 1701–1985

Figure 4.3 also provides some support for the idea that each successive system leader has access to a resource base of increasingly greater scope. Despite the higher absolute level of public debt, the relative debt level of the United States has remained at lower levels than that experienced by Britain. Similarly, Britain's relative debt level during its second leadership period (1816–1913) is noticeably different from that of the first period.

### The Restraints of Debt
The evidence for the relative persistence of debts induced by global wars appears compelling. The inescapable corollary to permanent increases in national debt principal lies in increases in interest payments. Between 1692 and 1714, for example, real British debt charges increased by a factor of approximately 14. By 1816, another sevenfold increase in interest payments

had taken place; and by 1919, debt charges had again risen 4.5 times. Expressed in constant 1913 values, British governmental expenditures in 1919 were about 193 times greater than in 1692. The level of interest payments had increased some 431 times in the same period. Perhaps, then, it should not be surprising that, if budgetary proportions can be used as a guide to governmental priorities, debt charges frequently constituted a primary concern of British governments between 1692 and 1853. The average peacetime budget of this 162-year period assigned about 48 percent of total expenditures to debt charges. During the postwar first half of the nineteenth century (1816–53), the proportion of the average debt charge was even slightly higher (53 percent).

Figure 4.4 plots the fluctuations in debt charges and military spending as proportions of British expenditures between 1692 and 1966. Prior to the Crimean War (1853–56), it is fairly easy to identify the periods of British warfare: every major debt interest payment trough before 1853 represents a period of either global or interstate war. When no such wars were being fought, the military proportion of the budget averaged approximately 34 percent annually through 1853. If we add this figure to the average peacetime debt charge (48 percent), it becomes clear that slightly more than four-fifths (81 percent) of British governmental expenditures were devoted to interest payments and the maintenance of the military—or past and future wars—with considerably more budgetary attention being paid to past wars.

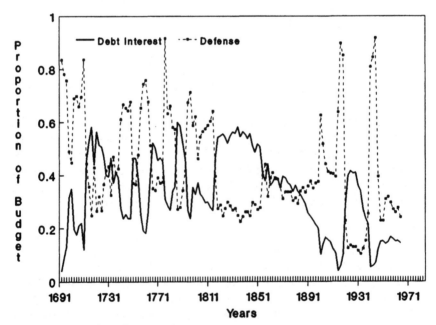

**Figure 4.4.** British Budgetary Priorities, 1693–1965

This is the point of the third generalization that attributes a historical restraining force to the public debt. Between 1714 and 1850, British decision makers chose to reduce governmental operating costs dramatically when no war was being fought. Consequently, debt charges dominated the budget in the years of peace, particularly in the years that followed global wars: 1714–27, 1815–53, and to a lesser extent 1920–30.

One concrete outcome of the retrenchment was the concomitant atrophy or attrition of absolute and relative naval capabilities. In 1714, Great Britain had 127 ships of the line. This figure was never exceeded or even matched until 1786. During much of the interval between 1714 and 1786, the number of capital warships was between 10 and 25 percent smaller than the number with which Britain had emerged as a world power after the 1688–1713 wars—despite the frequency of interstate wars in this period. Indeed, table 4.8 indicates that there was almost a steady 15 percent decline between 1714 and 1774. After the global wars that ended in 1815, the decline in absolute numbers of capital ships was even more pronounced, with a steady 42 percent reduction in the number of ships of the line conceivably available for war purposes. Moreover, many of the line ships that were counted as part of the British fleet in the first half of the nineteenth century were not ready for sea duty, and fewer than a score were normally at sea in any given year.

**Table 4.8**
**British Ships of the Line, 1715–1860**

| Year | Number of Ships | Relative Share of Global Power Total | Year | Number of Ships | Relative Share of Global Power Total |
|------|------|------|------|------|------|
| 1715 | 124 | .443 | 1790 | 137 | .334 |
| 1720 | 120 | .517 | 1795 | 131 | .349 |
| 1725 | 120 | .482 | 1800 | 132 | .401 |
| 1730 | 111 | .461 | 1805 | 130 | .413 |
| 1735 | 117 | .474 | 1810 | 151 | .500 |
| 1740 | 116 | .464 | 1815 | 134 | .523 |
| 1745 | 110 | .449 | 1820 | 118 | .567 |
| 1750 | 116 | .441 | 1825 | 100 | .543 |
| 1755 | 119 | .433 | 1830 | 86 | .551 |
| 1760 | 107 | .423 | 1835 | 81 | .533 |
| 1765 | 120 | .446 | 1840 | 78 | .538 |
| 1770 | 121 | .434 | 1845 | 73 | .507 |
| 1775 | 108 | .397 | 1850 | 70 | .483 |
| 1780 | 109 | .367 | 1855 | 80 | .530 |
| 1785 | 121 | .357 | 1860 | 76 | .517 |

*Source:* based on information in Modelski and Thompson (1988: 68–72).

Historically, then, a case can be made for an irregular cycle in governmental spending priorities of world powers. In periods of global and interstate warfare, military expenses escalate so sharply that normal and even extraordinary revenues are grossly inadequate to meet the rising costs. A significant proportion of the war-induced expenses must, therefore, be obtained through various borrowing techniques. Increased debt raises the fixed overhead of governmental operations. When the wars end and the immediate threat is dissipated, there is a noticeable tendency on the part of the maritime system leaders to cut governmental costs, especially swollen military spending, whenever possible. As a consequence, the impressive military strength marshaled for a global war is to some extent demobilized, and the remainder is permitted to erode in the interest of matching ordinary expenditures with ordinary revenues.

Not coincidentally, there is some parallel here to the destruction of industrial plants in Germany and Japan in World War II. Part of their postwar success is attributable to being forced to construct new and more modern plants to compete with the existing industrial infrastructure of the United States. Until competitive threats seriously alter the incentive structure, global war winners are apt to be confronted with obsolescence sooner than are defeated foes who are able to reemerge as competitors.[11]

We have qualified this interpretation of the interaction of restraints on the cost of world power and the fluctuations of the long cycle by labeling it a historical restraint. This means that the relationship is much more discernible in the period encompassing the pre-1945 period. Along converging lines, Parker (1979a: 208) points out that the "lack of money to pay for unlimited war was undoubtedly the critical restraint on military developments before 1800." In other words, financial restraints, in one way or another, were operative before, during, and after wars. Given time, however, state makers discovered schemes for overriding these restraints.

Despite funding inadequacies, Portuguese naval operations in the Indian Ocean succeeded to some extent largely by default, or because of the near-constant weakness of Portugal's sixteenth-century Asian opposition. Also, if the data were available, we would probably find large fluctuations in the number of Dutch ships actually being used as warships (as opposed to commercial vessels)—fluctuations that would certainly be associated with phases of war and peace. The Dutch fortunately rose to their lead status in an era when merchant ships could still be converted fairly easily to military uses. By the time they fell from leadership, that was no longer the case.

Where data are available (for the eighteenth and nineteenth centuries in the British case), the relationship between postwar retrenchment and the absolute decline of naval capabilities seems reasonably clear through the 1850s. After the Crimean War, the British were faced with French innovations in shipbuilding (the shift from wooden to ironclad and steel ships) and later with a more general increase in naval competition.

Accompanying these incentives for greater naval expenditures during peacetime was a gradual shift in governmental philosophy about state responsibilities vis-a-vis social and economic problems in an increasingly industrialized and complex society. These factors, in addition to the historical growth of the more advanced economies' capacity to generate revenues for governmental activities, have tended to soften some of the distinctions between maximal governmental activity during wartime and minimal activity during peacetime. Nevertheless, the relative and absolute decay of U.S. naval capabilities after World War II suggests that the high overhead costs of the world power role continue to contribute to the undermining of the world power's initial lead in military capabilities.

### Conclusion

In conclusion, global wars have been directly responsible for the creation and, through imitation, the eventual diffusion of modern public credit systems. The ability to generate and sustain the real discontinuities (as in the case of abrupt, permanent changes) in public debts historically has been significant for the financing of the political development and global successes of system leaders. As Braun (1975: 295) suggests, "the more advanced states are, the more deeply they are in debt without being insolvent."

So far, however, the high and somewhat persistent cost of winning has eventually exceeded the continued ability to pay the price. Public debt has a role to play in this relative decline process. Yet, no doubt, that role has diminished with the passage of time. Less prone to diminishing over time are the extractive processes relating to the expansion of state spending and revenues. These processes constitute the principal focus of chapter 5.

### Appendix to Chapter 4

The intervention component of the Box-Tiao models is represented by the transfer function parameters $\omega_0$ and $\delta$, which estimate the initial impact of an event $(I_t)$ on the observed $Y_t$ series and the rate of growth or decay in the level of the time series after the impact. The omega parameter $(\omega_o)$ reflects the initial impact of the intervention, an estimate of the difference between the preintervention and postintervention levels of $Y_t$; the delta parameter $(\delta)$, captures the dynamic response. Delta is a rate parameter in the sense that it specifies how quickly the postintervention series level continues to change (increasing or decreasing) by smaller and smaller increments (or decrements).

The size of $\delta$, which is constrained between $-1$ and $+1$, indicates how quickly (or slowly) the postintervention series reaches equilibrium. When $\delta$ approximates 1, the postintervention series returns to equilibrium very slowly. Conversely, when $\delta$ approximates 0, the postintervention series returns to equilibrium very quickly.

The parameters $\omega_0$ and $\delta$ provide the tools to assess whether an intervention has an initial abrupt or gradual effect on $Y$ and whether it is associated with a temporary or permanent change in the level of $Y_t$. The behavior of a time series generated from the impact of an event takes the form of either of two basic patterns, a step or pulse model of intervention. These models and their appropriate Box-Tiao intervention components are displayed in figure 4.5.

Step model A represents an abrupt, permanent impact pattern, where the event $(I_t)$ is associated with a significant shift in the level of the $Y_t$ time series from preintervention to postintervention. Model B characterizes a gradual, permanent impact. The onset of an event is accompanied by a significant initial change in the level of the postintervention series. However, the full impact of the event is not realized immediately. Instead, it has a gradual effect over a number of subsequent observations (or time periods) until the postintervention series reaches a new equilibrium.

Alternatively, model C illustrates a situation in which the event under study has a significant initial impact on a $Y$ series at one period (the onset of the event) and no residual effects on the rest of the observations. Finally, model D represents the case when an event is associated with an abrupt but temporary change in the level of the postintervention series.[12]

Summarily, the strategy of this approach is to identify the noise model (ARIMA structure) of the $Y$ series with the preintervention data. Then, an intervention component from figure 4.5 is selected based on theoretical notions about the type of impact that $I_t$ will have on the observed time series. These parameters, in addition to the ARIMA parameter(s), are estimated in a full model through iterative, nonlinear estimation procedures.

In most cases, parameters lacking statistical significance are removed from the equation, and the full model is reestimated. An important exception to this rule are cases involving deltas with values greater than 1 or where the confidence intervals associated with the deltas are not constrained within the $\pm 1$ range. This warning of model misspecification reflects what is called *explosive growth* (also known as a *ramp effect*) after the impact of the intervention. Intuitively, such an outcome is more likely to be interpreted as supporting a step function, permanent change than a delta-less, temporary, pulse function model.

In any event, an intervention model's ultimate goodness-of-fit is judged by the degree of correspondence captured between the observed and predicted

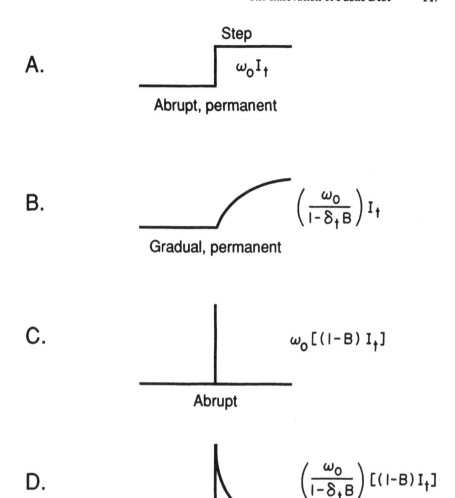

**Figure 4.5.** Models of Intervention and Impact

*Note:*

$\omega_0$ = An estimate of the difference between the pre- and postintervention process levels
$I_t$ = 1 during a war year and 0 during a nonwar year
$\delta_t$ = Rate of decay or increase
$B$ = A backshift operator that may be interpreted as $B(Y_t) = Y_{t-1}$

output series values, the residual mean squared error, the statistical significance of the model parameters, and the white noise or random character of the residuals.

# 5
## *Spending, Death, and Taxes in the Long Run*

We live in an era in which the appropriate scope of governmental activities is a subject of intensive political debate. Conservatives complain that governmental expansion and the encroachment of the public sector have gone too far and must be curbed. Liberals, on the other hand, complain that the process has not gone far enough to satisfy the demands of public welfare. Whatever one's ideological persuasion, it is clear that governments have expanded the scope of their activities and functions. Yet even if this statement enjoys consensus, by no means do we have a clear sense of how and why states have expanded their scale of operation. Toward the end of the nineteenth century, for instance, advocates of Wagner's Law contended that governmental activities would expand in roughly linear response to the development of growth-related social problems (see Bird 1971; Wagner and Weber 1977).

Peacock and Wiseman (1961), however, have stressed that governmental expansion has outpaced economic growth in the twentieth century. They attribute increases in the scope of governmental functions to the advent of national crisis. During crisis situations, they argue, the popular reluctance to accept tax increases can be overwhelmed by the need to respond. We agree that long-run governmental growth is discontinuous. We maintain, however, that, for the global powers, at least, the principal agent of change is a singular type of crisis—global war—and that the fundamental war-making–state-making process is much older than developments relatively unique to the twentieth century. Some support for this contention has already been provided in chapter

4. Further empirical evidence for this longer-term view is provided in this chapter by examining the long-term pattern of changes in governmental expenditures and revenues in relation to the onset of different types of war.

## The Expenditure Displacement Hypothesis

Expressed most simply, Peacock and Wiseman's (1961) displacement hypothesis states that governmental expenditures will increase during periods of national crisis. Although expenditures may decline in the postcrisis period, they will remain higher than precrisis expenditure levels. This permanent displacement effect on expenditures is attributed primarily to crisis-induced shifts in taxpayers' perceptions of tolerable tax burden levels. Depending on the governmental decision makers' attitudes toward the roles of public expenditures and their willingness to take advantage of the opportunity, major crises, especially wars, work to weaken or override normal (noncrisis) resistance to increased taxes. Tax revenues therefore are easier to raise. Wars, in addition, offer excellent opportunities to revise or overhaul the prevailing tax system and to create new sources of revenue. As a result, the widened tax base facilitates greater spending after the war or crisis than before.

Peacock and Wiseman (1961) present a detailed examination of Britain's principally twentieth-century expenditure patterns to test their hypothesis. Because their central hypothesis is attitudinally based, there are very real constraints on the extent to which expenditure data can be used to address their thesis. By visually examining a large number of spending series, however, they are able to demonstrate that World Wars I and II brought about major shifts in governmental spending that cannot be accounted for by population growth, inflation, or economic growth. Further support for their interpretation is produced by the finding that the expenditure increases were not due solely to increases in war-related and military costs. If this had been the case, the expenditure displacement process would represent merely the periodic augmentation of military spending and the gradual accumulation of war debts and pensions. Yet because nonmilitary and non-war-related spending increased as well, Peacock and Wiseman view this indicator as evidence of genuine governmental role expansion made possible by the involvement of a society in crisis or war.

Beyond the difficulty of tapping taxpayer attitudes with spending patterns, the Peacock-Wiseman evidence is also restricted by the small sample of one state and their exclusive reliance on the visual examination of longitudinal plots of numerous expenditure series. Even so, their hypothesis has stimulated a respectably extensive literature that sometimes uses more sophisticated empirical techniques or expands the number of countries surveyed or both. Although the most popular examples remain the British and American ones, the following states have also received some expenditure displacement effect attention: Brazil, Canada, Costa Rica, Dominican Republic, France, Germany, Guyana, Haiti, Honduras, Iceland, India, Japan, Panama, Sweden, and Taiwan. Viewed in the aggregate, the empirical outcomes represent decidedly mixed support for the original Peacock-Wiseman assertion. Four conclusions seem to have emerged. Crises associated with world wars:

1 bring about permanent changes in state expenditure levels (Emi 1963; Gupta 1967).
2 sometimes bring about permanent changes in state expenditure levels (Andre and Delorme 1978; Blondal 1969; Kaufman 1983; Tussing and Henning 1974).
3 create, at best, only temporary, impermanent shifts in state expenditure levels. The temporary impact may be attributed to the wartime higher priority given to military over civilian spending (Borcherding 1977a, 1977b; Musgrave 1969; Pryor 1968; Reddy 1970) or to postwar increases in civilian spending presumably related to addressing war damages and reconstruction (Bonin, Finch, and Waters 1967; Rosenfeld 1973).
4 may affect expenditure growth, but so do a number of other influences (Bennett and Johnson 1980; Meltzer and Richard 1978) including non-world wars (Emi 1963; Leff 1982; Nagarajan 1979), depression (Blondal 1969; Gupta 1967), and changes in governmental philosophies during peacetime (Goffman and Mahar 1971; Mahar and Rezende 1975; Reddy 1970).

Clearly, the four conclusions do not add up to anything resembling a consensus. Nor can the extent of disagreement be explained by the variety of countries examined. For example, all four conclusions have been arrived at by different analysts of the same or similar British and American expenditure data. To be sure, some findings should be viewed with more skepticism than others, owing to various research design problems.[1] Nevertheless, several questions deserve further investigation.

Does the war-induced expenditure displacement phenomenon apply to Britain? Alternatively, Peacock and Wiseman's explanation stresses "national crises," but their examination is restricted primarily to the effects of World Wars I and II. Yet, several authors contend that some interstate wars (e.g., the 1904–05 Russo-Japanese War for Japan or the 1962 Indo-Chinese War for India) had greater impacts on spending patterns than some of the twentieth-century's global wars. Other authors find significant impacts associated with World War I but not with World War II, and vice versa. Do all wars influence governmental spending in idiosyncratic ways and to varying extents? Or are some kinds of warfare, such as world wars, more likely than others to bring about permanent expenditure displacement effects?

## The War-making–State-making Interpretation

The variety of specification problems raised by the empirical studies that have followed Peacock and Wiseman do not exhaust the questions that need to be raised about the asserted displacement process. The Peacock-Wiseman emphasis on the crisis-induced stretching of tax burden tolerances is not implausible, and we see no need to reject it completely. Yet it is very much a twentieth-century explanation in flavor, just as it is based primarily on the examination of twentieth-century data. If the displacement phenomenon, however, predates the twentieth century, a more general or broader and less time-bound explanation is needed.

We are reluctant to argue that the twentieth century is an era generally characterized by more governmental sensitivity to taxpayer preference schedules. True, taxpayer revolts were once more common than they are now. Yet whether this generalization suggests greater taxpayer passivity, resignation, acquiescence, or all (or none) of the above remains debatable.

Nonetheless, we are suggesting that contemporary analysts are much more conditioned to emphasize popular constraints on governmental expansion than observers were likely to before the twentieth century. In a similar vein, the complete avoidance of the subject of war in Wagner's Law betrays a late nineteenth-century flavor. As Bird (1971: 4) notes, Wagner's late nineteenth-century generation did not expect wars to be common in the future. That expectation, although far off the mark, was somewhat justified; war in Europe was not frequent in the nineteenth century. Likewise, politicians do have some reason to be wary of voter hostility toward tax increases in the twentieth century. However, rather than focus exclusively on time-bound explanations, we should search for factors that operate over several centuries.

Support for our contention that the displacement process predates the twentieth century is not particularly difficult to find. As we and others have argued, a primary, if not the primary, imperative of state making has been the suppression of internal rivals and the defeat of external enemies. To remain in power at home and competitive abroad, military preparations have been essential and increasingly costly as military technology has improved. To pay for these seemingly ever-rising military costs, rulers have felt compelled to extract more and more resources from their populations. To collect and manage the increasing scale of these resource extractions, rulers have been forced or encouraged to create and expand their state's bureaucratic-administrative apparatus as well.

This version of the death-and-taxes cycle has been affected by change. Economic growth in general, and industrial development in particular, have made tax collections easier and more remunerative, but these same developments have also contributed to the likelihood of more intensive and costlier wars. The idea of a national debt was established to overcome shortfalls in tax revenues, especially in wartime. Yet the institutionalization of state debts also implies long-term debt accumulation and predictable debt interest payment schedules. Organizational fixed costs have increased as a result. Much more recently, and hardly isolated from other ongoing developments, the scope of governmental intervention in society and economy has also expanded. Yet although these developments may have modified the processes of state making, it is doubtful that they have been so radically transformed that we need to look for entirely new patterns. Interstate competition, wars, and the increasing costs of military preparations have not disappeared. Nor has the need to pay for these activities. Therefore, the historical connection between war making and state making and expansion has persisted.

The difference between this historical perspective on the growth of the state and the Peacock-Wiseman interpretation can be viewed as a matter of degree and emphasis. Peacock and Wiseman stress an image of contemporary state decision makers, who perceive a need to expand the scope of governmental activities, taking advantage of periods of crisis and war to expand their revenue base. The longer view does not preclude this inherently opportunistic possibility. It emphasizes instead a broader conceptualization of states owing their very organizational existence and raison d'etre to the need to survive, and to prevail, during periods of warfare.

Contronted with very real threats, decision makers have been compelled to mobilize human and material resources at their disposal in the interest of state security and military victory. At war's end, successful and unsuccessful states demobilize. Yet there is no reason to assume or to expect that the demobilization will be complete, except perhaps in cases of absolute defeat. Nor is it likely that state decision makers will insist on the strict restoration of the state's prewar role in national society. To the contrary, the following realities of wartime change will make turning back the political clock extremely difficult and unlikely.

1  New sources of revenue will have been created, and old sources will have been expanded, embellished, and perhaps made more efficient.
2  New social problems (e.g., price controls, provision for the homeless and refugees, concerns over inadequate diets and education for the draft-eligible portions of the population, the need to suppress racial tensions at home and in combat units, reconstruction) will emerge, and old problems will receive greater political attention than before.

3 New domestic political coalitions will emerge or have an improved opportunity to emerge as their constituencies' contribution to the war effort becomes more highly valued. The general resistance to social and political change, in any event, will more likely be weakened or even overwhelmed by the need to respond to the demands of the war effort.

4 New bureaucratic organizations will emerge to deal with novel war-related problems. Old governmental agencies will be expanded not only to deal with the increase in management problems, but also because the opportunity to invoke security-related justifications for bureaucratic expansion will be expanded as well.[2]

The significance of some of these war-induced changes may be eliminated or subsequently diminished in the postwar era. Nonetheless, it is most unlikely that all of the war-induced changes in expenditures, revenues, number of governmental agencies and personnel, salience of social issues and problems, and the nature and identity of political coalitions will disappear or even fade away. Wars thus induce direct domestic changes in the short run and also serve as catalysts and facilitators for direct and indirect domestic changes in the long run.[3] Thus, a respectable proportion of the war-induced growth of the global power state is not altogether a planned byproduct of making war.

Yet not all wars will have the same impact on state-making processes. Some wars will bring about very little change. Others will be associated with profound and wide-ranging impacts.

Although global wars are not defined in terms of scope, participation, or costs, they are unusually extensive and costly. It is reasonable to hypothesize, therefore, that the most important wars, the deadly turning points in modern political history for the global political system, should have the most important and significant impacts on the state-making processes of the participants. In contrast, interstate wars, as a rule, are less extensive and intensive affairs. Consequently, they are relatively less likely to exert significant impacts.

By focusing on the two categories of warfare as separate types of impact-producing interventions, our version of the war-making–state-making approach differs from the Peacock and Wiseman interpretation in several respects. First, Peacock and Wiseman restrict the temporal scope of their displacement argument to late nineteenth- and early twentieth-century British attitudinal and philosophical shifts toward greater state involvement in social policy arenas. Alternatively expressed, the two most recent world wars facilitated the expansion of the British state into new areas of government intervention. However, the distinction between global and interstate war presumably applies as far back as the initially crude emergence of the global political system in 1494, thereby encompassing nearly 500 years of state building and expansion.

Peacock and Wiseman (1961: 38) had noted that their emphasis on changing governmental attitudes would have been less tenable if crisis-related expenditure displacements had occurred before 1900. They then proceeded to demonstrate the absence of a permanent displacement effect on British spending after the Napoleonic Wars. If they are correct, the validity of our own historical argument is open to some question, unless the British pattern is exceptional. To ascertain what is a deviation from the norm requires an expansion of the number of states examined. However, we also believe that Peacock and Wiseman misread the early nineteenth-century British data. To explore this claim and to assess better the longer view on state building, the present examination needs to develop data series that extend back in time as far as is practical. The development of reasonably lengthy time series also facilitates the use of impact assessment models that measure the displacement impact of war as systematically as is possible.

Although our global war-making emphasis expands the temporal scope of the displacement explanation, the focus on the intervention agents is being narrowed considerably. Despite the fact that their own examination was restricted to the twentieth century's two world wars, Peacock and Wiseman equated their conceptualization of the opportunities for displacement with "social disturbances" or "national crisis." These broad categories imply the need to investigate the possible impacts of a relatively large list of candidate events. Nonwar crises, such as severe economic depressions, may indeed lead to the expansion of the state. Yet we doubt that any single type of crisis can compare over the long run to the ostensibly consistent, historical impact of global war.

Underlying our approach is the assumption that seeking information on war impacts for all states simultaneously is not a very efficacious strategy. Instead, given the disparities in types of states and historical experiences, a more selective and categorically homogenous state sample is desirable. Peacock and Wiseman's focus on a single state, of course, could be said to represent the extreme interpretation of this preference. Fortunately, there is a middle course between the extremes of single-state case studies and large-sample aggregations.

The logic of our hypothesis development suggests an actor focus on states that have participated in both global and interstate wars. However, all war participants do not participate fully or in the same way. For example, we might expect to find some differences in comparisons between strong and weak states or between persistent combatants and states defeated and occupied early in a war. On the other hand, we need to avoid eliminating all of the variance. Consequently, we confine our sample construction to the premise that the hypothesized displacement effects of global war should be most noticeable in the expenditures of those states most acutely involved in the succession struggles as contenders for systemic power. Ideally, then, our examinations would focus on the full set of global powers identified in chapter 1 (see table 1.5).

Unfortunately, continuous expenditure records from the sixteenth century on are not available for any global power state. We must also be careful to control for the possible complications of economic growth. Moreover, we wish to determine whether tax revenues follow the same historical course as do expenditures. In spite of the explanatory emphasis on tax revenues in Peacock and Wiseman's tax burden argument, these data are only rarely inspected vis-à-vis the displacement hypothesis.[4] Finally, we also wish to check whether any war-induced displacement effect that is uncovered can be explained solely in terms of increased military and war-related spending. A greater emphasis on the historical significance of warfare need not preclude the expansion of non-war-related activities, but the extent to which these governmental activities have expanded is probably subject to some degree of evolution.

The need for hard-to-come-by, continuous time series data on central government expenditures, tax revenues, military expenditures, and some measures of national wealth—all of which must encompass one or more global wars—forces some compromises on analysts.[5]

Longitudinal data that meet the requirements outlined in the previous paragraph are readily accessible for only a few global powers. Accordingly, we concentrate our most statistically sophisticated and comprehensive analyses on four global powers (Britain, the United States, France, and Japan). Given the need for continuous series on revenues, expenditures, military spending, and economic growth, these more comprehensive analyses must be relatively contemporary: post-1700 for Britain and roughly post-1815 for the other global powers.

Gains in accuracy and analytical power entail some sacrifice in the number of global war impacts that can be investigated. A post-1815 focus, for example, restricts the analysis to World Wars I and II. Even a post-1700 focus really adds only one more period of global war (1792–1815) for a single global power.

Although we are reluctant to dismiss these series as too short by the standards of social science (which usually makes do with substantially shorter series), gaining access to longer series would be most attractive and, ultimately, more persuasive. In this spirit, we have assembled partial, noncontinuous series for three global powers that permit us to inspect spending and taxing patterns before 1815 and even 1700. For England, we have royal revenue data extending back to the late twelfth century. Royal revenue data for Castile and Spain are available for portions of the fifteenth to the eighteenth century. Royal revenue and expenditure data for France are also available from the early sixteenth century.

With access to quasi series on preindustrial English, Spanish, and French state activities, what should we expect to find? If, as we claim, global wars are indeed the major historical source of perturbation in state making, the data, once some effort is made toward controlling for inflation, should demonstrate a clean upward staircase, with each consecutive global war creating a new step-level increase or expansion. If global wars are not distinguishable from nonglobal wars, we should find a number of increases that do not correspond in time with the global war combat.

Two important caveats apply to our expected findings. First, quite probably the impacts of global war have become increasingly stronger with the passage of time. In a vicious circle, global wars first encouraged state expansion. State expansion encouraged more deadly global wars. More deadly global wars encouraged more state expansion. Thus, we should not expect the impacts of the Italian-Indian Ocean Wars (1494–1516) to be as readily discernible (or as measurable) as the impacts of World War II.

A second preliminary consideration concerns the differences between maritime and continentally oriented global powers. Other things being equal, the more continentally oriented global powers should be involved in more frequent European interstate wars. Maritime powers should more likely do their nonglobal warring in the world economy's hinterlands. The maritime-commercial powers' state makers have also been consistently subject to more meaningful restraints on state expansion.

If these observations are accurate, they are grounds for anticipating two types of expenditure-revenue staircase patterns. The maritime-commercial state's staircase pattern should be relatively *clean*, with little in the way of increases occurring between bouts of global war. The staircase patterns of the continentally oriented powers, in contrast, are apt to be *messy*. That is, such states as Spain and France are more likely to expand between global wars as well as as a consequence of global wars. Figure 5.1 sketches our concept of clean and messy staircase-like expansion patterns.

The next section of this chapter examines the crude data available for England, Spain, and France. Merely discussing the various problems involved in analyzing these data is informative about the early expansion of the global powers. The next section also serves as a historical preface to the more exacting analyses to which we return after investigating the preindustrial evidence.

### The English, Spanish, and French Evidence

#### England
Roughly 525 years of English revenues, largely taken from Mann (1986), are summarized in table 5.1 and plotted in figure 5.2. Particularly helpful for

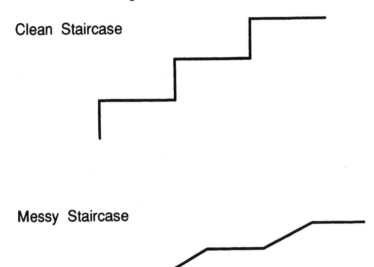

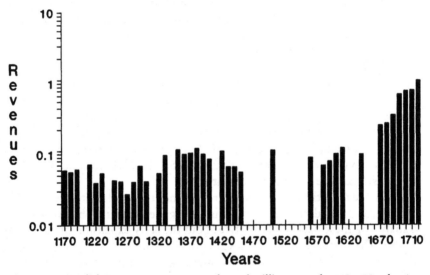

*Figure 5.1.* Clean and Messy Staircases

*Figure 5.2.* English Revenues, 1166–1720 (logged million pounds, 1451–75 values)

interpreting the English data is an unusually long price index, which permits the conversion of current revenue values to a constant series that minimizes the distortion of inflationary pressures. Mann's initial question was whether the English state was primarily oriented toward making and preparing for war or toward regulating domestic conflict. By examining the historical record

**Table 5.1**
*English State Revenues, 1155–1720*

| Years | Revenues in Current Pounds (thousands) | Revenues in Constant Pounds (millions) | Price Index |
|---|---|---|---|
| 1155–66 | 12.2 | | |
| 1166–77 | 18.0 | 0.060 | 30 |
| 1177–88 | 19.6 | 0.056 | 35 |
| 1188–98 | 17.1 | 0.061 | 28 |
| 1199–1214 | 37.9 | 0.072 | 53 |
| 1218–29 | 31.1 | 0.039 | 79 |
| 1229–40 | 34.6 | 0.054 | 64 |
| 1240–51 | 30.3 | 0.043 | 70 |
| 1251–62 | 32.0 | 0.041 | 79 |
| 1262–72 | 24.0 | 0.027 | 90 |
| 1273–84 | 40.0 | 0.040 | 100 |
| 1285–95 | 63.2 | 0.068 | 93 |
| 1295–1307 | 53.4 | 0.041 | 130 |
| 1316–24 | 83.1 | 0.054 | 153 |
| 1328–40 | 101.5 | 0.096 | 106 |
| 1340–51 | 114.7 | 0.116 | 99 |
| 1351–63 | 134.9 | 0.100 | 135 |
| 1363–75 | 148.4 | 0.104 | 143 |
| 1377–88 | 128.1 | 0.120 | 107 |
| 1389–99 | 106.7 | 0.100 | 107 |
| 1399–1410 | 95.0 | 0.085 | 112 |
| 1413–22 | 119.9 | 0.110 | 109 |
| 1422–32 | 75.7 | 0.067 | 113 |
| 1432–42 | 74.6 | 0.067 | 111 |
| 1442–52 | 54.4 | 0.056 | 98 |
| 1502–05 | 126.5 | 0.113 | 112 |
| 1559–70 | 250.8 | 0.089 | 279 |
| 1571–82 | 223.6 | 0.069 | 324 |
| 1583–92 | 292.8 | 0.079 | 376 |
| 1593–1602 | 493.5 | 0.100 | 496 |
| 1604–13 | 593.5 | 0.122 | 487 |
| 1630–40 | 605.3 | 0.099 | 609 |
| 1660–72 | 1582.0 | 0.251 | 630 |
| 1672–85 | 1634.0 | 0.269 | 608 |
| 1685–88 | 2066.9 | 0.353 | 585 |
| 1692 | 4100.0 | 0.693 | 592 |
| 1700 | 4300.0 | 0.773 | 556 |
| 1710 | 5200.0 | 0.790 | 658 |
| 1720 | 6300.0 | 1.090 | 578 |

*Source:* Mann (1986: 425, 451) is the source for the 1155–1688 data. The post-1688 revenue data are taken from Mitchell (1962). The constant revenues are expressed as million British pounds in 1451–75 constant prices. All revenue figures represent annual averages. Mann's sources for revenues are Chandaman (1975); Dietz (1923, 1928, 1964); Ramsay (1925); Steel (1954); and Wolffe (1971). Farmer (1956, 1957) and Phelps-Brown and Hopkins (1956) supplied the price information.

for state budgets, Mann sought an empirical answer to this occasionally debated proposition.

Although English state budgets are not without their ambiguities, especially in the earlier years, the historical record yields a fairly unambiguous response to Mann's question. Revenue increases were closely linked to war from at least the thirteenth century on. The increase in Tilly's "extractive state bulk," nevertheless, was far from impressive. Some 500 years were required in the English case for the size of state revenues to double. Clearly the impact of war on state making was only gradually realized, despite the extent to which the English state was focused on war-making activities.

The gradual impact of war on English revenues is less true after the mid-seventeenth century. As Mann expresses it, revenues rocket upward with each new war. We essentially agree and pursue this matter at greater length when examining Britain's post-1700 spending record later in this chapter. For now, we draw attention to another pattern emerging from the English data. Although every war may have some discernible impact, some wars have the abrupt, staircase-like impact for which we are searching. After these wars, revenues are permanently increased.

The first truly major impact found in table 5.1 is associated with the Hundred Years War (1337–1453), but even this impact appears to have been less than permanent, with constant revenues receding toward the prewar mean in the first half of the fifteenth century. Regrettably, there are major gaps in the series between 1452 and 1559. Yet revenues do appear to double between the 1450s and the turn of the century. They then recede in constant terms, possibly very slowly in the first half of the sixteenth century, only to increase again after the 1580s and through the first decade of the seventeenth century. Revenues rise again quite visibly in the 1660s (but probably also in the 1650s, which are missing from table 5.1), continuing on through the early eighteenth century.

What sort of staircase pattern thus emerges? We see major impacts in:

1  the fourteenth century,
2  possibly the end of the fifteenth and through the early sixteenth centuries,
3  the end of the sixteenth and through the early seventeenth centuries,
4  the mid-seventeenth century through the early eighteenth century.

Of the four steps, numbers three and four have the clearest association with global wars (1580–1608 and 1688–1713). The exact shape of the second step is not clear due to missing data, but part of it may coincide with the first global war (1494–1516). Only the first, somewhat tentative step is not accounted for by the global war hypothesis.

Is England a special case? From the European perspective, English military history was hardly typical. Storms, the English Channel, and the navy's wooden walls served to minimize the threat of foreign invasion for much of the period encompassed by our initial 525-year revenue series. Perhaps we are merely describing a staircase that happens to fit a single state, albeit one that has been unusually important in the annals of modern (post-1500) global power competition. At the very least, it must be conceded that England is unique in the sense that its revenue records have survived for a much longer period than those of other states. It is simply not possible to generate an equally long series for any other global power. Earthquakes, fires, and poor bookkeeping have all conspired to restrict the available data base. If we are willing to assume some risks of inaccuracy, however, it is possible to construct a long Spanish series and two French series.

### Castile/Spain

The Castilian/Spanish revenue data that we have been able to collect are listed in table 5.2 and plotted in figure 5.3. Nearly 400 years are encompassed by the admittedly spotty data. Regrettably, no controls for inflation appear to be available for this long period.[6] Yet even without the appropriate price controls, the historical pattern seems fairly clear.

Revenues in the fifteenth century began relatively high and declined into the mid-century internal wars. After 1481, they began to rise and continued to do so gradually into the next century. The missing data gap between 1511 and 1535 masks what may have been a doubling in revenues. In absolute terms, they had doubled again by the 1560s. By 1598 and in the midst of global war

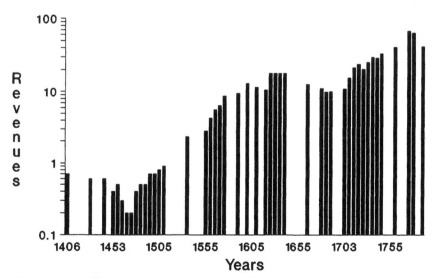

***Figure 5.3.*** Castilian/Spanish Revenues, 1406–1788 (logged million ducats)

**Table 5.2**
*Castilian/Spanish Revenues, 1406–1788*

| Year | Revenues | Year | Revenues |
|------|----------|------|----------|
| 1406 | 0.7 | 1598 | 12.9 |
| 1430 | 0.6 | 1608 | 11.5 |
| 1444 | 0.6 | 1621 | 10.5 |
| 1453 | 0.4 | 1625 | 18.0 |
| 1458 | 0.5 | 1630 | 18.0 |
| 1465 | 0.3 | 1635 | 18.0 |
| 1470 | 0.2 | 1640 | 18.0 |
| 1474 | 0.2 | 1667 | 12.7 |
| 1477 | 0.1 | 1680 | 11.1 |
| 1481 | 0.4 | 1687 | 9.9 |
| 1486 | 0.5 | 1689 | 10.0 |
| 1490 | 0.5 | 1703 | 10.9 |
| 1495 | 0.7 | 1708 | 13.7 |
| 1500 | 0.7 | 1710 | 15.5 |
| 1505 | 0.8 | 1713 | 20.8 |
| 1510 | 0.9 | 1720 | 23.9 |
| 1536 | 2.3 | 1725 | 20.5 |
| 1555 | 2.8 | 1730 | 25.5 |
| 1559 | 3.0 | 1735 | 29.8 |
| 1561 | 4.3 | 1740 | 29.0 |
| 1566 | 5.6 | 1745 | 33.5 |
| 1572 | 6.4 | 1761 | 40.9 |
| 1577 | 8.7 | 1774 | 68.1 |
| 1588 | 9.5 | 1778 | 64.4 |
| 1594 | 11.2 | 1788 | 41.9 |

*Note:* Revenues are expressed in million ducats.
*Sources:* Coxe (1813); Elliott (1963); Kamen (1969, 1980); Ladero (1970); Cooper (1970); Thompson (1976); Mackay (1981); Lynch (1984); Hillgarth (1978); Lovett (1986).

(1580–1608), revenues had doubled again. Although absolute revenues rose on the average during the seventeenth-century Thirty Years War, the increase was not all that dramatic. Only toward the end of the next global war phase (1688–1713) had royal revenues doubled over the 1689 figure of 10 million ducats—a figure that apparently approximated the revenue level throughout the 1588–1689 era. After 1713, revenues remained stable for only a decade or so before gradually escalating in the European wars of the eighteenth century.

Thus, we see a major step upward toward the end of the fifteenth century. Although it might be tempting to credit this rise exclusively to a global war effect, the major impetus was actually the Iberian war on Granada. Two step increases can be detected in the sixteenth century before a fourth step occurs, this time entirely attributable to global war (1580–1608). A fifth step increase is linked to the next global war (1688–1713), with revenues gradually rising throughout much of the eighteenth century.

### France

France is one European state that experienced destructive fires in its treasury archives. Despite the mishaps, one ironic problem in using French fiscal or spending information prior to 1789 is the survival of several conflicting series (see Legoherel 1965). Consequently, no one is in a sufficiently strong position to vouchsafe the authenticity of any of the existing series.

The problem is complicated further by some of the pathologies of French royal finances discussed in chapter 4: corruption, deficit spending, levied taxes that went uncollected, tax farming, secret royal accounts, and the usual ambiguities associated with interpreting the meaning of royal household accounts. Figure 5.4 illustrates one of these problems. One set of figures on French revenues pertain to gross revenues, or what the state expected theoretically to receive in any given year. The sums actually received (net revenues) invariably were much less than anticipated.

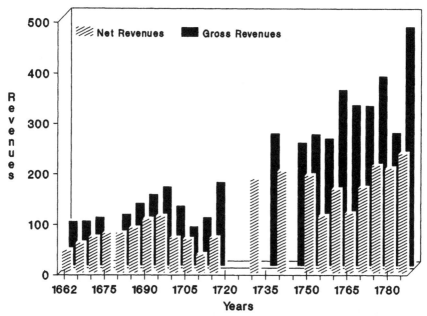

*Figure 5.4.* French Gross and Net Revenues, 1662–1785 (million livres tournois)

The records appear to be even worse for the transitional period from the Old Regime to Napoleon's empire (1789 to circa 1800), leaving a sizable hole to be filled for any series attempting to bridge the pre- and postrevolutionary eras. Currency equivalency problems (livres tournois versus francs) and the lack of price data on a par with the English case suggest additional reasons for considerable caution.[7]

**Table 5.3**
**French Revenues and Expenditures, 1250–1830**

| Years | Gross Revenues | Expenditures | Years | Gross Revenues | Expenditures |
|---|---|---|---|---|---|
| 1250 | 0.3 | | 1675 | 119.4 | 111.9 |
| 1418 | 0.7 | | 1680 | 107.7 | 96.0 |
| 1514 | 7.7 | 3.2 | 1685 | 125.0 | 103.0 |
| 1521 | | 3.9 | 1690 | 141.1 | 149.3 |
| 1523 | | 5.4 | 1695 | 156.7 | 187.7 |
| 1535 | | 4.2 | 1700 | 119.2 | 116.2 |
| 1546–47 | 15.7 | 6.2 | 1705 | 78.3 | 218.6 |
| 1548 | | 8.5 | 1710 | 115.0 | 225.9 |
| 1557 | 18.0 | 9.0 | 1715 | 169.4 | 146.8 |
| 1560 | | 8.8 | 1720 | 175.0 | |
| 1567 | | 8.7 | 1724 | 187.6 | 204.6 |
| 1575 | | 9.7 | 1730 | 195.7 | 183.0 |
| 1574–75 | 21.0 | 9.7 | 1735 | 258.0 | 206.6 |
| 1581–82 | 31.7 | 37.0 | 1740 | 210.9 | 197.6 |
| 1586 | 30.0 | | 1745 | 359.2 | 275.6 |
| 1588 | 27.9 | 16.1 | 1750 | 287.3 | 220.0 |
| 1596 | 23.0 | 16.3 | 1755 | 253.0 | 189.7 |
| 1600 | 20.5 | 20.5 | 1760 | 349.7 | 412.9 |
| 1605 | 26.9 | 26.9 | 1765 | 336.3 | 297.9 |
| 1610 | 33.3 | 33.6 | 1770 | 318.0 | 277.4 |
| 1615 | 22.1 | 24.6 | 1775 | 377.3 | 237.1 |
| 1620 | 25.7 | 36.7 | 1780 | 501.3 | 253.9 |
| 1625 | 34.7 | 49.5 | 1785–86 | 474.0 | 442.0 |
| 1630 | 23.9 | 41.9 | 1789 | 475.3 | 531.4 |
| 1635–36 | 79.9 | 68.4 | 1796 | | 637.0 |
| 1640 | 72.4 | 92.2 | 1801 | 547.0 | 550.0 |
| 1645 | 114.4 | 134.8 | 1805 | 678.6 | 704.0 |
| 1650 | 92.6 | 96.0 | 1810 | 795.4 | 859.0 |
| 1655 | 129.4 | 139.1 | 1815 | 729.0 | 931.0 |
| 1661 | 84.2 | 31.8 | 1820 | 933.0 | 907.0 |
| 1665 | 88.7 | 50.7 | 1825 | 979.0 | 982.0 |
| 1670 | 96.3 | 77.3 | 1830 | 971.0 | 1095.0 |

*Note:* Revenues and expenditures are expressed in current million livres tournois before 1790 and million francs after 1790.

*Sources:* The 1250 and 1418 figures are taken from Guenee (1971: 180). The 1514 through 1789 data are from Guery (1978) and Riley (1987). The remainder are taken from Sudre (1883); deKaufmann (1884); Marion (1914); and Mallez (1927).

In spite of all these reasons for not examining the French record, table 5.3 provides rather tentative information on French state spending and gross tax receipts between 1514 and 1830. As in the case of Spain, no adequate controls for inflationary pressures are available for this 400-plus-year series either. Price data on Paris grain (Baulant 1968) are sometimes used for this

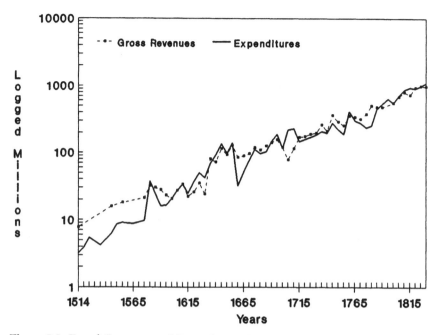

*Figure 5.5.* French Revenues and Expenditures (logged millions), 1514–1830

purpose. However, that series fluctuates too wildly from year to year to be of much use. The pattern that emerges from table 5.3 and figure 5.5 is less clearcut than its English counterpart. The sixteenth-century trend in current figures is gradual and positive through the 1570s. The first major spending increase occurs in or around 1582. For the next 100 years or so (through 1685), expenditures expressed in current values average roughly nine times the 1523–75 average spending levels. Some of this increase in average expenditure levels is due to French participation in the Thirty Years War, the fighting with Spain that continued through the decade after 1648, and the war with the Netherlands (1672–78). Nonetheless, a respectable increase in spending took place between 1685 and 1690 (approximately a 45 percent increase in current livres). Again on the average, table 5.4 indicates that spending levels between 1690 and 1780 were about three and a half times the level experienced between 1582 and 1685.

Table 5.3 and figure 5.5 show a continuation of this pattern, which might be described as a very rough or messy staircase, with ramps instead of stairs connecting each rising level. Not surprising, further spending increases are associated with the French Revolutionary/Napoleonic Wars (1792–1815), even though the scale of increase is not quite as great as one might expect. Another doubling effect, nevertheless, can be found by comparing the current expenditures of 1785 with those of 1815.

*Table 5.4*
**General Increases in French Expenditures**

| Years | Average Expenditure Levels Curent Million Livres |
|---|---|
| 1523–1575 | 7.3 |
| 1582–1685 | 64.3 |
| 1690–1780 | 223.3 |

In general, we regard the English, Spanish, and French evidence as decidedly supportive of our global war emphasis, even though each country displays a slightly different pattern. The common denominators are the serial upsurges associated with participation in global war. They deviate from a common pattern in what takes place between the global wars.[8] We interpret these inter–global war behaviors as roughly following the clean and messy dual paths predicted for maritime and continentally oriented global powers. The principal maritime global powers (the Netherlands, Britain, and, later, the United States) developed and operated with a variety of restraints and limitations on the expansion of their states. Indeed, the instinctive post–global war impulse was to try to force the newly expanded state to revert to its prewar size.

Their principal opponents (Spain, France, and, later, Germany) developed in different ways without the same type of domestic restraints, without the advantage of being able to tap the world economy's most dynamic economy, and without the advantage of winning the global wars. As a consequence, the intervals between global wars for the continentally oriented powers were usually characterized by catch-up activities. The combination of the greater interest in regional territorial affairs and the efforts to catch up with the more successful maritime powers meant more frequent and heavier involvement in Europe's land wars than was characteristic of the maritime powers. The leading land powers were, therefore, encouraged by systemic incentives to expand on an almost continual basis until, or unless, they were defeated decisively and removed from the ranks of principal contenders.

Although we suspect these conclusions would hold for the years not covered by the crude English, Spanish, and French data, there is no reason to base our argument solely on an exceedingly fragile data base. In the next section, we examine the continuous spending and revenue series (for which we can develop controls for inflation) of Britain, the United States, France, Japan, and, on a more qualified basis, Germany. Before we introduce these series, however, some methodological issues deserve our attention.

## Time Series Problems and the Utility of Box-Tiao
## Impact Assessment Models

Previous studies concerned with estimating the impact of war on various processes, such as economic growth and the increase in national and social welfare expenditures, can be divided into two groups. The first group basically relies on visual evaluations of the diferences between pre- and postintervention series in an attempt to assess war impact (Emi 1963; Mahar and Rezende 1975; Peacock and Wiseman 1961; Reddy 1970; Rosenfeld 1973). As a preliminary step or in instances in which an impact is acutely obvious, the eyeball technique may suffice; it certainly is always helpful. As the number of interventions and national series to be examined increases, however, visual plots quickly become cumbersome analytical and communication devices, especially if space is limited and not all the impacts are readily discernible. In general, but particularly in these circumstances, more objective tests are definitely desirable.

The second group, for the most part, uses regression techniques to estimate the changes in the level of prewar and postwar intervention series (Andre and Delorme 1978; Barbera 1973; Bonin et al. 1967; Gupta 1967; Kaufman 1983; Nagarajan 1979; Organski and Kugler 1980; Pryor 1968; Stohl 1976; Tussing and Henning 1974; Wheeler 1980). The ultimate validity of many of these regression-based findings, we feel, is handicapped by certain statistical problems related to an overemphasis on data-fitting operations and an underemphasis on controlling for autocorrelation and trend.

Most of the earlier expenditure displacement analyses exclude war period data in an effort to assess long-term effects without the results being unduly influenced by the war outliers. In the process, analysts have selected various time periods, ranging anywhere from 3 to 70 years or more, for the ad hoc prewar and postwar data intervals. To fit a least squares model to the data, prewar and postwar contortions in the original series, which might reduce the degree of fit, tend to be ignored.

In the presence of autocorrelation, a problem commonly encountered in time series and also frequently ignored, the data track for a period away from the equilibrium point. This tracking phenomenon results in unbiased but inefficient estimates of the parameters of a model. In linear regression, OLS estimates of $\beta$ will be unbiased while the variances of the estimators will be understated. In addition, the error variance of the regression model is minimized. If autocorrelation is ignored, the model will appear to provide a much better fit to the empirical data than is actually the case. Inferences based on sample $t$ and $F$-statistics will be misleading owing to the deflation of the true variance of $\beta$ and the regression model (Hibbs 1974).

Trend poses another obstacle in time series analysis. It produces a systematic change in the level of the series in such a way that it is difficult to interpret the short- and long-term effects of an intervention. The conventional method of removing trend has been to subtract a least squares trend line from the data. However, the OLS parameters cannot be estimated with much accuracy owing to their sensitivity to outliers as well as their somewhat static dependence on the positions of the first and last observations of the observed series.[9]

Perhaps an even more central issue with OLS detrending methods is the presumption by researchers that a time series is influenced by deterministic trend when it may be characterized by stochastic drift. A time series that is modeled as a fixed function of time (deterministically), when in fact the values vary in a probabilistic manner (stochastically), will result in errors in assessing the magnitude of an intervention's impact (McCleary and Hay 1980). In addition, because a time series can drift upward or downward for long periods owing only to random forces, it is not always obvious whether a progressive change in the level of a series is due to deterministic trend or stochastic drift.

To address the problems of fitting, autocorrelation, and trend, we use the impact assessment models developed by Box and Tiao (1975) and discussed in chapter 4. These models avoid the fitting problem because they use all the data in a time series to estimate parameters that are likely to have generated the series. The analyst has the opportunity to avoid excluding selected data points arbitrarily. Another advantage of Box-Tiao models is that they provide a parsimonious way to control for the effects of autocorrelation. An ARIMA scheme is used to model a noise component, which includes the random and deterministic effects of drift, trend, and autocorrelation. A linear filter(s) is then applied to transform the observed time series into white noise before estimating the actual effect of the intervention.[10] Moreover, the Box-Tiao models neutralize the problems associated with trend and drift, without a priori distinctions, through the use of difference equation models that can be used to differentiate between trend and drift and to provide dynamic estimates of trend.[11]

### Data Analysis

Our principal hypothesis states that for certain states, global wars are more likely to displace governmental expenditures and revenues than are interstate wars. In the Box-Tiao context, we would then expect to find significant, permanent impacts associated with the intervention of global wars and either temporary or nonsignificant impacts registered by interstate wars. To pursue this central hypothesis, we are in a position to analyze continuous revenue and expenditure series, expressed as proportions of gross national product, for Britain (after 1700), the United States (after 1792), France (after 1797), and Japan (after 1878). These series are plotted through 1985 in figures 5.6 through 5.9. Figure 5.10 plots an interrupted series for Germany for the sake of comparison. Table 5.5 lists the sets of global and interstate wars examined as interventions.

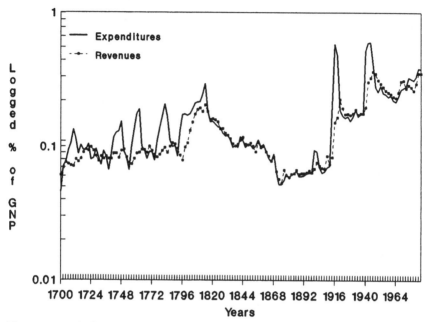

*Figure 5.6.* British Revenues and Expenditures (logged), 1700–1985

Gathering data on governmental expenditures and revenues, even the relatively contemporary variety, is subject to a host of pitfalls. Some of them we have failed to avoid. Whenever possible, we have attempted to use closed accounts as reported by governmental agencies or secondary and tertiary sources based on governmental abstracts. Occasionally, we have been forced to deviate from a reliance on official accounts in cases of overtly understated military spending figures. We have also attempted to exclude from the expenditure and revenue series spending for, and receipts from, public enterprises to enhance their longitudinal comparability.

The data sources used for France include Sudre (1883); deKaufmann (1884); Marion (1914); Jeze (1927); Mallez (1927); France, Ministere des Finances (1946); Marczewski (1961); Mitchell (1981); and France, Ministere de l'Economie (various years). For Britain, the sources are Deane (1955, 1968); Deane and Cole (1962); Mitchell (1962, 1981); Mitchell and Jones (1971); Feinstein (1972); United Kingdom, Central Statistical Office (various years);

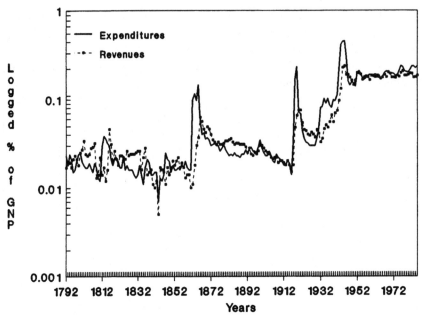

*Figure 5.7.* United States Revenues and Expenditures (logged), 1792–1985

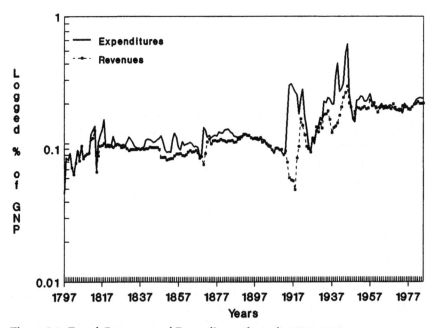

*Figure 5.8.* French Revenues and Expenditures (logged), 1797–1985

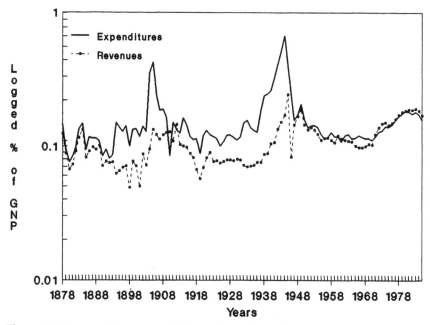

**Figure 5.9.** Japanese Revenues and Expenditures (logged), 1878–1985

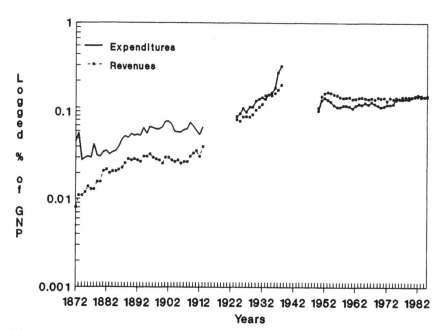

**Figure 5.10.** German Revenues and Expenditures (logged), 1872–1985

**Table 5.5**
**Interstate and Global Wars Examined**

| Interstate Wars | | Global Wars | |
|---|---|---|---|
| *France (1815–1979)* | | | |
| Franco-Spanish | 1823 | World War I | 1914–18 |
| Roman Republic | 1849 | World War II | 1939–45 |
| Crimean | 1854–56 | | |
| Italian Unification | 1859 | | |
| Franco-Mexican | 1862–67 | | |
| Franco-Prussian | 1870–71 | | |
| Sino-French | 1884–85 | | |
| Franco-Thai | 1940–41 | | |
| Korean | 1951–53 | | |
| Sinai | 1956 | | |
| | | | |
| *Britain (1700–1980)* | | | |
| Anglo-Swedish | 1715–19 | Spanish Succession | 1701–13 |
| Quadruple Alliance | 1718–20 | French Revolutionary | 1793–1802 |
| Anglo-Spanish | 1726–29 | Napoleonic | 1803–15 |
| Jenkin's Ear/Austrian | | World War I | 1914–18 |
| Succession | 1739–48 | World War II | 1939–45 |
| Seven Years | 1756–63 | | |
| American Independence | 1778–83 | | |
| Anglo-American | 1812–14 | | |
| Crimean | 1854–56 | | |
| Anglo-Persian | 1856–57 | | |
| Korean | 1950–53 | | |
| Sinai | 1956 | | |
| | | | |
| *United States (1792–1980)* | | | |
| Anglo-American | 1812–14 | World War I | 1917–18 |
| Mexican-American | 1846–48 | World War II | 1941–45 |
| Spanish-American | 1898 | | |
| Korean | 1950–53 | | |
| Vietnam | 1965–73 | | |
| | | | |
| *Japan (1878–1980)* | | | |
| Sino-Japanese | 1894–95 | World War I | 1914–18 |
| Russo-Japanese | 1904–05 | World War II | 1941–45 |
| Manchurian | 1931–33 | | |
| Sino-Japanese | 1937–41 | | |

and Cole (1981). The Japanese sources are Emi (1963, 1979), Ohkawa and
Rosovsky (1973), Mitchell (1982), and *Japan Statistical Yearbook* (various
volumes). For the United States, the sources are U.S. Department of
Commerce (1975), Berry (1978), and U.S. Office of the President (various
years). The incomplete German data are taken from Mitchell (1981) and

Germany, *Statistisches Jahrbuch* (multiple years). Finally, the wars listed in table 5.5 are based on information found in Wright (1965), Singer and Small (1972), Dupuy and Dupuy (1977), Small and Singer (1982), and Levy (1983).

The expected outcome is very close to that found and reported in table 5.6. All of the interstate war impacts reflect abrupt, temporary models, and only half of the omegas are significant. All of the global war omegas are significant, and all but one are associated with abrupt, permanent models.[12] The sole exception is the Japanese expenditures/GNP series, which requires the imposition of an abrupt, temporary model.

**Table 5.6**
**The Impact of War on Logged Expenditures/GNP and Tax Revenues/GNP[a]**

| State | Interstate Wars[b] $\omega_o$[d] | $\delta$ | Global Wars $\omega_o$ | Noise Model[c] $N_t$ | $\chi^2$ |
|---|---|---|---|---|---|
| Logged Expenditures/GNP | | | | | |
| Britain | 0.13* | 0.72* | 0.39* | white | 18.6 |
| (1700–1980) | (4.8) | (6.9) | (7.8) | noise | |
| United States | 0.15 | | 1.01* | white | 20.1 |
| (1792–1980) | (1.8) | | (7.6) | noise | |
| France | 0.07* | | 0.50* | white | 18.4 |
| (1815–1979) | (2.4) | | (6.7) | noise | |
| Japan | 0.27* | | 0.65* | white | 12.4 |
| (1879–1980) | (3.4) | | (5.2) | noise | |
| Logged Revenues/GNP | | | | | |
| Britain | 0.03* | 0.87* | 0.08* | white | 12.0 |
| (1700–1980) | (2.6) | (6.2) | (2.6) | noise | |
| United States | −0.06 | | 0.30* | white | 19.4 |
| (1792–1980) | (−1.2) | | (2.4) | noise | |
| France | −0.02 | | 0.27*,c | white | 12.4 |
| (1815–1979) | (−1.2) | | (5.7) | noise | |
| Japan | 0.05 | | 0.20* | $\theta_i = .41$* | 15.2 |
| (1878–1980) | (1.3) | | (2.3) | (4.3) | |

*Note:* No statistically significant trend parameters were encountered; *t*-values are reported in parentheses.
* denotes statistical significance at the .05 level.
[a] All data have been logged to achieve variance stationarity.
[b] The impact of interstate wars was abrupt and temporary. The impact of global wars was abrupt and permanent.
[c] The first seven noise models are white noise, first differenced series (0, 1, 1). The Japanese revenue noise model is a first differenced, moving average process (0, 1, 1). $\chi^2 \leq .05$ where H$_o$: residuals are white noise.
[d] The reported omega is based on a five-year lag for World War I.

In contrast to the evident British, French, and American displacements owing to global war, World War I had no visible impact on Japanese expenditures and revenues. This observation is underscored by comparing the effect of World War I to the disturbance in the expenditure series caused by the 1904–05 interstate war and the temporary expenditure spike during World War II. If it is fair to dismiss the first Japanese global war as a case of marginal participation (Small and Singer [1982] report 400 Japanese battle deaths for World War I), the second case suggests that defeat and occupation may interrupt the displacement effect, or at least alter the direction of displacement. Interestingly, however, Japanese revenues/GNP are permanently displaced by World War II even though expenditures/GNP are not.

Nevertheless, in three of the four expenditure cases and in all four revenue cases, the intervention outcomes are markedly different. The intervention impacts of the global wars are permanent or sustained, whereas the impacts of the interstate wars are either insignificant or transitory. Formally, we have not examined the twice interrupted German series. Nor did Germany participate in any interstate wars during the period for which we have data. Still, the step-level increases associated with World Wars I and II, especially in terms of revenues, are quite evident in figure 5.10.

It is possible to be more specific about the nature of the impacts for which we have continuous series. We could, for example, translate each logged omega parameter into estimates of percentage change before and after the interventions. The largest omega in table 5.6, for instance, is the 1.01 parameter associated with the impact of global wars on the United States expenditure/GNP series. In percentage change terms, the 1.01 parameter can be interpreted as an approximately 175 percent change in the expenditures-to-gross-national-product ratio. This figure can be compared to the insignificant and temporary 16 percent change ($\omega_0 = .15$) associated with the expenditure/GNP impact of the United States participation in interstate wars. However, we are modeling multiple interventions over fairly long periods of time and the omega parameters and percentage changes reflect average, as opposed to cumulative, effects. Calculating percentage changes in this context, therefore, does not really provide a more concrete numerical handle for interpreting and comparing the specific outcomes. Only the metric of the parameter is changed. Although such changes are helpful when the impact of a specific war is being analyzed, the interpretation advantage seems quite marginal when the average impact of wars is being assessed collectively.[13]

This generalization seems truer when the outcome is as clearcut as the findings summarized in table 5.6 indicate. The persistent effects of global war on both the expenditures and revenues of the states examined are simply of a different order of magnitude than are the impacts of interstate war. The logged parameter values also permit us to point out an interesting difference between expenditure and revenue outcomes. In the aggregate, global war tends to exert similar impacts on both types of series, that is, permanent and statistically significant. But wartime displacements of revenues are much less dramatic than are expenditures. In fact, revenue increases during wartime lag behind expenditure increases in terms of magnitude and timing. Revenue levels only begin to match expenditure levels toward the end, or after the end, of a war and only after expenditure levels have begun to decline.

This tendency could be viewed as somewhat contrary to expectations, based on Peacock and Wiseman's argument that wars increase tax burden tolerances. Alternatively, it could be argued that dramatic expenditure increases drag revenues upward and that the extent to which this occurs depends on the extent to which postwar expenditures decline, not the other way around. Unfortunately, one can push this counter-argument only so far with aggregate data. We need more detailed case studies of how wars bring about both temporary and permanent governmental expansion. See, for example, Marwick (1974), Burke (1982), Stein (1978), and Strickland (1983).

### The Permanence of Pre-Twentieth-Century British Displacements

Fortunately, however, these data do encompass the period used by Peacock and Wiseman to reject the presence of permanent pre-twentieth-century displacements. Our analysis, whether all British global wars are lumped together or examined separately, suggests that British participation in global wars, at least since 1700, has brought about permanent displacements.[14] How, then, do we account for the more general discrepancy between our findings and those of Peacock and Wiseman?

Table 5.7 lists Peacock and Wiseman's 1792–1890 data on expenditures/ GNP for selected years and contrasts it with our own corresponding data. Clearly, the numbers we use are not identical with those used by our predecessors, but the direction of movement is sufficiently similar to regard them as being in the same ballpark. However, there are two important differences. First, our series begins in 1700. This beginning date enables us to see a permanent displacement occurring between 1700 and 1720 (5 to 9 percent, which roughly persists in peacetime through the rest of the century), an impact that probably would be even more impressive if our series could be extended back through the 1680s.

The second difference is in Peacock and Wiseman's expenditure/GNP level returning to the 1792 level by 1841. Our series suggests that this does not occur until some 20 years later in the 1860s. Nevertheless, both series indicate an eventual return to the pre–French Revolutionary-Napoleonic Wars equilibrium level, thereby suggesting a less than permanent effect. Yet, how long is permanent? The disturbance to our series does not subside for some 45 years, and even Peacock and Wiseman's evidence indicates a 25-year effect, nearly a generation in length. The effect lasted sufficiently long, in any event, to be able to model the impact of the French Revolutionary-Napoleonic Wars as exerting a permanent effect on the British series.

Table 5.7
British Expenditures, GNP, and Expenditures/GNP

| Year | Expenditures/GNP (Percentage) Peacock-Wiseman | Rasler-Thompson | Expenditures | GNP |
|------|------|------|------|------|
| 1700 |    | 5 | 4 | 70 |
| 1720 |    | 9 | 8 | 67 |
| 1792 | 11 | 9 | 16 | 182 |
| 1800 | 24 | 17 | 28 | 166 |
| 1814 | 29 | 29 | 61 | 209 |
| 1822 | 19 | 15 | 51 | 350 |
| 1831 | 16 | 12 | 48 | 413 |
| 1841 | 11 | 11 | 47 | 428 |
| 1850 | 12 | 10 | 61 | 596 |
| 1860 | 11 | 10 | 65 | 621 |
| 1870 | 9 | 7 | 65 | 1013 |
| 1880 | 10 | 6 | 84 | 1446 |
| 1890 | 9 | 6 | 113 | 1890 |

Note: British expenditures and GNP are expressed in million 1913 pounds.

Regardless of how permanence is defined, it is clear that Britain enjoyed remarkable economic growth rates during the period in question. Between 1700 and 1792, the British economy expanded by roughly a factor of 2.5, although much of this growth was offset by population growth. In marked contrast, the size of the nineteenth-century British economy doubled approximately every 20 to 25 years. Any British government might have been hard pressed to expand their budgets at this same rate—particularly in an era consistently characterized (through the 1870s) by a conservative approach to governmental spending.

Thus, Peacock and Wiseman are not incorrect to treat the 1793–1815 displacement as less than permanent, but the nature of the evidence also requires careful consideration. In absolute terms or constant British pounds (see table 5.7), there is no doubt that British governmental expenditures were displaced upward. In relation to economic growth, this upward displacement ultimately proved to be temporary. How long the effect took to be regarded as temporary depends on whose data are used, but evidently the temporary status is as much, if not more, dependent on the intervention of the Industrial Revolution as it is on austerity budgets. Considered in conjunction with the permanent impact (on revenues/GNP, at least) of the second half of the 1689–1713 global war, we should be most reluctant to restrict permanent expenditure displacement to the twentieth century and the evolution of contemporary ideas about the appropriate scope of governmental activities.

## The Role of Military Spending

Our final question centers on the extent to which the permanent expenditure-revenue impacts of global war can be traced to military spending. The long view of state making stresses the role of military and war expenditures and preparations as the primary impetus to the growth of the state organization. Yet we do not infer from this emphasis that the growth of the state is predicated solely on the growth of military spending.

On the contrary, preparing for war and interstate competition has had a number of spillover consequences, ranging from the need for a permanent bureaucracy to collect taxes in order to pay for sporadic warfare to the war-related growth of social services administered by the state. Titmuss (1969), for example, has argued for a close link between the ascending intensity of war and the evolution of British social policy. As an increasing proportion of the population became involved in the warfare of the past few centuries, state makers were forced to expand their efforts to improve the health and morale of men available for combat. Later, the same attention was devoted to the next generation of recruits (especially children) and, ultimately, to the whole population as they too became more important to war efforts.

There seems little need to restrict the spirit of this argument to the British experience; this point of view is compatible with war- and state-making perspectives.[15] At the same time, it means that we have little basis, aside from the distinction about relevant crises, for expecting findings different from those advanced by Peacock and Wiseman. Global wars presumably should influence both military and nonmilitary expenditures.

In this examination, we initially pursue a minimal definition of military spending by restricting the concept to expenditures consumed directly by the state's armed forces. Accordingly, we confine our empirical attention to the differential impacts of interstate and global war on military (plotted in figures 5.11 through 5.15 for five global powers) and nonmilitary expenditures/GNP (reported in table 5.8 for four global powers).

The outcome reported in table 5.8 is not quite as clearcut as the findings in table 5.6. Except for the U.S. case, both interstate and global wars exert abrupt, temporary impacts on military spending. Only in the U.S. case is there a temporary-permanent split between the impacts of the two types of war. Further analysis, however, suggests that the categorical approach to war impacts requires some qualification, depending on which global wars are involved. When the impact of each global war is examined separately, the pre-1939 global wars are associated with temporary impacts. World War II, however, led to significant and permanent increases in British, U.S., and French military expenditures/GNP. Not too surprisingly, the Japanese experience requires the construction of a more complicated model—a temporary pulse

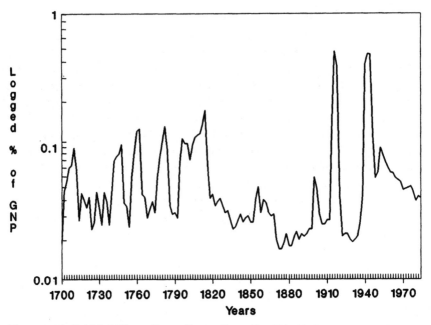

***Figure 5.11.*** British Military Expenditures (logged), 1700–1985

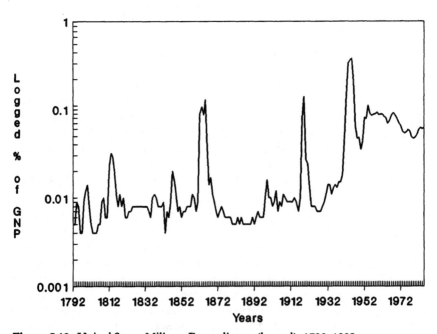

***Figure 5.12.*** United States Military Expenditures (logged), 1792–1985

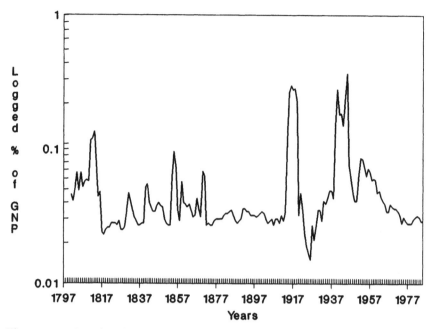

***Figure 5.13.*** French Military Expenditures (logged), 1797–1985

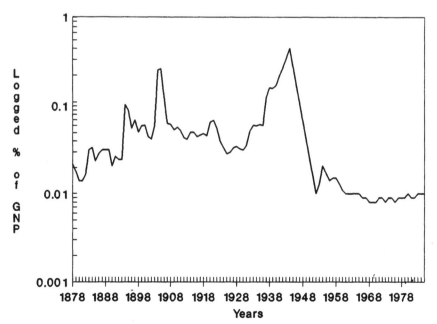

***Figure 5.14.*** Japanese Military Expenditures (logged), 1878–1985

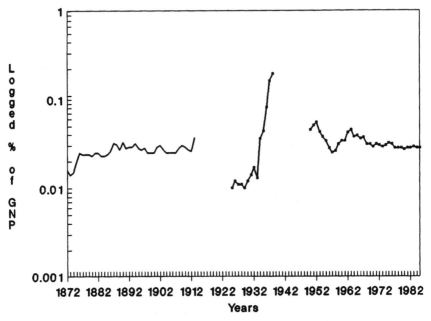

*Figure 5.15.* German Military Expenditures (logged), 1872–1985

model for war years followed by an abrupt, permanent model for the dramatic postwar decrease.

In contrast, the war-type distinction is operative for nonmilitary expenditures/GNP. The impact of interstate wars is nonsignificant for all four countries. Abrupt, permanent models apply in the British, U.S., and French global war cases. The unusual Japanese case takes a gradual, permanent model in this instance, reflecting increases in nonmilitary spending after both twentieth-century world wars. Ironically, then, it is nonmilitary, not military, spending that is more systematically influenced by periodic global warfare. Nor is this phenomenon an innovation of the twentieth century.

Still, dividing expenditures into military and nonmilitary spending categories constitutes a limited test of the extent to which global war expands non-war-related allocations. We can take this analysis one step further by removing some more of the war-related expenditures from the nonmilitary side of the ledger. Two prime war-related budgetary candidates for removal are interest payments on the national debt and veteran pensions. Series pertaining to the first item are relatively available for all four global powers. Data concerning veteran pensions, unfortunately, are somewhat less accessible for our long periods, but we were able to extract them for the Japanese and U.S. cases.

Table 5.8
The Impact of War on Logged Military and Nonmilitary Expenditures/GNP[a]

| State | Interstate Wars[b] $\omega_0$ | $\delta$ | Impact Type | Global Wars $\omega_0$ | $\delta$ | $\omega_0$ | Noise Model[c] $N_t$ | $\chi^2$ |
|---|---|---|---|---|---|---|---|---|
| Logged Military Expenditures/GNP | | | | | | | | |
| Britain | 0.32* | 0.69* | abrupt, | 1.60* | | | white | 11.9 |
| (1700–1980) | (4.0) | (4.9) | temporary | (9.6) | | | noise | |
| United States | 0.32* | 0.71* | abrupt, | 1.49* | | | white | 11.9 |
| (1792–1980) | (2.9) | (3.7) | permanent | (8.3) | | | noise | |
| France | 0.13* | | abrupt, | 1.10* | 0.47* | | white | 28.8 |
| (1815–1979) | (2.3) | | temporary | (8.9) | (5.8) | | noise | |
| Japan | 0.30* | | abrupt, | 2.32* | | | white | 29.9 |
| (1878–1980) | (2.1) | | temporary | (8.0) | | | noise | |
| Logged Nonmilitary Expenditures/GNP | | | | | | | | |
| Britain | 0.00 | | abrupt, | 0.33* | | | $\theta_i = -0.50*$ | 15.7 |
| (1700–1980) | (–0.5) | | permanent | (4.7) | | | (10.0) | |
| United States | –0.04 | | abrupt, | 0.52* | | | white | 18.4 |
| (1792–1980) | (1.8) | | permanent | (4.7) | | | noise | |
| France | –0.03 | | abrupt, | 0.27* | | | $\theta_i = -0.11*$ | 21.0 |
| (1815–1979) | (–0.6) | | permanent | (3.2) | | | (2.2) | |
| Japan | 0.08 | | gradual, | 0.35* | | 0.86* | $\phi = -0.35*$ | 32.8 |
| (1878–1980) | (1.9) | | permanent | (3.5) | | (9.5) | (–3.5) | |

Note: No statistically significant trend parameters were encountered; t-values are reported in parentheses.
* denotes statistical significance at the .05 level.
[a] All data have been logged to achieve variance stationarity.
[b] The impacts of the interstate wars were abrupt and temporary.
[c] Five of the first six noise models are white noise, first differenced series (0, 1, 0). The British and French nonmilitary noise models are first differenced, moving average processes (0, 1, 1). The Japanese nonmilitary noise model is a first differenced, autoregressive process (1, 1, 0).

Table 5.9 reports selected observations on two proportional series: (1) nonmilitary expenditures/GNP (nonmilitary expenditures equal total expenditures minus military expenditures, as analyzed in tables 5.6 and 5.8) and (2) nonwar expenditures/GNP (nonwar expenditures equal total expenditures minus [military expenditures plus debt interest payments plus veteran pensions] for the United States and Japan and minus [military expenditures plus debt interest payments] for Britain and France). The point of the exercise is not to compare the magnitude of the two sets of observations (the nonwar proportions must be smaller than the nonmilitary ones, by definition) but rather to check whether the global war changes in the nonwar series appear to behave much differently from the previously analyzed nonmilitary series.

The nonwar spending series do seem to exhibit the same patterns of discontinuous growth and permanent changes before and after global wars observed in the more broadly defined nonmilitary spending series. Equally worth noting is the 1790–1820 doubling of the proportion of GNP devoted to

Table 5.9
Selected Data on Nonmilitary and Nonwar Expenditures as a Percentage of GNP

| Year | Nonmilitary | Nonwar | Nonmilitary | Nonwar |
|------|-------------|--------|-------------|--------|
| | Britain | | France | |
| 1780 | .057 | .013 | | |
| 1790 | .070 | .013 | | |
| 1820 | .110 | .027 | | |
| 1830 | .088 | .021 | | |
| 1840 | .071 | .019 | | |
| 1850 | .076 | .022 | | |
| 1860 | .064 | .023 | | |
| 1870 | .045 | .019 | | |
| 1880 | .040 | .020 | | |
| 1890 | .038 | .023 | .096 | .047 |
| 1900 | .035 | .024 | .085 | .046 |
| 1913 | .042 | .035 | .061 | .037 |
| 1920 | .145 | .092 | .150 | |
| 1930 | .147 | .084 | .112 | .055 |
| 1950 | .192 | .155 | .219 | .207 |
| 1960 | .175 | .141 | .181 | .168 |
| 1970 | .227 | .202 | .235 | .212 |
| 1980 | .285 | .247 | .272 | .234 |
| | United States | | Japan | |
| 1890 | .019 | .008 | .063 | .049 |
| 1900 | .018 | .008 | .074 | .062 |
| 1913 | .010 | .005 | .083 | .052 |
| 1920 | .045 | .031 | .054 | .038 |
| 1930 | .027 | .018 | .081 | .051 |
| 1938 | .065 | .050 | .173 | .058 |
| 1950 | .104 | .076 | .160 | .158 |
| 1960 | .096 | .071 | .108 | .099 |
| 1970 | .119 | .094 | .103 | .096 |
| 1980 | .172 | .143 | .176 | .146 |

Note: The United States and Japan nonwar proportions exclude veteran pensions, whereas the British and French nonwar proportions are restricted to the common base (total expenditures—[military + debt interest spending])/GNP.

nonwar purposes in the British case. The proportions admittedly are quite small, in accordance with pre-twentieth-century austerity policies, and decline between 1820 and 1840. Unlike the nonmilitary series, however, the upward shift in the nonwar proportion reflects a permanent change. Thus, table 5.9 reinforces the support for the contention that the displacement phenomenon should not be dismissed simply as an artifact of postwar increases in war-related spending.[16]

## Conclusion

We have attempted to achieve several goals in this chapter. First, we have sought to reduce some of the empirical ambiguities about, and disputes over, the existence of a war-induced expenditure displacement phenomenon. In contrast to the divergence of opinion in the literature, the relationship between global war and permanent spending shifts in some of the world system's historically most powerful states (Britain, the United States, France, and Japan) is statistically and substantively significant. Nor are these war-induced displacements restricted to the twentieth or even the nineteenth centuries. They can be found at least as early as the fifteenth century. Moreover, the displacement that occurs is only partially a function of war-related expenditures. Non-war-related spending also is affected. Global war must, therefore, be considered one of the more important sources of the growth and expansion of the modern global power state.

Second, we have attempted to make a distinction between Peacock and Wiseman's hypothesized displacement effect and their tax tolerance explanation of the relationship. Demonstrating the existence of the displacements does little to confirm, or to disconfirm, the relatively independent idea that national crises provide opportunities for overcoming taxpayer resistance to greater revenue extraction efforts. Rather than seeking ways to compare taxpayer attitudes during war and peacetime, something about which we know very little (see Goetz 1977), our interpretive preference is to stress the broader, historical context of the reciprocal interactions between war and state-making processes. For the older and most powerful states at least, an appreciation for the persistent role of war is central to explaining the growth and expansion of the state, whether or not governmental leaders choose to pay much attention to citizen preferences on tax burdens.

Last, but not necessarily least, the outcomes of the data analyses again underscore the theoretical significance of a special category of warfare—the global war—that is much less appreciated than it deserves. There is no need to overstate our case by insisting that global wars are the only external events to have significant internal impacts. Other types of events, including the more frequent nonglobal wars, can and do have domestic repercussions. However, we have been able to demonstrate that the spending and tax revenue patterns and, more generally, the organizational expansion of some of the system's leading states are more likely to be displaced and displaced permanently by global wars than by interstate wars.[17]

In many respects, we suspect that we are only beginning to tap, in a systematic way, the domestic implications of global war as both a catalyst and as an agent of socioeconomic and political change.[18] Continuing the assault on this knowledge deficit, chapter 6 examines the direct impact of wars on economic growth rates. Increases in state extraction efforts certainly are not determined by economic growth. Yet there is a relationship. Economic growth has surely facilitated state expansion over the long term. In more recent years, the problems associated with the presence and absence of economic growth have probably encouraged state expansion as well.

To what extent, though, is economic growth itself a function of warfare? As is customary, opinion is divided, and for good reason. War's impact on economic growth is highly contingent on a variety of factors—an observation that we demonstrate in the next chapter. Nevertheless, it is possible to pinpoint the overall, differential impacts of interstate and global warfare on the economies of the main participants.

# 6
# War and the Economic Growth Question

Implicit in the expansion of debts, expenditures, and revenues is an economic base capable of supporting the financial extractions of state making. If, as we found in chapters 4 and 5, global wars are associated with significant changes in governmental borrowing, taxing, and spending patterns, then we need to know whether these same wars are associated with equally significant changes in national wealth and rates of growth that could independently influence the propensity, or ability, of state makers to expand their activities. However, pinning down the exact relationship between war and economic growth is not a simple task, even for a small subset of the universe of states, such as the global powers.

For some time now, scholars have debated the linkage of war to economic growth (Sombart 1913; Nef 1950; John 1954–55; Rostow 1962; Wright 1965; Dickson 1967; Gould 1972; Marwick 1974; Deane 1975; Parker 1975; Winter 1975). Whether the analytical focus is placed on specific wars, on a series of wars during a specific period, or on wars in general, however, the nature of the linkage continues to defy precise delineation. If we assume that all or most wars probably involve some obvious and subtle mixture of destructive and constructive effects on war participants, we are still left with the possibilities that the net war impact on economic growth can be positive, negative, variable (positive for some cases, negative for others), or insignificant. The range of possible outcomes is further complicated because any of these four effects can also be characterized as either temporary or permanent. Unfortunately, verbal arguments and, occasionally, empirical evidence can be found to support most if not all of the possible relationships. The problem is summarized cogently by Deane:

> Clearly, it is impossible to generalize usefully about the impact of war on the economic progress of nations for it has depended on the special circumstances of particular wars and of the countries concerned. To the extent that war involves: (1) physical destruction of real capital; (2) diversion of scarce labour, capital and raw material resources from productive to unproductive uses; and (3) an increase in the risks and uncertainties of mercantile or manufacturing enterprise, it must have a retardative effect on economic development. To the extent the demands of war: (1) draw into productive use underemployed factors; (2) stimulate output in industries whose expansion reduces costs or creates opportunities for other branches of industry; and (3) precipitate fiscal or financial or organizational developments which redistribute incomes or opportunities in favour of innovating enterprise, its effects are more likely to be growth-promoting than growth-retarding. For the countries concerned, success or failure in war may further affect industrialization by enlarging or diminishing their international markets for domestic produce or their access to crucial raw materials or other resources. (1975: 91)

No doubt, Deane's conclusion about the utility of generalization is unduly pessimistic. Her outline of the economic factors involved does suggest, nevertheless, why it has been so difficult to construct a definitive answer to the war-economic growth question. Given the correct mixture of circumstances prior to, during, and after a war, it is presumably possible that different wars have promoted, retarded, or made little or no net impact on the economic growth of various economies. In brief, none of the four possible outcomes need be regarded as incompatible with a fully specified theory (one that would include noneconomic factors not mentioned by Deane) on the economic impact of warfare—assuming such a theory were available.

In the absence of such a theory, two research strategies can be entertained. The first and most ambitious strategy entails developing the missing theory, perhaps along the lines suggested by Deane and perhaps incorporating other factors, such as warfare intensity, winner-loser status, global-nonglobal power status, territorial and population gains and losses, war duration, and combat location. Once a theory of the economic impact of war has been generated and specified, the appropriate data could then be collected for testing purposes. This first strategy thus is itself a major project.

If, on the other hand, information on the linkages between war and economic growth is sought as a subsidiary question to other interests, a second, less ambitious, and more provisional strategy can be pursued. Specifically, the economic impact of war question grants us another opportunity to investigate the differential impacts of different types of war and to test the hypothesized distinctiveness of global warfare's impacts. Accordingly, we propose to assess empirically, with the aid of time-series techniques, the net impact of global and interstate wars on the economic growth of five of the world system's leading actors (Britain, France, the United States, Japan, and Germany) of the past two to three centuries.

## Previous Empirical Assessments

Prior to elaborating and justifying the approach pursued in this examination, the research designs and results of four earlier efforts deserve some comment.[1] As a group, they are highly representative of the larger relevant literature. They provide useful information on the states in which we are most interested and, therefore, are suggestive about what we might expect to find in our inquiry. At the same time, their collective shortcomings should also alert us to some of the analytical problems we hope to avoid in this chapter. These same shortcomings also justify another examination of the economic impact question.

### Kuznets
Of the four, the most general study, for our purposes, is Kuznets's (1964, 1971) inquiry into the nature of modern economic growth patterns. Kuznets's broader interests relegate the impact of war to one of a number of research questions. In the process of inspecting the record of rates of growth aggregated on a decennial basis, however, Kuznets did conclude that active participants that experienced invasion during World War II (e.g., Germany, the Soviet Union, Japan, and France) suffered losses in total output per capita. The losses were rendered temporary, nevertheless, by rapid postwar growth. No major changes in output per capita were observed in the growth rates of active participants that were not invaded (e.g., Britain and the United States).

### Barbera
Barbera's (1973) monograph-length examination of the impacts of World Wars I and II on the socioeconomic development of some 70 states was oriented primarily to comparing, through trend correlations and regression, the stability of the development hierarchy before and after the two wars. A diverse number of findings emerged, and many of them were qualified by the introduction of level of development and degree of war participation control variables. Most pertinent for immediate purposes is Barbera's conclusion that the world wars, in general, neither accelerated nor interrupted per capita

growth. Yet, rather contradictorily, more developed states, more active war participants, and states that were occupied in World War II did experience faster growth than did less developed states, more marginal war participants, and nonoccupied states. Barbera also found little difference between the impacts of the two world wars except that rates of growth tended to be higher after World War II than after World War I. However one looks at these generalizations, their utility is definitely limited by Barbera's decisions to analyze a fairly heterogeneous set of states, to restrict his "trend comparisons" to six or fewer observations between 1913 and 1952, and to emphasize an indicator based on number of telephones per thousand population as his primary measure of development.[2]

### Wheeler

Wheeler's (1975, 1980) analysis of 60 cases (1816–1965) of the impact of war on industrial growth constitutes a third leg of the empirical foundation in this area. Focusing either on iron production or energy consumption series as measures of industrial growth, Wheeler contends that it is possible to compare observed postwar output with what might have been expected in the absence of war. The war-free expectation, in turn, is achieved by a projection of the prewar trend. Wheeler's approach thus consists of determining whether the trend line for the prewar to postwar period is significantly different from the separate trends for the prewar and postwar periods.

The general outcome is decidedly mixed. Significantly different trend lines were found in 44 of the 60 cases (73 percent). Of these cases of statistically significant shifts, 16 (approximately 27 percent of the original 60) represented positive effects in terms of increasing postwar output and/or accelerated growth rates. About the same number of cases (17), however, experienced negative effects. The remaining 11 cases were a mixture of negative (9 cases) and positive (2 cases) effects that were judged to be temporary due to the presence of decreased output but with accelerating growth rates or vice versa. Given the nature of this outcome, Wheeler concludes that war is likely to affect industrial growth but that the direction of change is difficult to predict. Positive and negative effects appear equally likely to take place.

Wheeler acknowledges thgat unusually poor prewar economic performances, as experienced in the pre–World War II period, establish awkward bases for projecting postwar expectations. This is simply one of the general liabilities of before-and-after trend comparisons. In the World War II example, one is therefore somewhat more likely to find a postwar positive effect than might otherwise be the case. And because 12 of the 16 cases of positive shifts involved World War II, Wheeler suggests that the evidence can probably best be interpreted as showing a marked tendency toward war-induced negative impacts.

Even if we ignore the World War II cases, the statistical outcome is still quite mixed. This problem is underlined by the global power cases extracted from the 60-case sample and reported in table 6.1. A few desirable cases, to be sure, are not represented in the study (e.g., World War I for Japan and World War II for Japan and Germany). Even so, the major power cases were only slightly more likely (59 percent) to be significant than insignificant. If the focus is restricted to the two world wars of this century, only 5 of 9, or 56 percent, were significant. Of these 9, the 4 nonsignificant cases marginally outnumbered either the positive (3) or negative (2) cases. As a consequence, Wheeler makes country-specific findings available, but generalization, as predicted earlier by Deane, is exceedingly difficult.

**Table 6.1**
*The Economic Impact of War: Wheeler's Findings for Global Powers*

| Global Power | War | Economic Impact |
|---|---|---|
| France | Sino-French | negative |
| | World War I | positive (temporary) |
| | World War II | positive |
| Germany | Franco-Prussian | negative (temporary) |
| | World War I | negative |
| Britain | Crimean | insignificant |
| | World War I | insignificant |
| | World War II | insignificant |
| Japan | Sino-Japanese | positive |
| | Russo-Japanese | negative |
| Russia/Soviet Union | Russo-Turkish | positive |
| | Crimean | negative (temporary) |
| | Russo-Turkish | insignificant |
| | Russo-Japanese | insignificant |
| | World War I | positive (temporary) |
| | World War II | negative |
| | Russo-Hungarian | negative |
| United States | Mexican-American | insignificant |
| | Spanish-American | positive |
| | World War I | insignificant |
| | World War II | insignificant |
| | Korean | insignificant |

*Note:* The threshold for statistical significance is the customary .05 level.
*Source:* Extracted from Wheeler (1980: 265–267, 273).

## Organski, Kugler, and the Phoenix Factor

Organski and Kugler's (1977, 1980) investigation of the *phoenix factor* provides the fourth set of findings considered here. Because the phoenix factor analysis has enjoyed favorable attention in the past few years, we need to review carefully its procedures and findings.

The crux of the phoenix factor is described by Organski and Kugler in the following way:

> While it is indisputable that losers suffer a good deal more than winners and are in a much worse position immediately after conflicts, in the long run they catch up with winners in terms of power capabilities. Moreover, levels of power distribution return reasonably soon to the patterns they would have followed had no war taken place. The mechanics of the change work in approximately the following way. After their defeat (and the plummeting of their capabilities), losers accelerate their recovery. Winners, in the wake of victory, show a rate of recovery in capabilities depleted by war which is substantially slower than that of losers. Neutrals are not affected. Within a relatively short period of time, all nations return to the levels of national capabilities they would reasonably expect to have held had there been no war. There is a convergence of winners and losers. The major reason for this seems to be the much more powerful acceleration by the losers during recovery; they appear almost literally to rise from the ashes of their defeat. There is a phoenix factor at work. (1980: 106–107)

Organski and Kugler's investigation of the phoenix factor is restricted to the twentieth century's two world wars.[3] Their procedural approach, not unlike Wheeler's, consists of extrapolating the trend observed in the 16 to 19 years prior to the outbreak of world war to the 20-year period following each war.[4] To deal better with the size diversities in war participants and their growth rates, the authors reverse the normal order of their dependent (gross national product) and independent (time) variables so that they attempt essentially to determine how many postwar years are required for belligerents to regain the output position predicted by the extrapolated prewar trend. Their findings are then expressed at the aggregate level, differentiating the categorical performance of active-occupied belligerent winners from that of active-occupied belligerent losers.

The reported findings do support the existence of a phoenix factor. Considering the outcome for both world wars, great power winners suffer an initial and roughly permanent postwar loss of 2 years in terms of their normal growth projection. Great power losers experience an initial 20-year loss, which is eventually overcome by the fifteenth postwar year. Treating each world war separately, the initial World War I losses are somewhat greater (5 years for winners and 22 years for losers), but the advent of the interwar depression handicaps an evaluation of long-run recovery. In World War II, the record of active winners is interpreted as suffering little in the way of loss of output and basically maintaining their expected growth patterns. Losers and occupied winners lost 20 years, but losers were able to complete their recovery process by the sixteenth postwar year.

Organski and Kugler thus conclude that the economic growth patterns of major power world war winners experienced only marginal impacts. Losers experienced intense losses in the short run, but they were able to regain the positions anticipated by prewar rates of growth. Organski and Kugler believe that in this sense the economic positions of winners and losers converge some 15 to 20 years after a world war and that systemic power distributions revert to what they would have been had no war occurred.

Organski and Kugler's analysis, of course, shares one problem encountered by Wheeler. Not only is it difficult to project growth rates with accuracy, but the interwar depression also intensifies the problem for post–World War II projections, just as it hinders the interpretation of post–World War I output levels and recovery. Moreover, the treatment of winners and losers as two categorical groups raises other problems of interpretation if members of these groups have experienced markedly different economic-war impacts. In addition to these awkward elements and other problems raised by Siverson (1980) and Stein and Russett (1980), Organski and Kugler's conclusions go beyond their own data manipulations. It is one thing to argue that winners' economic gains from wartime are marginal and that losers eventually realize a prewar projected position; it is quite another to say that the international system returns to the prewar distribution of power as if nothing had transpired.

Even putting aside objections about their equation of power with gross national product, determining whether winners and losers really converge and whether the postwar distribution of power actually returns to the prewar distribution of power requires an analysis of relative changes in capability positions—as opposed to aggregated absolute changes in economic output tendencies. Our own examination of twentieth-century global power concentration patterns in relative shares of gross domestic product per capita indicates that the extent of economic capability concentration did decline after World Wars I and II. In this sense, the overall distribution of economic capability returned to pre–world war levels of concentration. But this repetitive pattern of economic capability deconcentration after global war, depicted in figure 6.1, can be deceptive.

The preeminent winner of each global war, especially since the Napoleonic Wars, has emerged with a substantial economic lead over the other members of its own victorious coalition, as well as of the members of the losing coalition. Despite the material benefits of leadership, the economic leads do not last forever. As other states improve their own relative standings, the leader's position decays in relative terms. Yet, the rank order of the global powers has tended to remain reasonably stable between global wars.

For example, the following global power rank order (in terms of shares of GDP per capita) prevailed in 1913, 1920, 1940, and 1946: (1) the United States, (2) Britain, (3) France, (4) Germany, and (5) Japan. The information reported in table 6.2 suggests that, more recently, there have been some shifts

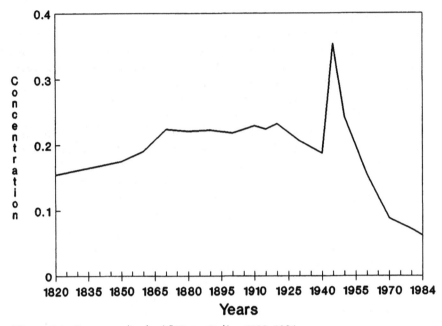

*Figure 6.1.* Concentration in GDP per Capita, 1820–1984

in the second through fifth positions. But the most significant changes, aside from Britain's downward slide, have occurred in the narrowing of the gap between first place and the other four positions. Since 1946, Germany and Japan have definitely improved their relative positions vis-à-vis the United States, but then so has France. These movements do not quite sum to a clear-cut, 15- to 20-year convergence between winners and losers, in either relative or absolute standings. This observation seems all the more appropriate in an era when important economic powers are no longer, or not currently, equally important military powers.

However one chooses to interpret the phoenix factor, it is not simple to construct inductive expectations, based on the relevant empirical literature, about the net economic impact of wars. Still, we are left with the general impression that the twentieth-century impacts have been relatively marginal for global power winners and fairly transitory for global power losers. There also are extremely awkward problems in determining how generalizable earlier findings are, given their collective, if difficult to avoid, empheses on the two most recent world wars, the heterogeneity of the states examined, and the acknowledged technical limitations on projecting postwar normal growth based on prewar growth patterns. Whatever else might be said, the question of how wars affect participant economies remains open to further inquiry.

**Table 6.2**
**The Stability of Gross Domestic Product per Capita Rankings**

| 1913 | | 1920 | | 1940 | |
|---|---|---|---|---|---|
| United States | .325 | United States | .347 | United States | .313 |
| Britain | .257 | Britain | .259 | Britain | .263 |
| France | .220 | France | .187 | France | .162 |
| Germany | .113 | Germany | .100 | Germany | .147 |
| Japan | .086 | Japan | .107 | Japan | .076 |
| Concentration | .224 | Concentration | .232 | Concentration | .187 |

| 1946 | | 1970 | | 1984 | |
|---|---|---|---|---|---|
| United States | .434 | United States | .256 | United States | .243 |
| Britain | .276 | Germany | .204 | Germany | .204 |
| France | .171 | France | .198 | France | .194 |
| Germany | .073 | Britain | .175 | Japan | .188 |
| Japan | .046 | Japan | .167 | Britain | .170 |
| Concentration | .354 | Concentration | .087 | Concentration | .061 |

*Source:* Based on GDP and population data in Maddison (1982, 1987). The degree of concentration is calculated with the formula developed in Ray and Singer (1973).

## A Different Strategy

### Statistical Techniques

Instead of comparing projected prewar behavior with observed postwar behavior, we propose to regard wars as interventions in the process of economic growth and to employ Box-Tiao (1975) intervention models to measure the systematic impact of war. The Box-Tiao models should prove quite useful in the war-economic growth context. Previous studies have tended to rely on various regression strategies that are associated with at least three types of limitations. Most of the earlier studies have emphasized fitting and comparing least squares models to pre- and postwar series. Yet we have no analytical guidelines for determining what are adequate or appropriate bases for comparison. How long in duration, for instance, should a reasonable pre- or postwar series be? Alternatively, to what extent does the length of the pre- and postseries measurements influence the analytical outcome? Or, for that matter, what are the consequences of removing the war year outliers from the analysis? Box-Tiao models enable the analyst to avoid these vexing problems by using the entire time series to model the underlying process that is assumed to generate the observed values. Consequently, the analyst is in a position to estimate both the immediate and longer-term effects of a hypothesized intervention, without being required to carve the series into relatively ad hoc slices.

One problem that Box-Tiao models cannot overcome completely is the potential overestimation of a war impact when it is closely preceded by unusually depressed economic conditions, as in the case of the 1930s and World War II. By estimating the war-induced change in the level of economic growth in comparison to nonwartime observations, some confounding of the effects of war mobilization and destruction and slow prewar growth is probable. The only recourse is, as usual, a careful examination of serial behavior and the pertinent data plots. Fortunately, the most obvious example of this type of problem in our examination involves such an intensive war (World War II) that a significant impact could be anticipated in most cases, even in the absence of a preceding depression.

Autocorrelation and trend constitute the other two major sources of problems in regression analyses of time-series data. In the presence of autocorrelation, ordinary least squares (OLS) estimates of $\beta$ may be unbiased, but the variances of the estimators will be understated. The error variance of the regression model will appear to provide a much better fit to the series than is actually the case. Inferences based on sample $t$ and $F$ statistics, furthermore, will be misleading due to the deflation of the true variance of $\beta$ and the regression model (Hibbs 1974; Gottman 1981).

Trend poses another potential stumbling block by producing a systematic change in a time-series level that creates difficulties in interpreting short- and long-term impacts. The conventional approach to this problem involves subtracting a least squares trend line from the observed series. But, as we argued in chapter 5, this strategy constitutes a peculiarly static approach to a dynamic problem in that the first and last observations of the observed series are likely to make the greatest contribution to the trend sum of squares function, regardless of how well the middle observations fit. More important, it may be erroneous to assume that a time series is influenced by a deterministic fixed function of time. Because a time series may drift upward or downward for long periods of time due only to random forces, it is not always obvious whether a progressive change in the level of a series is due to deterministic trend or stochastic drift.

Box-Tiao models are appealing because they provide a parsimonious way to control for the effects of autocorrelation, trend, and drift while modeling the impact of an intervention in a time series.

### Actors, Wars, and Temporal Focus

Our interest in the relationship between war and the state-making processes of the world system's leading actors dictates a focus on a much narrower set of states than those investigated in many of the earlier examinations. Although we are prepared to consider the entire post-1500 "modern" period as a germane temporal focus, for empirical purposes we are clearly restricted to a shorter period by the absence or paucity of economic growth data. It is possible, nevertheless, to gather sufficient information on gross national product per capita, a conventional indicator of economic growth, to construct the following series: Britain, 1700–1979; the United States, 1792–1980; France, 1800–1979; Germany, 1870–1979; and Japan, 1879–1979.

Readers familiar with the problems of quantitative economic history will appreciate the difficulties inherent in constructing series encompassing long-term economic fluctuations. The gross national product concept is of fairly recent origin. Consequently, the series reflect reconstructed estimates that have frequently been generated for specific periods of time. A desire for continuous series thus often requires the splicing together of different estimates created at different times by different analysts. Moreover, to control for inflationary fluctuations, a problem of particular importance for both longitudinal and war-related research, one must also transform each series in terms of constant price indexes, which are themselves subject to many of the problems associated with reconstructions of total output series. The series analyzed in this investigation are expressed in 1913 wholesale prices and the country's own currency unit (i.e., pounds, francs, dollars, yen, or marks).

In every instance, however, we have attempted to use series (GNP, wholesale prices, and population) developed by economic historians for their own purposes and to incorporate the latest known modifications or adjustments to these series. The sources consulted include the following: (1) Britain—Deane (1955, 1968); Deane and Cole (1962); Mitchell (1962, 1981); Banks (1971); Mitchell and Jones (1971); Feinstein (1972); United Kingdom, Central Statistical Office (multiple volumes); and Cole (1981); (2) France—Marczewski (1961); France, Ministere du Travail (1966); Banks (1971); Mitchell (1981); Carre, Dubois, and Malinvaud (1975); Caron (1979); and France, Ministere de l'Economie (multiple volumes); (3) United States—Banks (1971); U.S. Department of Commerce (1975); Berry (1978); and U.S. Office of the President (1982); (4) Japan—Emi (1963); Banks (1971); and Ohkawa and Rosovsky (1973); and (5) Germany—Hoffman (1965); Banks (1971); Mitchell (1981); and Maddison (1982).

Table 6.3 lists two types of warfare encompassed by the available GNP per capita series. Global wars, defined by their systemic function, are the decisive contests fought over the issue of succession to world leadership. As highly significant structural turning points for the global political system, global wars tend to be the most extensive wars and the most costly. Therefore, it seems reasonable to hypothesize that this distinctive class of warfare should have the most important and influential impacts on the economic growth processes of its participants. Interstate wars, in contrast, are relatively less

*Table 6.3*
*Interstate and Global Wars Examined for Their Impact on Economic Growth*

| Interstate Wars | | Global Wars | |
|---|---|---|---|
| *France* | | | |
| Franco-Spanish | 1823 | Napoleonic | 1803–15 |
| Roman Republic | 1849 | World War I | 1914–18 |
| Crimean | 1854–56 | World War II | 1939–45 |
| Italian Unification | 1859 | | |
| Franco-Mexican | 1862–67 | | |
| Franco-Prussian | 1870–71 | | |
| Sino-French | 1884–85 | | |
| Franco-Thai | 1940–41 | | |
| Korean | 1951–53 | | |
| Sinai | 1956 | | |
| *Britain* | | | |
| Anglo-Swedish | 1715–19 | Spanish Succession | 1701–13 |
| Quadruple Alliance | 1718–20 | French Revolutionary | 1793–1802 |
| Anglo-Spanish | 1726–29 | Napoleonic | 1803–15 |
| Jenkin's Ear/Austrian | | World War I | 1914–18 |
| Succession | 1739–48 | World War II | 1939–45 |
| Seven Years | 1756–63 | | |
| American Independence | 1778–83 | | |
| Anglo-American | 1812–15 | | |
| Crimean | 1854–56 | | |
| Anglo-Persian | 1856–57 | | |
| Korean | 1950–53 | | |
| Sinai | 1956 | | |
| *Japan* | | | |
| Sino-Japanese | 1894–95 | World War I | 1914–18 |
| Russo-Japanese | 1904–05 | World War II | 1941–45 |
| Manchurian | 1931–33 | | |
| Sino-Japanese | 1937–41 | | |
| *United States* | | | |
| Anglo-American | 1812–14 | World War I | 1917–18 |
| Mexican-American | 1846–48 | World War II | 1941–45 |
| Spanish-American | 1898 | | |
| Korean | 1950–53 | | |
| Vietnam | 1965–73 | | |
| *Germany* | | | |
| Franco-Prussian | 1870–71 | World War I | 1914–18 |
| | | World War II | 1939–45 |

extensive and intensive affairs and, therefore, less likely, we hypothesize, to exert significant impacts. Consequently, we treat the two kinds of wars as separate types of interventions, and we expect that the assessment of their impacts will yield different results according to the types of wars examined. The long-cycle perspective does not exactly predict whether the impacts will be positive or negative, temporary or permanent, or abrupt or gradual, but it does give us reason to anticipate that the global war impacts will more likely be substantively and statistically significant than will the impacts associated with interstate wars.

There are also good theoretical reasons to anticipate that if anyone profits from global warfare, it is most likely to be the maritime winners and not the more continentally oriented losers. These states have tended to be more distant from the battlefields and thus less exposed to the more destructive wages of war. By definition, moreover, at least one maritime winner emerged from global war with the system's most dynamic economy. As argued in Thompson (1988), global war helps put system leaders "over the top" in certain leading sectors. Whether this boost is translated into absolute growth (as opposed to gains in relative position) remains to be seen. Otherwise, previous research strongly suggests that we should expect to find fairly abrupt and temporary war-induced impacts.

## The Impact of War on Economic Growth

Figures 6.2 to 6.6 provide general visual summaries of the fluctuations in global power economic growth. Tables 6.4 and 6.5 summarize the more specific statistical outcomes of applying Box-Tiao impact assessment models to the five continuous series of historical economic growth. Based on the previous analyses reviewed earlier, we expect that interstate and global wars will have primarily temporary effects on economic growth. The question is whether the growth is significantly increased (or decreased) and, if so, how long it is sustained over time. Of the four Box-Tiao impact models presented in figure 4.5, the two pulse models (C and D) represent the competing theoretical effects.

In the interest of parsimony, the simplest pulse model, model C, is used initially to fit the impacts of interstate and global wars. Should the $\omega_o$ parameter, which represents a numerical estimate of the impact, prove statistically significant, the analyst moves on to fit the more complex abrupt, temporary model. In this instance, if both the $\omega_o$ and $\delta$ parameters yield statistically significant estimates, wars have had a short-term influence on economic growth, which eventually returns to a postwar equilibrium. On the other hand, a nonstatistically significant $\delta$ estimate would indicate that war impacts have been shortlived and are best specified as a simple pulse model.

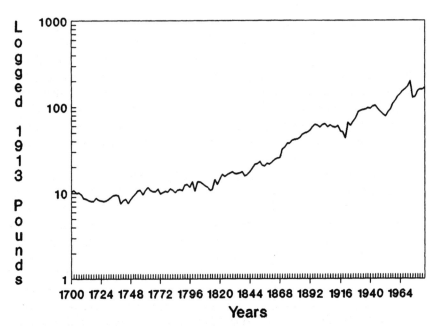

**Figure 6.2.** British Economic Growth (GNP per Capita in Logged 1913 Pounds), 1700–1985

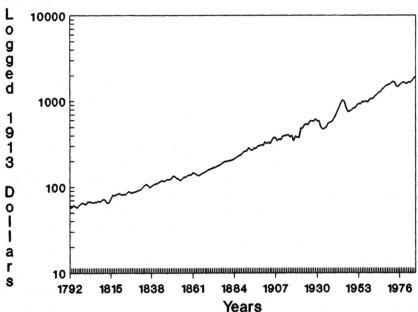

**Figure 6.3.** United States Economic Growth (GNP per Capita in Logged 1913 Dollars), 1792–1985

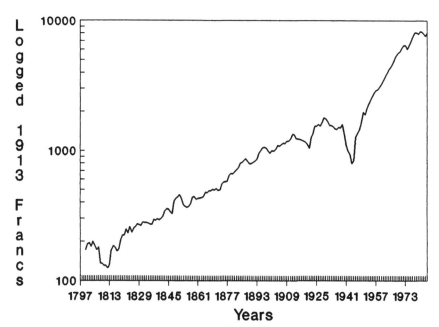

*Figure 6.4.* French Economic Growth (GNP per Capita in Logged 1913 Francs), 1797–1985

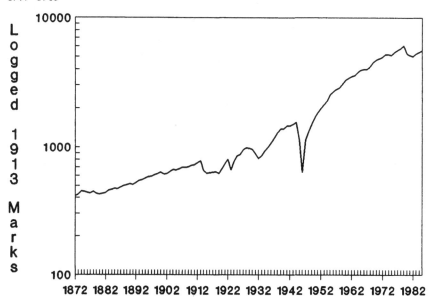

*Figure 6.5.* German Economic Growth (GNP per Capita in Logged 1913 Marks), 1872–1985

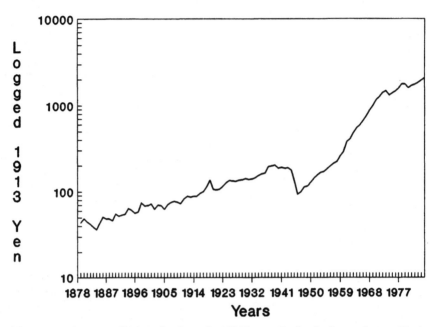

**Figure 6.6.** Japanese Economic Growth (GNP per Capita in Logged 1913 Yen), 1878–1985

One point of clarification involves the question of the timing of war impacts. Because there is no reason to anticipate that the influence of war on economic growth will be particularly discernible immediately, we have examined the war impacts at $t_0$, $t_{+1}$, $t_{+2}$, and $t_{+3}$. In many cases, the outcome does not differ greatly according to the lag examined, but in a few cases it does make some difference. Unless otherwise noted, we have reported impact parameters at $t_{+1}$ in tables 6.4 and 6.5.

For convenience of calculation, two separate equations have been generated for each state's history of economic growth. The first set of equations examines the collective impact of interstate wars as one separate class of warfare. In other words, interstate wars are specified in a pulse model as a single collective impact for each nation-state. Table 6.4 provides the results derived from the estimation of these models. It shows that, in general, these wars have no statistically significant impact on economic growth.

Nevertheless, the German and Japanese cases do represent near exceptions to this statement. Although there is only one German interstate war (the Franco-Prussian) in this series, quite conceivably one or more of the Japanese interstate wars (e.g., the Russo-Japanese War) did have some significant, albeit temporary, economic impact that could be isolated.

**Table 6.4**
**The Impact of Interstate Wars on Economic Growth**

| State | Interstate Wars $\omega_0$ | Noise Model[b] $N_t$ | Noise Model Type[a] |
|---|---|---|---|
| France | 0.01 | −0.33* | (0, 1, 1) |
| | (0.01) | (0.08) | |
| Germany | −0.18 | white | (0, 1, 0) |
| | (0.09) | noise | |
| Britain | −0.01 | white | (0, 1, 0) |
| | (0.01) | noise | |
| Japan | 0.14 | −0.28* | (0, 1, 0) |
| | (0.08) | (0.10) | |
| United States | 0.002 | white | (0, 1, 0) |
| | (0.01) | noise | |

*Note:* All data have been logged to achieve variance stationarity; standard errors are reported in parentheses below the parameter coefficients.

* denotes statistical significance at the .05 level.

[a] (0, 1, 1) denotes a first-differenced, first-order moving average process; (0, 1, 0) denotes a first-differenced series.

[b] A constant parameter was estimated initially to check for the presence of any systematic trend in the series. Because this parameter proved statistically insignificant in all cases, a trend component is not included in the final noise models. The $\chi^2$ tests for residual autocorrelation in the final noise models were statistically insignificant.

The second set of equations treats each global war separately. Specifically, individual pulse models for each global war are estimated simultaneously in an equation. The global wars are thus represented as multiple interventions in the economic growth series of each nation-state. The estimation results presented in table 6.5 show that, except for Germany in World War I, global wars have significant but short-lived influences on economic growth. Subsequent estimations of abrupt, temporary models of global wars for these cases yield statistically insignificant $\delta$ parameters. The implication is that global wars are associated for the most part with significant changes in economic growth during the context of war, but that the postwar period is characterized by a rapid return of economic growth to prewar levels. Only the impact of World War I on Germany's economic growth series is represented best as an abrupt, temporary model. The relatively large size of the parameter (0.86) indicates that the initial decrease in economic growth was accompanied by a slow return to prewar levels.

In the final analysis, table 6.5 produces a markedly different set of outcomes from those reported in table 6.4. Eight of the 13 global war $\omega_0$ parameters are statistically significant.[5] One Japanese parameter (World War I) borders on significance; however, the net impact no doubt reflects marginal Japanese participation in World War I as much as anything else. Similarly, the

*Table 6.5*
*The Impact of Global Wars on Economic Growth*

| State | Spanish Succession $\omega_o$ | French Rev./ Napoleonic $\omega_o$ | World War I $\omega_o$ | $\delta$ | World War II $\omega_o$ | Noise Model[b] $N_t$ | Noise Model Type[a] |
|---|---|---|---|---|---|---|---|
| Britain | 0.01 | 0.06* | -0.19* | | -0.03 | -0.15* | (0, 1, 1) |
| | (0.03) | (0.03) | (0.04) | | (0.03) | (0.07) | |
| France | | -0.11* | -0.02 | | -0.28* | white | (0, 1, 0) |
| | | (0.05) | (0.04) | | (0.05) | noise | |
| Germany | | | -0.08* | 0.86* | -0.29* | white | (0, 1, 0) |
| | | | (0.04) | (0.18) | (0.07) | noise | |
| Japan | | | 0.13 | | -0.21* | -0.24* | (0, 1, 1) |
| | | | (0.07) | | (0.05) | (0.10) | |
| United States | | | 0.11* | | 0.13* | white | (0, 1, 0) |
| | | | (0.05) | | (0.04) | noise | |

*Note:* All data have been logged to achieve variance stationarity; standard errors are reported in parentheses below the parameter coefficients.
* denotes statistical significance at the .05 level.
[a] (0, 1, 1) denotes a first-differenced, first-order moving average process; (0, 1, 0) denotes a first-differenced series.
[b] A constant parameter was estimated initially to check for the presence of any systematic trend in the series. Because this parameter proved statistically insignificant in all cases, a trend component is not included in the final noise models. The $\chi^2$ tests for residual autocorrelation in the final noise models were statistically insignificant.

absence of a significant impact in the preindustrial Spanish Succession case (Britain) presumably reflects the more limited extent of societal commitment in war that the British once enjoyed. If we discount these last two cases as less than curious exceptions, only two deviant cases remain—France in World War I and Britain in World War II.

A closer examination of the growth records applicable to the two other deviant cases suggests much less deviance than is indicated in table 6.5. Data on aggregate French economic performance during World War I are scarce and must be estimated. Our own estimates suggest that between 1913 and 1918 French GNP per capita declined 12.2 percent, with about half of this loss (7 percent) taking place in the first year of the war.[6] After 1918, French GNP per capita continued to decline through 1921, but the postwar 1918–21 loss (12.8 percent) actually exceeded wartime losses. British GNP per capita, on the other hand, fluctuated during World War II. It rose in the first year of the war, fell in the second, and then rose through 1943 before falling during the last two years of warfare. By the end of World War II, British GNP per capita was roughly equal to the level attained in 1938. However, per capita British output then proceeded to decline in each successive year through 1951, at which point it had returned briefly to the GNP per capita levels associated with the late 1920s. Consequently, we are most reluctant to dismiss these two cases as situations involving insignificant economic impacts. Most likely, they are, at least in part, products of our need to focus on first differences with relatively crude dichotomous intervention specifications.

One other caveat deserves mention. Our reliance on the ratio of GNP to population does raise a potential index validity threat. Conceivably, a state's war-induced economic losses could be accompanied by a sufficiently substantial loss in population to the extent that little or no change in GNP per capita might be registered. In our global power sample, only the post–World War II division of Germany approximates this hypothetical situation. Between 1938 and 1947, Germany (focusing on West Germany after 1946) experienced a nearly 40 percent decline in output, a 32 percent decrease in population, and only a 12 percent decline in GNP per capita. Although this GNP per capita decline was quite short-lived (or temporary), the important question from an index validity perspective is whether the output and population losses were more permanent. Of the two, population has yet to match the 1938 figure. The 1938 output figure, on the other hand, was surpassed in the early 1950s. Consequently, we do not consider the German case a serious threat to the validity of our dependent variable or findings.

In any event, however one chooses to qualify it, the statistical outcome favors the general interpretation that global wars are more likely than interstate wars to affect the economic growth of major powers; however, the economic impact of global war, for both winners and losers or invaded and noninvaded, is of relatively temporary duration. The rare positive war impacts translate into short-lived growth spurts. Negative war impacts, by far the more common outcome, tend to be nonterminal setbacks in the historical development of national economic growth. Despite the increasing destructiveness of global warfare, the economies of the global powers, the core of the world economy, have demonstrated remarkable resilience in adjusting to the shock of world war—at least so far.

## Implications and Conclusions

It is difficult to imagine a less controversial generalization than the assertion that economic processes are susceptible to the effects of war. Yet for all the absence of controversy, we remain uncertain about the ways in which wars have influenced patterns of economic change. Table 6.6 illustrates this claim by contrasting two recent sets of findings on the impact of world wars on the economies of five global powers. Of the seven to ten possible opportunities for agreement, consensus is actually obtained in only one cell (Britain and World War II). To be sure, differences in research designs, including choices pertaining to statistical techniques and dependent variables,

*Table 6.6*
**A Summary Comparison of Two Recent Sets of Findings on the Economic Impact of World Wars**

| State | World War I | | World War II | |
|---|---|---|---|---|
| | *Wheeler Findings* | *Present Findings* | *Wheeler Findings* | *Present Findings* |
| France | positive (temporary) | not significant | positive | negative (temporary) |
| Germany | negative | negative (temporary) | none reported | negative (temporary) |
| Britain | not significant | negative (temporary) | not significant | not significant |
| Japan | none reported | not significant | none reported | negative (temporary) |
| United States | not significant | positive (temporary) | not significant | positive (temporary) |

*Source:* The Wheeler findings have been extracted from Wheeler's (1980) more extensive analysis.

help account for some portion of the disagreement. Yet more fundamental reasons underlie our collective problems in assessing the consequences of war.

Economists, for instance, routinely exclude war from their theoretical explanations and econometric modeling of economic processes. Wars come and go and, it is argued, can best be viewed as intermittent and exogenous shocks to the normal functioning of economic systems. Historians and political scientists must share the blame as well by emphasizing the study of what factors bring about specific wars and wars in general. Only rarely is equal attention bestowed on the consequences of war (Stein and Russett 1980).

Then, too, there is a tendency to treat war as a generic phenomenon, as if all wars are of, or should have, equivalent social science significance. As a consequence, findings concerning minor wars are apt to be mixed with findings pertaining to major wars. This same tendency, however, is partially contradicted and also partially augmented, by the tendency to focus on the most recent wars because of their presumed greater relevance to contemporary problems. The picture is confused even more by another tendency—the popular inclination to give every war a unique identity in time, place, and meaning.

Obviously, we prefer not to subscribe to any of these three tendencies. All wars by definition involve the mobilization of armed forces and the destruction of lives and property; but some wars are more important than others. From the perspective of the global political system and its primary actors, the global powers, a functional distinction needs to be made between global and interstate wars. In the present case, it is global and not interstate wars that tend to exhibit significant impacts on the economic growth patterns of the system's leading actors.

It is true that every global war may not affect every actor's economic system in precisely the same fashion, but the general probability of impact remains much greater than in the case of nonglobal warfare. Nor is this tendency a novel feature of the past 50 years or even of the twentieth century. In terms of measurable economic growth, we are able empirically to trace it back to at least the 1793–1815 period of global combat. Even more consistent is the temporary nature of global war's economic impact. However, we should not infer from this finding that all global powers have survived global warfare relatively unscathed. To the contrary, there are definite winners and losers in both the short- and long-run sense, and short-run victors are not necessarily long-run winners (see table 6.5). After all, Portugal, Spain, the Netherlands, France, Germany, Japan, and Britain are no longer contenders for global military power in the world system.

Nevertheless, the temporary nature of global war's economic growth impact underscores the inherent instability of a system that determines its leadership by trials of global combat. To the extent that economic power has evolved (especially after the advent of the industrial revolution) into serving as a, if not the, platform for military and political power at the global level, the immediate postwar lead enjoyed by the global war winners and the global system's leadership will tend to be temporary too. Stated another way, global wars, historically, have not been sufficiently destructive to stabilize the postwar capability imbalance that seems so conducive to world order. The long cycle of relative capability concentration and deconcentration continues. The ability of most global powers to overcome economic losses in the aftermath of global war is thus a contributing element in the persistence of one of the system's most fundamental political processes.[7]

The domestic implications of the temporary economic impacts of global war should not be overlooked either. One reason we are particularly interested in this economic impact of war question is our related interest in the effects of war on state-making processes. If one wishes, for example, to assess the relative contributions of war and economic growth to increasing revenue extraction levels, it is useful to know whether the two main independent variables are also interrelated. If they are related, the modeling process is made more difficult. If war and economic growth are essentially unrelated, the problems of analysis are less imposing. As our investigation demonstrates, global war and economic growth are related, but apparently, the relationship is quite transitory. Evidence on the permanent impacts of war, consequently, cannot be dismissed as mere artifacts of domestic economic growth.

Less abstractly, the evidence indicates that global war does not seem to pay in terms of directly augmenting net national wealth and that this verdict holds for both winners and losers. Yet it is equally clear that global war does cost, not only in the painfully obvious currency of lives and property, but also in terms of permanently increasing the costs of maintaining and operating competitive states. Global war increases national debts, state spending, and state taxes without discernibly expanding the collective material base for meeting the ratcheting overhead costs of the global powers. The fact that global wars are expensive is hardly new information, but the more interesting question is whether we appreciate fully (or know) just how expensive global wars really are.

Three final caveats are in order. First, changes in GNP per capita cannot be viewed as encompassing all that is worth knowing about economic impacts. It is highly conceivable that wars in general, and global wars in particular, do influence some economic processes in a permanent fashion (either positively or negatively). Our single indicator suggests only that if this is the case, other offsetting effects, when combined with the more permanent effects, lead to net temporary gains and losses. A focus on less aggregate indexes may help clarify the full extent of the economic impact of global war.

Inevitably, the use of a less conventional technique, such as the Box-Tiao models, raises the question of whether the empirical results we have found are simply a statistical artifact of the methodology used. In this study, it is reasonable to assume that this is not the case. Box-Jenkins time-series techniques, of which Box-Tiao models are a distinct subset, are viewed as a conservative approach to dynamic modeling. Primary criticisms have centered on the issue of first differencing a time series, which some econometricians feel takes out too much variation (Pierce and Haugh 1977; Feige and Pearce 1979). But in our experience, the crux of the problem is that Box-Tiao model estimation tends to yield statistically significant results only in the context of a sizable change in level of a $Y$ series during an intervention. If there is a discernible change in the $Y$ series that does not involve a dramatic change, Box-Tiao models may not be likely to capture it. Because these models err on the conservative side, it is safe to conclude that global wars have a stronger effect on economic growth than do interstate wars.

Whether interstate wars have a significantly small or nonexistent effect on economic growth is a question not as easily resolved. However, a visual inspection of the data reveals only negligible changes in the economic growth series during periods of interstate wars. Hence, we feel confident that Box-Tiao results for interstate wars are an accurate depiction.

Although previous theoretical and empirical evidence led us to model abrupt, temporary impacts, we have also estimated alternative forms of impact (abrupt, permanent) to avoid the possibility of misspecification. In situations in which the theoretical expectations are weak and/or the outcome of the statistical criteria (parameter estimates, residual mean square error, and the behavior of white noise residuals) is mixed, analysts will be forced to rely primarily on their judgment. However, in this investigation, the statistical criteria helped us rule consistently in favor of the abrupt, temporary models.

Finally, the findings of the present analysis have been restricted explicitly to general categories of warfare and, more important, to the historical experience of the relatively small universe of global powers. Unfortunately, it is most unlikely that our temporary impact findings can be projected as a prediction about the effects of a future global war. Moreover, our generalizations do not preclude the possibility of significant economic impacts being associated with specific interstate wars. Nor are we able to say much about the economic impacts of nonglobal power warfare. Hence, there should be little quarrel with the contention that a great deal more can be learned about the question of exactly how wars affect economic and other processes. Having answered our immediate question, we have only scratched the surface on this more fundamental question.

Notwithstanding the need for additional work in this area, we now move away from the financial, fiscal, and economic resource extraction emphases of the past three chapters. Chapter 7 focuses on a different, but related, dimension of state making, that is, the need to make new coalitions and concessions in crisis situations. The following questions are addressed. Under what conditions are global power governments more or less likely to reach new accommodations with groups whose resources are valued? To what extent must these same groups resort to violence to gain governmental attention? Finally, if wars represent the most serious crises for global power states, to what extent are wars associated with violence and group accommodations?

# 7

# Accommodation and Violence

Preceding chapters have focused on seemingly largely impersonal factors—wars; geopolitics; the shifting tides of political-economic fortune; the historical manipulation of debts, revenues, and spending; and the long-term progression of global power economic growth. These factors can be, and often are, discussed as if they represent abstract, disembodied processes. But they do not. As processes and variables of some significance in state making, they have no meaning if, ultimately, they do not impact on people.

Tracing precisely how these forces impact on decision makers and the rest of the populations whom decision makers claim to represent is not always a straightforward task. One way to manage the complexities of the task is to simplify the problem by ignoring some dimensions of reality while concentrating on other dimensions. Our approach has hitherto been restricted principally to how elite state makers have responded to systemic processes and have created states often by default. Yet we do not mean to convey the impression that global power states are like pieces of metal shaped and pounded on historical anvils by systemic hammers alone.

Certainly the pounding and shaping takes place, but the hammers come from within the state as well. The historical development of Spain and France discussed in chapters 2 and 3 suggests some ways that domestic forces historically have influenced state making and systemic processes. In particular, though, political groups engaging in various forms of collective behavior are increasingly capable of swinging their own state-making hammers.

Nor are state makers themselves, situated between the systemic and subsystemic pressures, powerless to influence how these forces are perceived to be interacting. How state makers cope with these internal pressures while struggling to survive external crises affords another angle on the war–state-making nexus, one we explore in this chapter.

Although we could adopt any number of different spatial and temporal foci, we concentrate on U.S. governmental responses to violence during the twentieth-century periods of war and postwar demobilization. The choice of the United States focus is somewhat arbitrary. However, the availability of interesting data on U.S. violence had something to do with the choice. The twentieth century, moreover, is especially interesting because it reflects the cumulative effects of several hundred years of interactions between war and global power state making. We began our inquiry by examining eleventh century Iberian conflict; it is only fitting that we conclude with an examination of contemporary American labor unrest, racial violence, and political dissent.

## *War, Governments, and Civilians in the Twentieth Century*

Writing about World War I, Michael Howard emphasizes some of the fundamental changes that took place in the relationships between governments and various subsets of the populations.

> The burdens which this kind of warfare imposed on the civilian populations were accepted without complaint. Immense war loans were raised. Women took the place of men in the factories and the fields. Civilians forfeited luxuries, submitted to increasingly severe rationing of necessities, tightened their belts as consumer goods disappeared from the shops. In the process fundamental changes took place in the belligerent societies themselves. Governments acquired control over new areas of social and economic life. Pressure for wider participation in government increased and had very largely to be accepted. Trade unions had to be accepted as partners with governments and exacted a price—much as the aristocracy had two centuries earlier—in terms of recognition of privileges and status within society. War taxation levelled out the major inequalities of wealth inherent in the old order. (1976: 114)

As Howard indicates, the political gains realized in the twentieth century by labor and women in the combatant states resembled earlier gains made by European nobility. To wage war, kings had needed elite support in terms of acquiescence, troops, money, and supplies. One way these resources could be obtained was by making political concessions. Contemporary legislatures, as a result, owe much of their original stimulation to these older, war-induced or war-related exchanges of elite privileges for elite support of the state in times of external conflict.

The deals struck between monarchs and nobility were not duplicated exactly in every state. For instance, nobles were not exempt from taxation everywhere—only in some states, such as France. Nor were the arrangements arrived at smoothly. Two steps forward and one step backward characterized the historical evolution of a number of European representative institutions. In such states as France and Spain, there were long periods in which parliaments took more steps backward than forward.

Ultimately, however, the nature of external threats continued to evolve, becoming in the process more intense and pervasive. As a number of authors have argued, late eighteenth-, nineteenth-, and early twentieth-century changes in international conflict patterns increased state-maker incentives for encouraging greater popular participation in war-making activities.[1] The size of national armed forces (see table 3.2) had continued to expand exponentially. Eighteenth-century armies had been counted in the thousands. Late nineteenth-century armies numbered in millions, augmented by equally substantial reserves. Warfare had also become increasingly dependent on technology and industrial production. The political significance of factory workers and their contribution to the war effort increased accordingly. The level and extent of taxation, noted in chapter 5, had to increase accordingly. Somebody had to pay for the expansion in the number of military personnel and the goods they consumed.

Greatly simplified, increasingly greater war-making activities meant that state makers would have to learn how to extract even greater resources from their populations. The greater the enthusiasm of the population, the easier the subsequent extraction of resources. Other factors were involved in the closer identification of individual citizens with their states, to be sure, but one, if not the, paramount factor was interstate warfare and the increasingly continuous preparations for future warfare. As one student of public opinion puts it:

> Taken together, these factors encouraged, indeed impelled, rulers to seek popular support for the maintenance of their military power. Huge permanent armies of citizen-soldiers could be raised more easily and could be induced to fight more vigorously if imbued with enthusiasm for their cause. Popular support facilitated military conscription and ultimately made soldiers more willing to endure hardship and danger. (Ginsberg 1986: 21)

Nonetheless, the sociopolitical impact of war continued to operate spasmodically and unevenly in the twentieth century. World War I (World War II for France) probably accelerated the extension of suffrage to women in most of the major states. Yet, as suggested in figure 7.1, suffrage extensions have been influenced by factors other than global war. Not shown in figure 7.1 are the political gains made by women prior to the advent of war in 1914. No doubt women eventually would have won the right to vote without a global

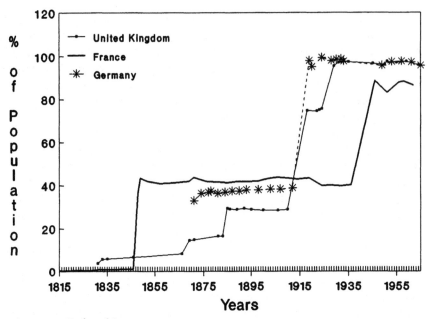

*Figure 7.1.* Enfranchisement

war from 1914 to 1918. Still, the war effort created an environment in which resistance to women voting was easier to defeat than it had been before the war.

The gains achieved by women in several states, however, were not paralleled by American blacks who, nevertheless, hardly went unaffected by the same war. World War I interfered with the inflow of immigrant labor from Europe when war-related business was prospering and expanding. One direct outcome of this war was a tremendous boost in the number of blacks leaving the South for the northern industrial cities. Between 1870 and 1910, the average South–North migration of blacks had approximated 67,000 per decade. Between 1916–17 and 1920, the number may have swollen to as many as 300,000 to 500,000 (Wynn 1986: 180). They came from more places in the South than ever before and ended up in more northern cities than previously had been the case. Perhaps most important, the number of blacks employed in manufacturing rose dramatically. Even so, several more wars had to be fought before these war-induced changes made genuine political gains for blacks more feasible.

As these two examples suggest, it cannot be taken for granted that modern war participants will necessarily benefit in terms of the exchanges sometimes made between states and their populations in order to enlist support for foreign wars. Some groups may profit; others suffer. Their relative political value may also fluctuate from war to war. So, too, will the relative political vulnerabilities of the governments faced with opportunities, welcome or otherwise, for widening political participation and governing coalitions.

We are tempted to argue that war is most likely to expand political participation in the more democratic, maritime-oriented global powers. In a decidedly circular fashion, more open political systems should be more open to further democratization. Real gains in participation seem least likely in the more repressive, continentally oriented powers. In these states, popular revolutions have been more likely to devolve into greater concentrations of power, as exemplified by the ascension of Bonaparte in one global war and the Bolsheviks in the next one. Along lines hinted at in chapter 3, the incentives to survive and catch up in a menacing world override the more general trends toward greater public participation, however symbolic, in domestic political arenas.

Because we are arguing that several factors may intervene between war mobilization and domestic coalition building, we must be careful not to overgeneralize about processes that certainly vary with space and time as well as with the type of regime. We also need to keep in mind that the gains for democratization that were achieved in relation to the last global war were probably greatest in Germany and Japan, thanks to their absolute defeats and subsequent transforming military occupations.

Given the complications associated with exploring the subject of state-population interactions during and immediately after war, let alone the enormous difficulties involved in pertinent data collection, we do not pursue the cross-national comparative dimensions of this aspect of state making. Instead, we concentrate on one global power, the United States, and its twentieth-century experiences with two global wars and the domestic responses to them. To make the analysis even more manageable, we confine our focus on domestic responses to the salient category of violence.

### War, Accommodation, and Violence

In this chapter we analyze the three-sided relationship among war, state accommodation, and the level of internal violence for the United States from 1890 to 1970. We contend that the observed linkages between war and domestic conflict depend on the position of governing elites vis-à-vis the claims advanced by internal political groups. Governments willing to accommodate the demands of domestic political contenders weaken the link between external and internal levels of violence. In contrast, nonaccommodating governments, unconvinced of the potential merits of reforms, are more likely to rely on coercive resources to suppress domestic challenges. In that event, the linkages between war and domestic conflict are expected to be strong and positively associated.

The hypotheses reflect the view that domestic violence is the byproduct of a sequence of actions and reactions between state officials and dominant and nondominant political groups. To the extent that government officials are the primary agents of civil conflict, it follows that their behavior is a crucial intervening variable in the overall relationship between war and domestic violence. Therefore, the theoretical task is to find out how state makers respond to internal challenges during difficult periods of national management. To what extent do their actions contribute to reducing or escalating internal violence? Is internal violence more or less likely to be reduced during periods of external violence? More generally, how is state making channeled by the interaction of officials and groups in the context of war?

These questions are hardly new. There is, for instance, a large literature on the interactive influences of domestic conflict on foreign conflict, and vice versa, that speaks to some portion of the problem we are addressing. A brief review of the pertinent literature on foreign-domestic conflict linkages can help set up the theoretical and empirical analyses that follow.

### Previous Empirical Assessments

After reviewing 30 studies on the linkages between foreign and domestic conflict, Stohl (1980: 312–13) finds only five (Denton 1966; Denton and Phillips 1968; Flanigan and Fogelman 1970; Sorokin 1937; and Tanter 1969) that systematically assess the specific relationship between involvements in war and large-scale internal violence.[2] Based solely on visual impressions of longitudinal data, three of these studies (Denton 1966; Denton and Phillips 1968; and Tanter 1969) assert that there is a linkage. The remaining two (Flanigan and Fogelman 1970; and Sorokin 1937) declare that there is none. To complicate matters further, these studies do not overlap in their choice of samples, data, time periods, and temporal units of analysis. Yet, as an ensemble, they present an excellent overview of the larger maze of empirical research in this area.

Theoretically, these five studies have been criticized for specifying overly simple relationships without regard for the role of intervening variables.[3] The strategy of reducing the question to ingroup-outgroup forms of conflict has made it easy to ignore such factors as political integration, repression, regime structure, and internal changes in the distribution of power.

Another problem is the implicit assumption that the theoretical linkages between external and internal conflict will always be positive. Conceivably, relationships could take either sign. Or the association might operate in some contexts and not in others. Despite the demonstrable evidence for this notion, many analysts either ignore it or interpret it as an indication of no genuine relationship. Such reasoning, of course, points out the lack of çonsideration for intervening influences and the weak specification of previous theoretical frameworks.

The most sophisticated illustration of this problem is Stohl's (1975, 1976) quasi-experimental analysis of American domestic violence between 1890 and 1970. As the most systematic empirical investigation of the effects of war on domestic violence, Stohl's studies eschew both the ingroup-outgroup propositions and the simple bivariate approaches of other analyses. Nevertheless, they postulate principles in favor of consistent unidirectional relationships. Specifically, Stohl hypothesizes that U.S. war involvements (the Spanish-American War, the two world wars, and the Korean and Vietnam Wars) have influenced the mobilization of new domestic groups by enhancing their economic and social positions in American society. This mobilization, in turn, stimulates general demands for a redistribution of power and resources between lower and upper strata and also generates an escalation of domestic conflict.

Stohl's two studies depart from previous research by quantifying the frequency, duration, and intensity of conflictual events involving 20 or more persons, as listed in the *New York Times* and *New York Times Index*. A total of 2,861 domestic violent events have been identified for the years 1890–1906, 1913–23, and 1935–70. Using an interrupted time series design and an ordinary least squares estimation, Stohl investigates whether nonrandom changes occur in these events at the start, during, and after U.S. war involvements. He finds step-level changes in civil violence both at the start of all five wars and in the postwar periods. However, no uniform pattern (in terms of statistical significance or positive and negative effects) holds for any of the five wars or for any of the dimensions of violence. Despite the unsupportive outcome, Stohl concludes the data generally support the contention that war escalates domestic political violence.

In contrast, we argue that the linkage between war and domestic violence is likely to be inconsistent. Whether it is positive, negative, or nonexistent ultimately hinges on the governmental elites we have been describing as state makers. As repositories of tremendous economic and political power, they have some capacity to influence the course and direction of domestic violence. Although wars can result in mobilizing new and old domestic political contenders, this does not automatically have to end in violence. Elites can ignore or appease these groups in a variety of ways—particularly through compromise, reform, imprisonment, or execution—all of which may stimulate or diffuse domestic conflict. Even in cases in which state officials are weak, their ineffective responses will have a substantial impact on civil conflict. Along the way, the shapes of states will also be affected. Therefore, the following hypotheses inextricably tie the behavior of state makers into the theoretical relationships between war and domestic conflict.

## Hypotheses

### The Role of the State as an Intervening Variable

The central question is how war influences the political context in which government elites view domestic challenges. Does its appearance facilitate the development of flexible political environments in which government elites make concessions to domestic groups? Or does it sustain environments in which governments are determined to pursue status quo policies, regardless of public demands? With either of these possible outcomes, the linkages between war and domestic violence can be positive, negative, or nonexistent.

For instance, war-inducing internal reforms may subsequently preempt or nullify domestic violence. According to Block's (1977, 1981) and Skocpol's (1979, 1980) analyses of structural change in political systems, wars and postwar demobilization periods free governing elites from the typical constraints of dominant political groups. Because they have a fundamental role in maintaining order and political peace, which wars jeopardize, state makers are apt to grant concessions, even though these concessions may be at the expense of powerful groups. Such actions reflect the government's primary interests in extracting economic resources, recruiting military personnel, and diffusing potential violence during a difficult period.

Therefore, the emergence of accommodating political regimes may account, in one instance, for defusing the linkages between wars and domestic violence. Yet the same regimes can be equally responsible for facilitating violence if new political and social rights derived from recent concessions catalyze the mobilization of large numbers of people and economic resources into political organizations. With a new or renewed sense of efficacy and the perception that the government favors their claims, these groups may challenge other political elites and groups not willing to embrace them (Tilly 1978: 145–46). Meanwhile, sympathetic officials, reluctant to take punitive measures against these emerging constituencies, are likely to resist the demands of powerful groups seeking repression. If the outcome is a direct confrontation between the contenders, the probability of conflict will increase and result in a positive association between war and domestic violence.

Because the internal effects of political reforms are difficult to foresee, state makers may be conservative about undertaking major internal reforms when their positions in the global political system are threatened. Instead, they may take repressive measures (deportations, arrests, censorship, and restrictions on public assemblies) against the leadership of opposition groups posing potential sources of challenge and instability. If the repression is consistently and effectively applied, officials will be able to wear down the position of domestic groups by making the costs of engaging in collective action too high (Tilly 1978: 101–06). In this case, the intervening effects of a nonaccommodating political environment can account for a negative or nonexistent relationship between wars and internal violence.

However, if the government's coercive sanctions are weak and poorly directed, they may intensify antagonism and conflict among groups that fail to be inhibited by threats of retaliation (Gurr 1970: 239). The act of committing military forces abroad, for example, may weaken the government's capacity to suppress internal challenges. These circumstances could become revolutionary if domestic groups continued to press their claims by seeking the overthrow of the established order (Tilly 1978: 209–11).

Finally, circumstances may contribute to the rise of conservative policies after a time of political and economic reform. Such a pattern is typical of postwar demobilization periods. During the war years, governments are able to expand the resources and powers of the state. In the interest of preserving domestic peace, they may extend new economic resources and political concessions to internal groups. During the postwar recovery period, however, available resources may contract, particularly if there is a recession, leaving state makers responsible for reconciling the commitments made to old and newly favored domestic groups. In that event, they are faced with two choices: (1) increase the state's coercion against segments of the population to maximize the yield of resources for reallocation, or (2) break the commitments that will incite the least dangerous opposition. Either step could lead to a defensive mobilization by internal groups and to a subsequent escalation of domestic conflict (Tilly 1978: 207). Although this generalization could apply to cases of victory or defeat, military defeats are apt to represent the worst cases of contraction.

These scenarios illustrate how domestic political regimes can mediate the effects of war involvement on the series of actions leading to internal violence. By understanding how national crises, like war, act on the political contexts and perceptions of governing elites, it is possible to isolate some of the political processes that account for the fluctuations in the level of domestic violence. Even so, the array of possible linkages complicates the problem of generalizing the directional relationships between war (or any other crisis) and domestic violence. It is difficult to advance propositions when the variation in the intervening variable, namely, the presence or absence of government accommodation, can be responsible for the same empirical outcomes.

An alternative approach is to start with the presumption that wars and other crises stimulate the mobilization of domestic political contenders who decide to press their claims at a propitious moment. Because the claims advanced by these contenders are likely to be at odds with at least one other domestic group (not excluding state makers), the preconditions for internal violence are not only established but also intensified in comparison with nonwar periods. As central actors in the political system, state makers play a crucial role both in resolving these claims and in countering the effects of domestic instability. Whether they decide to repress these challenges through the coercive capacities of the state or to make concessions through government-sponsored reforms, the consequences are likely to result in some domestic violence. The fundamental issue is the degree of severity. In other words, under what circumstances do wars generate levels of domestic violence atypical of previous nonwar periods?

Nonaccommodating political regimes, it has been contended, are most liable to be associated with these kinds of severity because of their greater propensity for repression. Repression, in turn, has been linked empirically to escalating civil conflict (Snyder and Tilly 1972; Stohl 1976). In contrast, reform-oriented regimes are less likely candidates. They have a better chance of deflecting what could be serious quantities of internal violence by creating political climates that discourage attacks on and by domestic challengers. The actions of state makers and the political context influencing the flexibility and range of potential policy responses are the keys to understanding the linkages between war and domestic violence.

The explicit hypotheses under investigation are:

1  The presence of accommodating governments will account for weak, insignificant linkages between war, their postwar demobilization periods, and internal violence.
2  In the presence of governmental nonaccommodation, strong, substantial linkages between war, their postwar periods, and internal violence are more likely.
3  Wars (and postwar periods) that sustain nonaccommodating governments will be associated with higher levels of repression than will wars that induce reform-oriented regimes.

Given the variation in war attributes, it is impractical to assume that all wars will have similar impacts on domestic violence. However, the lack of available data and the inherent constraints in this type of study make it infeasible to isolate these effects and the role of accommodation at the same time.

Nevertheless, the additional influence of war intensity can be addressed indirectly by distinguishing American war involvements as either global or nonglobal. Global wars (World Wars I and II) are fought on a larger scale and result in the major expansion of new domestic institutions and state powers.[4]

Linkages between external and internal conflicts are expected to be strongest for these wars, because the foreign and domestic agendas will bring governing elites into more serious opposition with domestic groups over basic aspects of the economic, political, and social arrangements of their society. On the other hand, nonglobal wars (the Spanish-American, Korean, and Vietnam conflicts) present fewer problems of domestic mobilization for state makers; hence, they are expected to produce, at the most, weak conflict linkages.

If the two types of wars generate similar linkages, intensity will no longer be an important conditional variable, and the role of accommodation will become the central explanatory variable. In the event nonglobal wars engender consistently weak (or nonexistent) conflict linkages and the global wars yield mixed linkages, the subsequent analysis will concentrate on connecting the presence or absence of accommodation with the observed linkages of the global wars. Thus, war intensity will be held constant as the variation in the intervening variable is left to account for the fluctuations in the conflict linkages.

Operationalizing governmental accommodation is a relatively difficult task in lieu of obvious quantitative measures. One way to tap into this concept involves scanning historical records for evidence of reform activity undertaken by the executive, judicial, and legislative institutions of the U.S. government. Substantive reforms will indicate an accommodating national administration. Their absence will denote nonaccommodation. Ultimately, the findings will be based on two components: (1) a qualitative analysis of governmental accommodation during the relevant U.S. political administrations, and (2) a quantitative assessment of the effects of war, and their postwar demobilization periods, on American domestic violence from 1890 to 1970.

### Data and Indicators

Fortunately, the availability of data on American violence in Stohl's (1976) analysis makes empirical testing of our hypotheses possible. However, the annual domestic violence data in that study cover only the periods of 1890–1906, 1913–23, and 1935–70. Because Stohl's (1976) data collection procedures are outlined clearly, the task of expanding the annual data for the missing periods of 1907–12 and 1924–34 is relatively straightforward. The present analysis uses an annual measure of the magnitude of domestic violence. The frequency of all violent events is multiplied by their duration to yield four time series under investigation: economic, social, and political violence, and total violence (a combined measure of all three). Plots of these series are provided in figures 7.2 and 7.3.

The decision to maintain Stohl's economic, social, and political classifications is based on the view that conflict linkages may be contingent on the type of

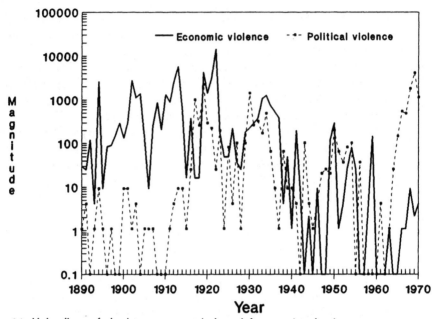

0.1 added to all scores for logging purposes; magnitude equals frequency times duration.

***Figure 7.2.*** U.S. Economic and Political Violence, 1890–1970 (Logged Values)

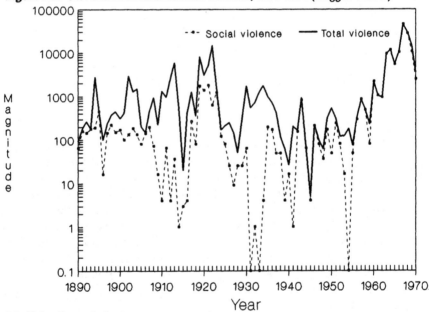

0.1 added to all scores for logging purposes; magnitude equals frequency times duration.

***Figure 7.3.*** U.S. Social and Total Violence, 1890–1970 (Logged Values)

domestic challenge being made. As an example, the state's wartime interest in preserving economic stability for the production of war materials may lead to concessions to labor unions. At the same time, other groups considered to be unacceptable threats to the state (e.g., anarchists, International Workers of the World, and the Communist Party) are likely to be repressed. Such discrimination inevitably will affect the observed conflict linkages.

Stohl (1976) identifies economic-related violence by the types of issues (collective bargaining, wage increases, unemployment) at stake and the groups participating in the conflict (management versus labor, landlords versus tenants, farmers versus bankers, and agricultural laborers versus landowners). Social-related violence comprises racial, ethnic, religious, and educational disputes (whites versus blacks, Indians, and Orientals; native Americans versus foreign immigrants; and students or faculty versus university administrators). Finally, political-related violence involves disagreements over governmental policies or ideological differences (Republicans versus Democrats, right-versus left-wing groups, government actors versus antiwar protestors, Communists versus Socialists, and government actors versus Communists and Socialists).

In addition to these dimensions, Stohl (1976) distinguishes among prosystem (events initiated by status quo groups), antisystem (events initiated by groups seeking to reform or challenge the status quo), and clash (events identified as either pro- or antisystem) activities. Because a large proportion of the data is identified as clashes, an extensive examination of each series is unnecessary. Nevertheless, the magnitude of prosystem violence is used to discern whether repression (initiated by either the government or other powerful groups) is indeed higher in wars involving nonaccommodating political regimes than in wars involving conciliatory regimes.[5]

### Statistical Specifications

The impact of U.S. war involvements on domestic violence is estimated for each violence time series in the form of three interventions: one encompassing the combined effects of the Spanish-American, Korean, and Vietnam Wars, and a second and third reflecting the separate influences of World Wars I and II.[6] The influences of the interstate wars are combined because of the expectation that they will not have strong statistically significant associations with internal violence, either separately or jointly. In cases where the parameter estimates indicate otherwise, the separate influences of each war will be calculated. The same approach is used to estimate the postwar effects. Each postwar demobilization period will equal the number of years involved in actual warfare.[7]

## The Impact of War on Domestic Violence

Table 7.1 summarizes the statistical results of applying Box-Tiao impact assessment models to the four continuous series of domestic violence. The collective impacts of the interstate wars are expected to yield statistically insignificant impact parameters. The two global wars should be associated with statistically significant estimates. Considering that some levels of violence occur in any political system, statistical significance is an important criteria for identifying historical deviations from the norm. Even though the short-term consequences of wartime influences on internal violence are important, our primary interest centers on whether these influences are responsible for unusual levels of severity in comparison to nonwar years. Table 7.1 indicates that the only significant impacts of war are associated with World War I. Except for economic-related violence, the direction of these impacts is positive for the remaining forms of violence.

Our initial strategy was to isolate the effects of global and interstate wars on internal violence. Mixed results, if any, between the global wars were to be accounted for through the intervening effects of government accommodation. Because the evidence does reflect contrasting conflict linkages between World Wars I and II, the parameter estimates for economic, social, and political violence are interpreted below.[8] Particular attention is paid to the wartime policies pursued by national elites.

**Table 7.1**
**The Impact of War on U.S. Domestic Violence, 1890–1970**

| Violence Series | Intervention Component[a] | | | | Noise Component | | Goodness of Fit[c] | |
| | Interstate Wars $\omega_0$ | World War I $\omega_0$ | $\delta$ | World War II $\omega_0$ | ARIMA Parameters | Type of Noise Structure[b] | $\chi^2$ | RMSE |
|---|---|---|---|---|---|---|---|---|
| Economic | 0.19 (1.1) | –3.7* (2.6) | | –0.69 (0.66) | $\theta_1 = 0.76*$ (9.5) | (0, 1, 1) | 16.1 | 2.9 |
| Social | –0.14 (1.1) | 2.1* (2.4) | | 0.29 (0.56) | $\theta_1 = 0.49*$ (4.4) | (0, 1, 1) | 13.8 | 2.8 |
| Political | 0.51 (1.5) | 4.1* (2.7) | –1.1* (3.6) | –0.09 (0.14) | $\phi_1 = -0.51*$ (5.1) | (1, 1, 0) | 9.4 | 3.1 |
| Total | –0.15 (0.35) | –0.07 (0.87) | | –0.88 (1.2) | white noise | (0, 1, 0) | 19.3 | 1.9 |

*Note:* All data have been logged to achieve variance stationarity; *t*-values are reported in parentheses.

* denotes statistical significance at the .05 level.

[a] All intervention models are the abrupt, temporary type with the exception of abrupt, permanent models for economic violence during World War I.

[b] (0, 1, 1) denotes a differenced, first-order moving average process; (1, 1, 0) denotes a differenced, first-order autoregressive process; (0, 1, 0) denotes a differenced process.

[c] Chi-square values indicate residuals are white noise with 11 degrees of freedom; RMSE represents residual mean square error.

*Economic Violence*

Although World War I is associated with the only statistically significant decline, the findings suggest that economic violence, a large proportion of which derives from labor-management disputes, did not increase when national officials would have been most vulnerable. According to labor historians, the two world war experiences offered extraordinary opportunities for American labor leaders, who were normally locked out of the political process, to gain access to the inner circles of national decision making.

During the world wars, the Wilson and Roosevelt administrations made a concerted effort to enlist labor's cooperation to smooth and sustain the process of economic mobilization. Their policies led not only to major reforms on behalf of labor, but also to the sponsorship of labor participation in the national government.

Both Wilson and Roosevelt established National War Labor Boards (NWLB), involving the participation of prominent labor officials, to formulate a comprehensive set of rules to guide labor-management relations during the wars. Many of the new principles involved significant labor reforms. During World War I, these reforms included the recognition of workers' rights to join independent trade unions, the preservation of the union shop and union conditions where they existed, an eight-hour workday, and equal pay for women (Dubofsky 1975: 122). During World War II, the reforms disposed of any remaining barriers to collective bargaining and extended labor-management issues beyond wage topics to include fringe benefits, wage-rate inequalities, piece rate computation, and geographical differentials (Brody 1980: 112–16). In exchange, the AFL (in World War I) and the CIO (in World War II) agreed to no-strike policies, actively squashed strikes, and aided the government in purging disloyal, subversive elements—members of the International Workers of the World (IWW) and of the Socialist and Communist parties—from the labor movement.[9] See figure 7.4.

Although the war years were characterized by greater government flexibility regarding labor issues, there was still a substantial rise in labor strikes. Between 1914 and 1916, an average of 2,195 work stoppages occurred, in comparison with 4,450 in 1917 and 3,353 in 1918 (U.S. Department of Commerce 1975: 179). Yet our empirical findings and figure 7.4 indicate economic violence declined significantly during World War I. This phenomenon can be attributed partially to the efforts of federal mediation in labor-management disputes and the influence of AFL officials in persuading workers to return to their jobs. In cases where these options failed, the government repressed union leadership, for example, in the IWW-led strikes in copper, lumber, and food grains (Dubofsky 1975: 115–21).

The pattern is similar in World War II, though less dramatic. The average

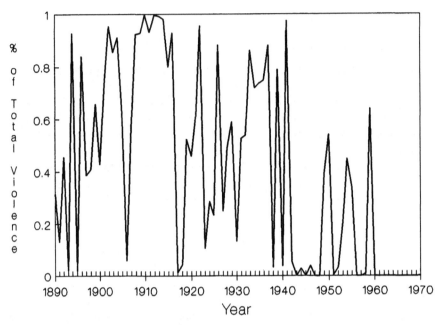

**Figure 7.4.** Economic Violence as a Proportion of Total Violence, 1890–1970

number of work stoppages in the four years preceding the war (1938–41) was 3,045; this increased to an average of 4,107 during the war years (1942–45) (U.S. Bureau of the Census 1975: 179). Nevertheless, there was an empirical decline, albeit weak, in economic violence. Again, the harmonious labor-management relations fostered by the government's support of collective bargaining was probably a crucial factor. In the final analysis, the political contexts of World Wars I and II, in addition to the quantitative evidence, contribute support for the hypothesis that accommodating political regimes will contribute to weak or nonexistent conflict linkages.

*Social Violence*

The empirical evidence in table 7.1 indicates that World War I is associated with a statistically significant, major increase in social violence. World War II demonstrates a statistically weak increase. Bearing in mind that 95 percent of the social violence events for the 1890–1970 era involve racial violence, the role of governmental accommodation needs to be analyzed in terms of the Wilson and Roosevelt administrations' wartime record on black civil rights issues.[10]

During World War I, the Wilson administration failed to undertake significant reforms on behalf of blacks. It ignored basic demands by blacks for the elimination of military segregation, federal employment discrimination, and Jim Crow practices in the federally controlled railroad system (Scheiber and Scheiber 1969: 454–57). Prewar discriminatory practices by employers and white union officials were sustained during the war (with the approval of the federal government), and black workers had little or no opportunity to advance from unskilled to semiskilled occupations (Foner 1982: 133–34). An examination of the U.S. Supreme Court civil rights decisions from 1876 to 1955 reveals a significant decline both in the volume of cases and the number of pro–civil rights outcomes between 1916 and 1920 (McAdam 1982: 85). In sum, national political elites were far from accommodating to the political and social interests of blacks in American society.

The concomitant rise in social violence during this period, readily apparent in figure 7.5, is attributed in large part to the conflict between blacks and whites over urban issues of housing, transportation, recreational facilities, and the competition for jobs and wages. Despite pleas from black leaders, Wilson refused to take public positions denouncing the practice of lynchings and failure of local authorities to protect black citizens (Scheiber and Scheiber 1969: 455–57).

The Roosevelt administration, in contrast, undertook some major reforms during World War II to accommodate the interests of blacks. In 1943, the National War Labor Board outlawed wage differentials based on race;

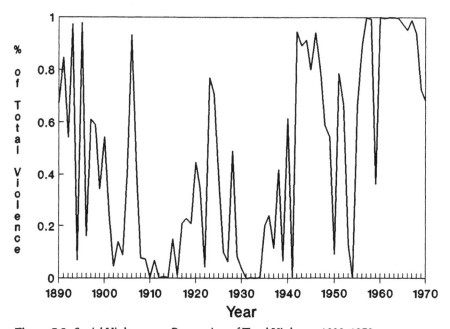

*Figure 7.5.* Social Violence as a Proportion of Total Violence, 1890–1970

the U.S. Employment Service reversed existing policy by refusing to honor requests specifying the race of applicants; and the National Labor Relations Board stated it would refuse to certify unions excluding minority groups. By the end of the war, the federal government had increased the number of its black employees from 60,000 to 200,000, and more often in higher classifications (Polenberg 1972: 116). Finally, the volume of U.S. Supreme Court decisions on civil rights cases, many of which were aimed at striking down Jim Crow practices, and the number of favorable outcomes increased from 1941 to 1945 (McAdam 1982: 85). In short, the political accommodation during World War II is associated with a statistically weak conflict linkage. The lack of accommodation in World War I is linked with a statistically strong conflict linkage.

### Political Violence

The empirical evidence indicates that World War I is associated with a strong increase in political violence and that World War II has only a rather weak, negative association.[11]

Much of the political violence between 1917 and 1918 was the result of actions taken by government agencies and other status quo groups against leftists, farmers, and pacifists protesting the war and selective service laws (Peterson and Fite 1957; Stohl 1976: 91–95). Members of the Socialist Party and the International Workers of the World were prominent targets because their organizations took strong public stands against the war. Their rallies, parades, and assemblies often precipitated attacks at local levels. The IWW was an especially popular target of repression by local and national authorities. They used its antiwar position to justify eliminating its disruptive labor union operations (Peterson and Fite 1957: 48–60).

The limited political violence during World War II shown in figure 7.6 was due to the impact of Pearl Harbor on public consensus and the absence of major violence in interning the Japanese-American population. The presence of the Soviet Union as a major American ally, which helped to unify leftist support, was also a factor (Brooks 1979: 314–15). The lack of opposition to the war, in contrast to the 1917–18 years, makes it difficult to pin down the role of accommodation during the Roosevelt administration. Because national elites were never required to respond to any large constituency, it is not possible to link the position of government officials to the weak, negative relationship between World War II and political violence.

The only other significant finding in this section is the strong positive impact of the Vietnam War on political violence. Because the estimation of the collective influences of interstate wars yielded contradictory estimates, the intervention components were respecified to calculate the separate influences of the Spanish-American, Korean, and Vietnam Wars on political violence.

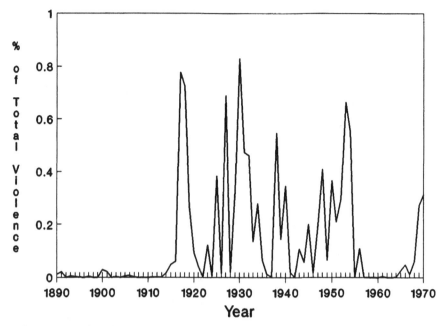

***Figure 7.6.*** Political Violence as a Proportion of Total Violence, 1890–1970

The results indicate that the Vietnam War is accompanied by a statistically significant change in the level of the series. This finding supports earlier evidence of a positive association between the escalation of U.S. troop levels and the rate of increase in the number of antiwar protests from 1964 to 1968 (Tanter 1969: 557). However, the violence data fail to cover the entire period of American war involvement, making it premature to analyze the statistical results without first updating the violence series. This task must be left to subsequent analyses.

## The Postwar Impact of Demobilization on Domestic Violence

### Economic Violence

The parameter estimates in table 7.2 show that the post–World War I period (1919–20) is accompanied by a statistically significant, albeit unstable, increase in the level of economic violence. The post–World War II era (1946–49) is linked with a statistically weak increase.

In comparison with the major reforms on behalf of labor during World War I, the postwar period was characterized by a return to national conservatism. By mid-1919, labor unions had lost many of the reforms gained

Table 7.2
The Impact of Postwar Demobilization on U.S. Domestic Violence, 1890–1970

| Violence Series | Intervention Component[a] | | | | | Noise Component | | | |
|---|---|---|---|---|---|---|---|---|---|
| | Interstate Wars $\omega_o$ | World War I $\omega_o$ | $\delta$ | World War II $\omega_o$ | ARIMA Parameters | Type of Noise Structure[b] | | Goodness of Fit[c] $\chi^2$ | RMSE |
| Economic | −0.37 | 3.9* | −1.0 | 0.58 | $\theta_1 = 0.63$* | (0, 1, 1) | | 17.4 | 4.1 |
| | (0.73) | (2.3) | (3.6) | (1.1) | (6.2) | | | | |
| Social | 0.78 | 3.6* | −0.97 | 0.31 | $\theta_1 = 0.46$* | (0, 1, 1) | | 12.3 | 2.8 |
| | (1.5) | (2.1) | (3.9) | (0.56) | (4.2) | | | | |
| Political | −0.76 | 1.4* | | 0.69 | $\phi_1 = -0.45$* | (1, 1, 0) | | 4.5 | 3.0 |
| | (1.3) | (2.0) | | (1.1) | (4.1) | | | | |
| Total | 0.13 | 3.2* | −1.0* | 0.22 | white | (0, 1, 0) | | 19.8 | 2.0 |
| | (0.20) | (2.3) | (2.5) | (0.30) | noise | | | | |

Note: All data have been logged to achieve variance stationarity; *t*-values are reported in parentheses.
* denotes statistical significance at the .05 level.
[a] All intervention models are the abrupt, temporary type with the exception of the abrupt, permanent models for economic violence during World War I.
[b] (0, 1, 1) denotes a differenced, first-order moving average process; (1, 1, 0) denotes a differenced, first-order autoregressive process; (0, 1, 0) denotes a differenced process.
[c] Chi-square values indicate residuals are white noise with 11 degrees of freedom; RMSE represents residual mean square error.

during the war. Both the U.S. government and management no longer endorsed and maintained agreements on wage levels, the length of the workday, and codes on industrial safety. Most significantly, collective bargaining was no longer embraced by governmental officials (Dubofsky 1975: 122–31; Hawley 1979: 45–52).

Therefore, when labor-management disputes occurred between 1919 and 1920, the resulting labor strikes generated an increase in the level of economic violence. It is difficult to overlook the decline in economic violence accompanying the large number of work stoppages during World War I (mean = 3902), when a relatively equal number of work stoppages between 1919 and 1920 (mean = 3521) is associated with a statistically significant increase. The absence of a government promoting and enforcing policies of collective bargaining removed an important avenue for avoiding potential violence.

The post–World War II years (1946–49) are also characterized by a large number of work stoppages (mean = 3926); and though there is an increase in economic violence, the change is statistically weak from a historical perspective.[12] As between 1919 and 1920, the post–World War II era saw a return to public and Congressional conservatism regarding the economic position of labor unions, federal spending, and U.S. foreign policy. Nonetheless, national administrative elites worked against these trends in their efforts to regenerate the American economy and supervise the European Recovery Program.

Truman made every effort to co-opt major American labor leaders in an attempt to obtain internal economic stability and enlist their aid in mobilizing domestic support for the Marshall Plan (Freeland 1972; Godson 1976; McClure 1969). Stimulated by the reasoning that future economic growth would produce abundance and material gain for all classes without a redistribution of economic power, CIO and AFL labor leaders endorsed the administration's policies (Hamby 1974: 66; Milton 1982: 154–55). They compromised on labor-management battles designed to expand their role in management decisions and accepted the proposition of pegging wage increases to cost-of-living and economic productivity levels (Brody 1980: 173–213).

As representatives of the U.S. government, they also participated in selling the merits of the Marshall Plan to the West European trade unions. Eventually, they succeeded in splitting the European labor movement between Communist and non-Communist elements, contributing to the development of European political institutions on a more centrist political path (Maier 1978: 40–46). According to labor historians, these actions would lead to labor's loss of political independence and ensure labor peace over the course of the next 25 years (Brody 1980: 229–55; Milton 1982: 154–67). This position is supported by the quantitative evidence in figure 7.2, which shows a decrease in the overall level of economic violence from 1946 to 1970.

### Social Violence

The Box-Tiao estimates in table 7.2 indicate that the post–World War I era is accompanied by a statistically significant increase in the level of social violence. The post–World War II era is linked with a statistically weak increase.[13] The political climate for blacks in 1919 and 1920 was far from favorable. Blacks in America went into the war with high morale generated by the belief that a new democratic order would be achieved on the home front. Instead, black soldiers met with discrimination and segregation, and when they came home, they faced Jim Crow and unemployment. They also found the Ku Klux Klan revitalized, a denial of suffrage and residential segregation as before, and a gathering of racial tensions that led to the "Red Summer" of 1919. In one year, 77 blacks were lynched and 26 American cities suffered race riots (Scheiber and Scheiber 1969: 455–58).

Despite the post–World War I years, America's rise to world leadership status after World War II had unintended consequences for internal policies of racial discrimination. Locked in what was perceived to be an ideological struggle against communism, national leaders viewed racial discrimination as a major handicap in the Cold War competition for influence over nonwhite Third World nations (Berman 1974: 186; Bernstein 1974: 58; Myrdal 1970: 35). Furthermore, the strategic location of black voting blocs in northern states with large electoral votes made blacks an important element in Truman's bid for the presidency in 1948 (Berman 1974: 186).

These international and domestic realities prompted Truman to take increasingly progressive actions that led to (1) the desegregation of the armed forces, (2) the appointment of a Civil Rights Committee, and (3) the establishment of a Fair Employment Board within the Civil Service Commission. In February 1948, Truman introduced the first comprehensive civil rights program to the Congress since the post–Civil War years. Three years later, he closed out his term by establishing a Committee on Government Compliance, aimed at preventing discrimination in employment by private firms holding government contracts (McAdam 1982: 83–84).

*Political Violence*

According to the Box–Tiao estimates in table 7.2, the post–World War I years are charged with a statistically significant increase in political violence. The post–World War II years, on the other hand, are associated with a statistically weak increase.

The substantial levels of post–World War I political violence were due, in large part, to the sustained concern of national governmental elites with repressing groups and individuals espousing communist, socialist, or anarchist views. Public distaste for such radical groups as the Socialist party and the IWW intensified with exaggerated threats of bolshevism spreading from Europe to the United States. Public demonstrations continued to be attacked by local populations with the tacit approval of local and national officials (Peterson and Fite 1957: 285–306).

The role of governmental accommodation during the post–World War II years is difficult to discern closely because, as with the war years, there was very little organized political activity protesting or making public demands for or against government policies. Although the political climate became more antagonistic toward communists (or alleged communists), the reactionary elements of anticommunism did not dominate public attitudes until after 1947 and the intensification of the Cold War. Truman's national security concerns vis-à-vis the Soviet Union shaped domestic priorities toward a preoccupation with radical subversion, both abroad and at home. The federal employee loyalty program and the trials of American communists during these years fostered rigid conservatism among national elites and contributed to the rise of Joseph McCarthy in the 1950s (Theoharis 1970: 197–232). Nevertheless, there was no sustained level of organized political activity similar to the Socialists and Wobblies (IWW) during and after World War I. Consequently, governmental accommodation cannot be linked in any obvious way with the empirical findings.

## Linkages between Repression and National Accommodation

The final hypothesis in this chapter associates nonaccommodating political administrations with higher levels of repression than reform-oriented regimes. Nonaccommodating governments are more likely to use coercion to suppress domestic challenges, thus escalating the level of internal violence. Reform governments, on the other hand, are less likely to rely on repressive measures, thereby reducing potential levels of violence. A test of the hypothesis is based on a comparison between the levels of violence initiated by prosystem groups during World Wars I and II and their postwar periods. Unfortunately, the outcome is inconclusive because the prosystem violence includes the actions of both governmental elites and dominant political elites. However, if nongoverning elites take cues from the behavior of national officials regarding appropriate and inappropriate responses to new contenders, there is apt to be a correlation among their actions. Therefore, prosystem violence is still a useful measure for comparing levels of repression among U.S. administrations.

Table 7.3 tabulates the average magnitude of prosystem violence for each decade from 1900 to 1959 (including the war years) in comparison with the average magnitude of prosystem violence for each war period. The evidence suggests two things. First, the overall levels of repression are higher during the war-related years than during the non-war-related periods, regardless of accommodation.[14] This is not unexpected, in view of the greater insecurity among governing and nongoverning elites during critical periods.

Second, a rank order of the repression during the crisis periods shows that two of the three nonaccommodating regimes (1917–18 and 1919–20)

*Table 7.3*
*A Comparison of the Average Magnitude of Prosystem Initiated Violence
during War and Nonwar Years*

| Nonwar Years | Prosystem Violence | War Years | Prosystem Violence |
|---|---|---|---|
| 1900–09 | 6 | 1917–18[a] | 183 |
| 1910–16 | 29 | 1919–20[a] | 1215 |
| 1921–29 | 54 | | |
| 1930–33 | 302 | | |
| 1934–39 | 143 | | |
| 1940–41 | 23 | | |
| | | 1942–45[b] | 89 |
| | | 1946–49[b] | 58 |
| 1950–59 | 35 | | |

*Note:* No national accommodation toward major economic, social, and political group (with the exception of reforms on behalf of labor during 1917–18) occurred during periods marked *a*. National accommodation did occur during periods marked *b*.

are associated with the highest levels of repression. Two of the three conciliatory regimes (1942–45 and 1946–49) are linked with the least amount of repression.

## Conclusion

This chapter shows that the search for positive statistical associations between war and domestic violence can overlook substantively important evidence that has broader theoretical implications. In particular, our analyses aim at demonstrating how the relationship between war and internal violence is conditioned by two potential factors: the severity of the war and the presence or absence of governmental accommodation. Table 7.4 shows that the isolation of these variables during the critical periods of World Wars I and II, and their postwar eras, is associated in eight of ten cases with increases in American domestic violence. However, the crucial test involving the statistical significance of Box-Tiao parameter estimates indicates that five of these eight cases depict historical periods of unusual levels of domestic violence, all of which

**Table 7.4**
**U.S. Governmental Accommodation and the Linkages between War and Domestic Violence**

| Type of Contenders | Accommodation | | Nonaccommodation | |
|---|---|---|---|---|
| | War | Conflict Linkage[a] | War | Conflict Linkage[a] |
| Economic | World War I | strong, negative | Post–World War I | strong, positive |
| | World War II | weak, negative | | |
| | Post–World War II | weak, positive | | |
| Social | World War II | weak, positive | World War I | strong, positive |
| | Post–World War II | weak, positive | Post–World War I | strong, positive |
| Political | World War II | no test | World War I | strong, positive |
| | Post–World War II | no test | Post–World War I | strong, positive |

*Note:* Governmental administrations that implement major reforms on behalf of less powerful economic, social, and political groups are labeled as accommodating; otherwise, administrations are considered nonaccommodating.

[a] Based on Box-Tiao parameter estimates indicating statistical significance (strong/weak) and the directional impact of war and postwar demobilization on economic, social, and political forms of violence.

are linked with nonaccommodating political environments. Conversely, all of the five cases indicating a decline or weak positive increase in domestic violence are associated with accommodating U.S. political administrations. Overall evidence supports the hypotheses that link nonaccommodating and reform-oriented regimes with statistically significant and insignificant conflict linkages.

Although the levels of repression tend to be higher during and after wars than during non-war-related periods, nonaccommodating U.S. political administrations are associated more frequently with higher levels of repression than are conciliatory ones. The theoretical implications are that conservative political regimes are likely to generate higher amounts of repression during and after wars, thereby escalating the magnitude of internal violence. When governmental elites recognize the legitimacy of the claims advanced by domestic groups (at least symbolically) they are less prone to use repression, thereby breaking the cycle of intensive violence. When elites are willing to negotiate the claims of domestic contenders, conflict is likely to be preempted or substantially reduced. This outcome is demonstrated by the decline in economic violence with the appearance of government-supervised collective bargaining in labor-management disputes during World Wars I and II.

Nevertheless, decisions to support political reforms, no matter how limited, can be very risky. If there is concern with maintaining internal stability during critical periods of management, state makers are faced with establishing crucial policies that may open up a Pandora's box of unexpected outcomes. Their tendency to rely on status quo policies and repression becomes somewhat more understandable. Therefore, the context that ultimately supports political change becomes an important issue. Under what conditions are war-related crises likely to support governing elites who are willing to sponsor political reforms? As the evidence suggests, the presence of a global war alone does not automatically ensure political concessions, regardless of the magnitude of domestic violence.

In our view, general crises like global wars that coincide with fundamental transformations in domestic political environments are more likely to facilitate important, long-lasting concessions. For instance, there is the culmination of the long-term growth in the northern black electorate that coincided with major reforms on behalf of blacks during and after World War II (Dalfiume 1974: 181–84; McAdam 1982: 81–86).

So, the lesson seems to be that governments become sensitized to the issues put forth by domestic challengers but are only motivated to support them when the political environment makes it advantageous to do so. In short, domestic concessions come when governmental officials receive something in return, whether it is labor peace, elected office, or support for international policies. Therefore, Block's (1977) and Skocpol's (1980) thesis that crises open up political space for new reforms appears to have some validity, but only if their timing intersects with other fundamental changes in domestic social and political arrangements. At least that appears to be the case in the American experience.

The most significant aspect of this chapter has been the theoretical benefits derived from linking the behavior of state makers with the empirical relationships between war and internal violence. It reconfirms the necessity of thinking about domestic violence in terms of a process of actions and reactions among multiple actors (governmental and nongovernmental), and about how the process is affected by the appearance of war and postwar demobilization. Nevertheless, the extent to which the evidence presented in this chapter is a reflection of other, non-American, global power experiences depends on future investigations.

The evidence also reminds us that choices made by state makers are influenced simultaneously by forces emanating from outside and within the state. The structural shape of states and their standard operating procedures reflect the serial outcomes of choices made under internal and external pressures.

# 8
# War Making and the State

Arthur Stein and Bruce Russett (1980: 418) have observed that we still do not know whether wars "involve real discontinuities in historical development," or whether "they simply cause ripples in a basically continuous process of a development that is fueled by other determinants." We cannot speak for all cases. By now, however, there can be little doubt on which end of the impact continuum global wars and global power state making belong.

We have not found that many ripples. Some aspects of war's impact on economic growth do resemble this description. In comparison to the effects of global wars, for instance, a good number of interstate wars are more likely to create ripples than discontinuities in global power state making. Yet the state-making processes of the global powers, in general, have been more discontinuous—in the global war-induced staircase sense—than continuous.

Other determinants no doubt are at work. Still, it is difficult to overlook the direct and indirect impacts of global war on extraction and other dimensions of state making. Expanded, more effective, and more deadly states have returned the favor by making increasingly more devastating global wars, as the casualty ledger in table 8.1 demonstrates.

Global wars and global power state making, therefore, are inextricably bound together. We need not dwell on the distant origins of states in general. Multiple simuli have contributed to the origins of these central political organizations. In particular, though, the origins of the global powers and their states are heavily indebted to war. Portugal, France, Spain, Germany, and

Table 8.1
Global War Battle Deaths

| Global War | Battle Deaths (millions) | As Percentage of Battle Deaths in: |
|---|---|---|
| Italian/Indian Ocean Wars | 0.1 | — |
| Dutch-Spanish Wars | 0.2 | 1517–1609: 20% |
| Wars of Louis XIV | 2.0 | 1610–1713: 37% |
| French Revolutionary/Napoleonic Wars | 2.5 | 1714–1815: 40% |
| World Wars I and II | 20.7 | 1815–1945: 95% |

Source: based on Modelski (1987b: 47) which, in turn, is based on battle death data in Levy (1983: 88–92).

Russia were the products of expansionary war and state makers. The forceful creation of France helped make England the distinctive country that it eventually became. The Dutch and the Americans, too, were only able to create their states as a consequence of winning wars of independence against Spain and Britain, respectively. Even the isolated Japanese state was first unified by force in the late sixteenth century and then forced into the nineteenth-century world system by the threat of a war it could not hope to win.

Once these states were territorially consolidated, what might have occurred in the absence of the intermittent war shocks of the grand and small varieties is extremely difficult to forecast. Would France and Spain eventually have devolved into the smaller units from which they were carved? Would the Dutch have rebelled in the first place? Would England have remained a small island always on the fringe of the continental action? Or would it have been another large European state with territory on both sides of the Channel? Would there have been a second geoeconomic restructuring centered on the British industrial revolution? Without Napoleon and British economic dominance, would there have been a united Germany? Would Japan have been pulled so rudely from its comfortable isolation? How would the Europeans have established their dominance over so much of the Third World without the partially war-induced gains made in military and industrial technology? Might there still be a Czarist regime of some sort in Russia? Would there have been another economic restructuring, this time with an American focus?

Merely raising these speculative questions suggests an obvious answer. War has so dominated the historical development of the global powers that the past 500 or more years become inconceivable without acknowledging its impact. Once the competitive state-making process began to gain momentum after 1500, war, particularly global war, continued to dominate the political development of the global powers. More and bigger wars, coupled with changes in military technology, meant larger armed forces. More armed forces meant more and bigger wars, as well as greater military expenditures. Greater military expenditures meant greater and gradually more efficient extraction efforts on the part of the states. More extractive agents were needed as well.[1]

Long-term public debts emerged as one answer to the competitive state's war-induced financial problems. Increased revenues based on a more extensive and intensive tax base constituted another. Emerging somewhat as a lagged corollary to these increases in resource extractions was the principle of expanding rights for members of the state's population who might be expected to contribute to a future war effort. Enfranchisement and broader forms of governmental protection followed sporadically and rather spasmodically. Yet by the end of the nineteenth and into the twentieth century, a global power's entire population had become relevant to the competition among the global powers. At least partially in consequence, state makers began to worry more about improving the mental and physical health of potential draftees. Less directly, it can be argued, these developments also contributed to the gradual shift of advanced industrial states from nightwatchmen states to welfare states.

These observations have been made before. Analyses of the war-making facet of state making have become more frequent, particularly in the last two decades. As much as is practical, we have integrated the findings of these earlier analyses into our investigations. We have also made a few critical comments along the way. Yet one of the more intriguing aspects of this line of inquiry is the continuing, often unconscious resistance to incorporating or even exploring the implications of war making and state making.

Some suggestive evidence relating to this assertion is demonstrated by the fact that several aspects of the perspective argued for in the earlier chapters and elsewhere have existed in the literature for quite some time. In 1906, a German historian, Otto Hintze, delivered a lecture in Dresden on the relationships between state and military organizations. Among a number of points made in that lecture, the following seven paraphrased statements apply to our present purposes:

1   Prior to the expansion of agricultural cultivation, all state organization was initially military organization or organization for war. The more frequently wars were fought, the stronger was the coerciveness of the governments involved.
2   To best ascertain the relationships between military and state organizations, two sets of phenomena provide the most explanatory power: (1) the structure of social classes, and (2) the external positioning of states to one another and, more generally, in the world.
3   If forced to rank order the two explanatory sets, the external positioning of states and the ensuing interstate conflict have been much more important. Moreover, external pressure and conflict have been more influential on internal social structure than the other way around.

4  As feudal kings found themselves campaigning farther and farther from their home bases and, relatedly, found themselves needing a better formula to control their nominally vassal troops in the field, new means were sought to recruit soldiers for pay. Gradually, monetary payments were increasingly substituted for feudal obligations to provide military service.

5  By the fourteenth and fifteenth centuries, preparations for war had become a question of finances. The consequent royal preference for taxes and other fiscal extractions rendered feudal military service obsolete. One prime byproduct was the development of corporative participatory assemblies (estates, parliaments, *etats generaux*, and *landtage*) to facilitate the extraction process and as part of a general centralization of political authority.

6  To enable France to fight Spain and Austria, Richelieu had to overwhelm provincial particularism. In the process, a new standard of state absolutism was achieved. More generally, the constant rivalry and tensions among the great powers, dating back to the Valois-Habsburg rivalry, was responsible for establishing the international system, absolutist governments, and standing armies—which, for Hintze, equalled "the foundations of modern Europe."

7  By and large, external pressures brought about a progressive extension of political rights because more and more soldiers were needed.

In the same lecture, Hintze said the following about sea and land powers:

A military system whose center of gravity is in sea power will influence the organization of the state in its own peculiar way, different from the way of the Continental military system. Land forces are a kind of organization that permeates the whole body of the state and gives it a military cast. Sea power is only a mailed fist, reaching out into the world, it is not suitable for use against some "enemy within." Land forces have stood since the beginning in more or less intimate alliance with the propertied classes; they still carry something of a feudal transition in them. Sea power lacks all feudal vestiges. To an eminent degree it serves the interests of trade and industry. Its place is with the modern forces in life, simply by virtue of the vital importance that technology and capital have in its development. Sea power is allied with progressive forces, whereas land forces are tied to conservative tendencies. (1975: 214)

Hintze's arguments were not exactly stillborn. We have been inexcusably slow, though, to appreciate the value of his insights. We have been equally slow to appreciate the pervasive role of warfare in state making. We have been even slower to admit that a special class of wars, the global wars, occupy a unique niche in the annals of war-making consequences.

There is no reason to attempt to generalize to all states. For the global powers, however, global wars have dominated the expansion of the state. The impact of these special wars was not easily discerned at the beginning of the global war sequence. Table 8.1 suggests one reason. The passage of time and other developments were required for the impacts to become increasingly more impressive. The reciprocal interaction of war making and state making contributed a great deal. By the end of the seventeenth century, global wars had become readily discernible watershed events for the global powers and the development of their political organizations. The outcome reflects the broader theoretical point that global wars, in general, became critical watershed events for the world system beginning in the 1490s.

Table 8.2 summarizes the bulk of the results of our analysis of multiple time series relevant to the historical expansion of the global power state and the state-making impact of global wars. None of the series behave in precisely the same way. Not all of the global powers or, alternatively, not all of the time period of interest (post-1494) is amenable to this type of analysis. Even so, the outcome is fairly consistent with our expectations. Public debt, total expenditures and revenues, and nonmilitary expenditures (controlling for economic growth) have been ratcheted upward repeatedly by global wars. Once these increases have occurred, the post–global war level often subsides. Yet it rarely returns to pre–global war levels. Instead, a new, higher mean level of state-making activity is established. This does not mean that interstate wars have had no impact whatsoever—only that their impact pales in comparison to the impacts of the global wars.

Somewhat ironically, military expenditures as a proportion of GNP

*Table 8.2*
*Permanent and Relatively Permanent Global War Impacts*

| Series | Britain | United States | France | Japan | Germany |
|---|---|---|---|---|---|
| public debt | + | + | not analyzed | not analyzed | not analyzed |
| total expenditures | + | + | + | + | not analyzed |
| total revenues | + | + | + | + | not analyzed |
| military expenditures | mixed | + | mixed | mixed | not analyzed |
| nonmilitary expenditures | + | + | + | + | not analyzed |
| economic growth | mixed | + | mixed | mixed | − |
| violence | not analyzed | mixed | not analyzed | not analyzed | not analyzed |

*Note:* a + or − indicates a positive or negative impact. A mixed entry signifies that the impact was not consistent across time.

give the appearance of deviating from this permanent racheting pattern. Only the United States shows up as an exception in the summary table. Yet such an interpretation is misleading. World War II, if not World War I, brought about significant changes in the military spending patterns of the other states analyzed. To some extent, as well, the appearance of insignificant changes prior to World War II reflects the substantial economic growth of the nineteenth century and, in some ways, the depression of the early twentieth century.

The contemporary impacts of war on economic growth and violence are mixed.[2] In some circumstances, global war provides a temporary boost; it is also responsible for temporary setbacks. In the twentieth century and among the global powers, only the United States has been a consistent winner.

The interaction of war and violence, limited as we are to the U.S. evidence, is more complicated because it very much depends on the previous history of government relations with the groups in question. War-related violence is always contingent on the strategies and concessions that emerge from state-group interactions. State strategies, in turn, are partly a function of how serious the external threat is and/or of how valuable domestic peace and cooperation are perceived to be. Of course, we have examined these questions only in the context of the U.S. experience between 1890 and 1970. More work is needed to determine how modal the American findings really are.

Wars are not the only influence on state making that we have examined. If wars are important, then so is the geopolitical-economic context in which wars occur. Context makes a difference in that it predisposed certain areas, namely Rokkan's west European zone, to develop states early. Some states in that region were encouraged to give territorial control first priority. A few other states were largely precluded, by size and location, among other factors, from European territorial ambitions.

From this basic split in strategic orientations, two types of global powers emerged. One type, the maritime-commercial powers, won the global wars. Both the maritime-commercial orientation and the military victories influenced the direction of subsequent state making. The other type, the continentally oriented land powers, vacillated over how much emphasis to give sea power and long-distance trade. As a consequence, the occasional geoeconomic restructuring that takes place in the world economy placed the land powers at a decided disadvantage. Their economic disadvantages combined with the mosaic quality of their territorial consolidation strongly influenced the ways in which their states were shaped. Later, these early influences were supplemented and aggravated by the efforts to catch up with the maritime-commercial powers. Not unrelatedly, these same states frequently found themselves within the losing camps of the intermittent global wars.

Over the past 500 years, the global power subset has encompassed Portugal, Spain, England/Britain, France, Russia/the Soviet Union, the

United States, Germany, and Japan. While they number only a small minority of the states currently in existence, their wealth, military power, and general historical importance suggest that we should not dismiss them too quickly as anachronistic exceptions to some general rule on how the state is shaped. On the other hand, it is clear by now that the concept of the state is an analytical myth. This does not mean that every state is unique. We have generalized, for example, about the nine global powers as members of a distinctive category.

Their wars, their geopolitical-economic contexts, and their state-making activities, all reciprocally interconnected, have made them distinctive. These same phenomena have also blurred the meaning of internal and external distinctions. Wars and geopolitical-economic contexts may belong to the external realm. Yet the nominally internal process of state making cannot be profitably analyzed without considering their many and manifold influences. Indeed, the more time spent with these topics, the more the inherent utility of internal and external conventions fades completely.

Non–global power states share some of the history and some of the influences associated with the global power state-making experience. If only because of the example set by the global powers as pioneers of modern state making, other states cannot be separated entirely from the factors highlighted in this study. In any event, the global powers have not been a passive reference group. They have literally forced their example on the rest of the world. Consequently, a number of locations around the world might be better off without states if only their populations could find a way to dispense with them.[3] Nevertheless, we need to be careful about generalizing beyond the global power subset. Although we strongly suspect war and geopolitical-economic context are important for other types of state making, ultimately, non–global power states need to be explained in their own terms.

We began chapter 1 by noting that the role of war seemed largely to be missing from the literature on political development. We then demonstrated in several chapters that war cannot be overlooked if the goal entails tracing the political development of the global powers. Indeed, it is one of the most indispensable explanations that we possess. What, then, does this tell us about our images of political development and the state—whether global or nonglobal powers?

## War Making and Images of the State

The model of the state that has dominated postwar American political science emphasizes both pluralism and modernization. The pluralistic dimension focuses theoretical attention on individual political actors and representative groups and organizations that aggregate the collective preferences of individuals. One of these organizations happens to be the state. Its political functions, as one of a system's several centers of authority, include responding to popular demands and resolving conflict where necessary to maintain stability and consensus. Above all, the state and its various institutions are supposed to operate as mediator in the authoritative management of public problems.

Mediation can be accomplished in a variety of ways. Dunleavy and O'Leary (1987: 41–49) perceive three variations on how contemporary pluralist states are interpreted.[4] In the *weathervane* version, the state operates as if it were a political abacus. Groups press for policies that favor their interest. The strongest groups win, and their demands become state-legitimated law. For state expansion to occur in this context, only an increase in the level of pressure group demands is needed.

In the *neutral* variant, the state is granted a margin of autonomy, but largely for the purpose of playing the unbiased bystander. Occasionally, these referee states may be forced to intervene in domestic conflict as third parties to ensure compliance with the prevailing rules of the political game. The expansion of such states remains a direct function of group demands. The only difference is that state personnel must first translate the meaning of the multiple pressures confronting them. The demonstration of some element of creativity in assessing where the public interest lies is to be expected. Steering the ship of state requires some independent judgment.

The third state model is the *broker*. As in the first two images, public policy continues to be a function of group interest demands. The state, however, is more than a neutral referee or dispassionate abacus. In this version, it has its own interests to pursue. These states are most likely to expand when the direction of group pressures coincides with or overlaps the interests of the state bureaucrats.

The modernization dimension links political development to the evolutionary and progressive transformations of a social division of labor. In response to such forms of societal change as those brought about by technological innovation and industrialization, all roles and institutions must become increasingly specialized and differentiated. After all, change introduces new problems that must be managed.

The emergence of the state is a product of this evolutionary trend toward increased specialization and differentiation. One implication of this perspective is the notion that political demands lead unilinearly to better, improved state models. Most versions equate some form of democratization with their idea of improvement. Therefore, political development should lead to more accessible states that facilitate and encourage widespread participation in their mechanisms, deliberations, and responses to demands.

Another implication is that state-building activities are relatively purposeful. Political leaders set out to build political organizations in explicit response to societal changes, group demands, and the functional needs of their systems. A third, perhaps related implication is that state making should be emphasized as an endogenous response to endogenous problems. The functional maintenance of stability, consensus, and order through mediation, of whatever stripe, and conflict resolution is very much an internal concern.

A fourth implication of this perspective is that the modern state is a universally applicable concept and universally desirable. The newer, less developed states should, therefore, look to the older, more developed states as models to emulate and work toward their replication in Third World environments. The possibility that these Third World environments do not parallel the historical contexts from which older states emerged is a factor that analysts have been reluctant to acknowledge.

There is always the risk of indulging in caricature when attempting to characterize mainstream models and assumptions. The four implications of modernizing pluralism as sketched may seem to border on caricature, but the outline is not that exaggerated. If the implications seem overstated, it is probably because of their tendencies to remain implicit assumptions. The mere act of rendering them more explicit undercuts their validity because they seem so unappealing.

If they do not appear unappealing, many of the arguments and much of the empirical work of earlier chapters have fallen on deaf ears. A basic intellectual flaw of modernizing pluralism, as Badie and Birnbaum (1983: 49) point out, is one of converting the process of institutional differentiation into a universal law of social change, growth, and maturation. Social change occurs; institutions undergo differentiation. Why we must link the two teleologically and depict the state that emerges as a functional and highly desirable result and agent of change is less than clear. Putting other theoretical and methodological objections aside, an exceedingly fundamental criticism must be raised. The images and implications of modernizing pluralism simply do not correspond well with the historical state-making activities of the global powers.

Certainly, we do not see war and war preparations as *the* cause of all state making. Nor do we view war as the sole determinant of global power state making, even though this moderation may not have been that evident in the preceding chapters. Our view is that war and its more continuous preliminaries are a paramount, if not the paramount, factor in global power state making. This was an accurate observation in the sixteenth century. It remains an accurate observation in the last quarter of the twentieth century. Regrettably, it will no doubt retain its accuracy well into the twenty-first century.

Nonetheless, an interpretation that promotes war as the principal stimulus to the state making of certain very powerful states does not preclude other state activities. States and their managers have engaged in domestic conflict mediation and resolution, both historically and currently. We hasten to add that states and state making have also constituted an important source of domestic conflict. If one were somehow to subtract all the acts of domestic political violence associated with resistance to centralization, tax collection, and military conscription, a considerable dent would have been made in the history of national (as opposed to international) conflict. Because the state itself is an important source of conflict, it seems only fair that states occasionally mediate and resolve conflict as well.

In contrast, interpretations that promote interest aggregation and conflict resolution as the principal functions of state making and that downplay the state as an autonomous political actor and source of conflict distort historical realities. Interpretations that also ignore war and its consequences as integral components of the most developed states' state-making processes overlook the glaring historical facts of political life.[5] If we had to choose between an interpretation that minimizes the impact of internal-external conflict and one that overstates it, we would select the latter. The probable degree of analytical error is reduced significantly.

The ideas of unilinear and progressive political development stem from the notion that change in the complexity of political institutions will mirror or follow increased complexity in the social division of labor. Economic change creates new problems that require political attention. The state is expected to respond to the new demands by growing incrementally and, through differentiation, by creating ever more specialized institutions: legislatures to make laws, executives and bureaucracies to enforce them, courts to referee disputes, and so forth.

However, the political development of the global powers reads a bit differently when a war-making focus is adopted. State-making executives seeking, often desperately, to improve their ability to extract resources created and expanded bureaucracies so that they could make war. The development of legislatures was also a function, in part, of the extraction problem. Legislatures at the very least have legitimized resource extraction activities. In some geopolitical-economic settings, executive weaknesses enabled legislatures to develop degrees of independence and autonomy. In other settings, they functioned more like symbolic window dressing.

Yet what the image of specialization and differentiation misses most are the continuous elite conflicts within the state organization, which are fought to establish and maintain the relative political power of the state's various subagencies. The socioeconomic setting may or may not grow more complicated over time. What happens in the political realm, and, in particular, how the organization of the state is shaped, will depend as much, if not more, on who wins and loses the internal state-making battles. As we have maintained consistently, who wins and loses the external battles also makes some difference.

Whatever else it may have been, the political development of the global powers has not proceeded in a unilinear, straight-lined fashion. Depending on the type of global power, and the outcomes of the global wars, a more appropriate metaphor for the direction of historical political development is a staircase, and a rickety one at that. Maritime-commercial global powers have developed along a more abrupt, steep staircase pattern. The increments in the more continentally oriented global powers' staircases tend to be less abrupt, only because their states are expanding in between the global wars major steps.

Whether these states somehow became better states in the sense that they were more responsible to their respective populations and better able to aggregate and service their demands is debatable in each case. Less debatable is the contention that improved responsiveness is not exactly what global power political development has been about. Creating more competitive organizations for making war is much closer to the mark, but even this statement probably gives state makers too much credit for pursuing specific, long-term goals. Coping with and surviving short-term problems and crises is a more appropriate description of what most state making is about.

Another element that emerges quite strongly is the highly inadvertent, ad hoc quality of so much of global power state making. More generally, Poggi notes:

> The concrete historical processes leading to the emergence of a state have typically been protracted, tentative, and circuitous, and have presented a wide discrepancy between *undertakings* and *outcomes*.
> All this makes doubtful the "state-building" imagery, the notion that the historical events involved actualized a conscious purpose, an explicit design. (1978: 99)

Or, as Finer puts it:

> It could be said that the Normans and the Plantagenets, the Capetians, and the Valois were lines of monarchs—each one of whom was setting out on his own individual adventure in self-aggrandizement, a kind of blind progress which only we, with our hindsight, recognize as constituting successive milestones in state-building. (1975: 110)

Did Ferdinand fully comprehend the implications for Spanish state making of resisting the French invasion of Italy in 1495? Did Henry VIII fully understand the implications for English state making of seizing monasteries to finance European wars in the sixteenth century? We will never be able to answer these questions to everyone's satisfaction. Yet no matter how clearly historical state makers perceived the long-term consequences of their actions, the more telling question may be whether they would have done anything different to resolve their short-term problems.

Would the Spanish *tercios* have stayed away from the French if someone had argued that continental entanglements might eventually preclude Spain's ability to remain among the world system's leading powers? Would Habsburg administrators have thought twice before insisting that Netherland towns develop long-term borrowing procedures if they had known the implications for the subsequent financing of the Dutch Revolt? Would Henry VIII have hesitated if he had been told that seizing monasteries would serve his immediate purposes but create long-term problems for his successors?

Again, these questions are highly speculative, and any answers must be equally speculative. Our hunch, however, is that short-term problems will almost always receive priority over conjectures of the long term. The former are concrete and, from the view of the decision makers involved, often inescapable. The long-term phantoms can always be postponed to someone else's watch. State makers have attempted to resolve their short-term problems, especially those pertaining to war; only in the long run have their short-term actions added up to what we like to call state making.

Just as a goodly portion of global power state-making seems to have been a byproduct of coping with short-term crises, democratization can be viewed more as a byproduct than as an explicit goal of state making. Coalitions and participation eventually were broadened. Citizenship rights were extended. Some representative institutions did become stronger. Yet the question is not simply who fought for these changes. Somebody had to, or they would not have occurred. Equally important is why state makers felt compelled to make concessions at various times. Granted, this is a seemingly cynical interpretation of democratization, and one that has not been fully explored in this study. Yet it does seem to match the global power historical records better than does the rival image of increases in political participation coming about primarily as a consequence of socioeconomic modernization and subsequent demands for more open political systems.

Should the global power states then be regarded as worthy role models for newer states to emulate? Do their political development records reflect universal laws at work that we can extract and apply to different settings? The two questions are not identical, but their answers are similar. Because our study is limited to the global powers, we are not in a position to test the universality question. For that matter, our decision to look only at the global powers reflects an initial bias against the likelihood of discovering universal laws of political development. Otherwise, our sampling procedures should have been subject to greater randomization.

Bias or no bias, we are hard pressed to imagine how the highly contingent, global war-related, political histories of the global powers could serve as much of a predictive base for non–global powers. Given the war-induced nature of so much global power state making, we are equally hard pressed to understand why any groups of people should have to repeat the global power development experiences that relied so much on bloodletting as a principal organizational stimulus. This does not mean that some Third World states will not escape the martial path to political development. Indeed, war may continue to be a crucial ingredient in successful state-making stories. What we are balking at is developing a theory that commends war stimuli, however unwittingly, as a desirable approach to building bigger and better states.

Nor does the image of war-making state makers correspond very well to neo-Marxist interpretations that regard class dynamics as supreme. We need not fixate on the old-fashioned, reductionist version of the state that dismissed it as an executive committee of the ruling class. More recent versions, however, are not always so distant from this variation on the weathervane model of the state as their authors would have us believe. A good case in point is the work done by Wallerstein (1974) on the European emergence and development of a capitalist world-economy. Wallerstein's analyses are hardly ahistorical. Much of what we say about France in chapter 3, for instance, overlaps much of what Wallerstein has to say about France. Yet old habits are difficult to break. When Wallerstein writes abstractly about the emergence of strong states, he falls back on the notion that states exist primarily to serve the interest of the dominant classes.

For Wallerstein, some states must emerge that are strong in comparison to (1) other states, (2) local political units within the state's boundaries, and (3) specific social groups. They must emerge in the core because capitalists need politico-military mechanisms to protect their interests (as in guaranteeing property rights). Without these protections, the capitalist system eventually would disintegrate. For the same reason, strong states must be prevented from rising in the periphery where they would constitute obstacles to core exploitation.

State strength facilitates the development of some level of autonomy from internal and external pressures. Somebody, of course, has to desire the autonomy. State managers and bureaucrats with their own interests to pursue, therefore, must also be present. Yet strong states and their managers emerge for reasons other than their existence is functional for the maintenance of the system.

> [State managers and state bureaucracies] emerge within the framework of a capitalist world-economy because a strong state is the best choice between difficult alternatives for the two groups that are strongest in political, economic, and military terms: the emergent capitalist strata, and the old aristocratic hierarchies.
>
> For the former, the strong state in the form of the "absolute monarchies" was a prime customer, a guardian against local and international brigandage, a mode of social legitimation, a preemptive protection against the creation of strong

state barriers elsewhere. For the latter, the strong state represented a brake on these same capitalist strata, an upholder of status conventions, a maintainer of order, a promoter of luxury. (Wallerstein 1974: 355)

In this functionalist variation on Dunleavy and O'Leary's (1987) pluralist broker model, strong states are equated with the absolutist regimes of continentally oriented Europe. In fact, these states had rulers with powers that were not that absolute. Monarchs who do not know how much revenues they can extract or even how many soldiers they have stationed throughout their territories should not have their strength exaggerated. Nor did they prove to be very strong in combat with the presumably not as strong, commercial-maritime powers.[6]

These observations aside, an explanation for the emergence of strong states that focuses exclusively or even primarily on endogenous class standoffs is, in the end, not that different from pluralist models that equally restrict the independent significance of states and their state makers. Such models share as well an underappreciation for the state-making impact of war that, we have suggested, misses much of the very essence of global power state making.

## A Concluding Comment

It is sometimes suggested that the state is no longer the optimal way to organize national political life. As the world becomes more interdependent and wars more difficult to survive, the state is said to have become more obsolete. Conceivably, the state could wither away, or it could give way to other forms of political organization at the supranational or subnational level. Cities could resume their one-time significance as foci of political loyalties. Political parties have already subordinated states in some places. Whether this phenomena proves to be a permanent feature of the political landscape remains to be seen. States could also give way to corporate organizations, if corporations continue to assume some of the functions traditionally reserved to states (e.g., foreign policies, welfare, protection).

That some type of change will occur seems predictable enough. Precisely what changes will occur is much less predictable. Yet there is one nagging problem with the argument that the state is no longer politically optimal. One may well ask whether the state was ever optimal? And, if so, for what sorts of activities was it optimal? In a world of competitive state organizations, some states prospered from warfare. A good number simply disappeared. As far as the global powers are concerned, only a few states proved to be optimal in profiting from periodic global and interstate war and geoeconomic restructuring. In the very long run, even most of these successes have turned out to be transitory.

So when the optimality of the state question is raised, we should immediately ask a number of preliminary questions. Of which states or types of states are we speaking? Assuming it makes some difference, are we talking of optimality for war activities or protection activities? Moreover, we should also ask for whom is the state optimal or less than optimal? State makers, who historically have been the principal arbiters of optimality, are likely to have a different perspective on this question than are the people who pay the taxes, provide the military manpower, or generate the productivity basis for economic competitiveness.

Whether or not the state is judged optimal today for whatever reason, it is not clear that the global power state has been equally optimal for all members of its population. In some respects, the question is historically moot. During much of the past 500 years or so, the alternatives have been eliminated or subordinated. In the increasing absence of competition, except from similar political organizations controlling other territories, the question of optimality becomes not only moot but also academic.

As to whether the state some day will wither away, the question to pose is what type of context would facilitate the dismantling of organizations initially designed with the short-term purpose of making war in mind? Has the interstate context changed that much from the time when war-making states were first encouraged to develop and become the predominate form of political organization? Without a sufficiently radical change in context, it is difficult to envision a withering away of the state in the near future. Unfortunately, it is much easier to envision the state as a war machine persisting indefinitely, gradually adding new activities to its organizational repertoire but always remaining a war machine at the core. Yet an indefinite persistence somehow seems preferable to another alternative—the self-destruction of a competitive state system, and presumably the organizational predominance of the state itself, in the impact of one last global war.

# Notes

## Notes to Chapter 1

1 Taylor (1987) suggests that historically war has been quite important in shaping Burmese political development. Chan (1987) also finds war important to development in Asia. See Gurr's (1988) argument as well.
2 We return to some of Hintze's specific arguments in chapter 8.
3 Rosenau (1988: 24) notes that a large number of different types of state categories has been discussed in the literature on the state.
4 Prominent examples are Small and Singer (1982) and Levy (1983, 1985).
5 These issues of actor identification are discussed further in Singer and Small (1972: 24); Levy (1983: 24–49); and Modelski and Thompson (1988: 316–37).
6 Naval capabilities are emphasized because, for so many of the past 500 years, sea power has been the principal, if not the exclusive, tool for exerting global reach. See Modelski and Thompson (1988) for a more extensive justification of this theoretical emphasis.
7 Different approaches to introducing systemic–international–external considerations to the war–state-making equation can be found in Zolberg (1980, 1981) and Kimmel (1983).

## Notes to Chapter 2

1 A bibliography of Rokkan's work is available in Saelen (1981). We have focused primarily on Rokkan (1975, 1980, 1981).
2 Kiernan (1965: 25–26) comes close to this argument when he observes that towns enjoyed the greatest freedom in between a western zone (Spain to Scotland) and an East European zone. In the west, the early rise of fairly strong feudal monarchies constrained the possibilities for urban independence. In the east, towns tended to be dependent garrison centers. Only in between ("northern Italy, western Germany, the Netherlands, the Baltic") did the towns really flourish politically, commercially, and culturally. Even so, most lacked what Kiernan refers to as the necessary amalgam of urban and feudal elements essential for nation–state development.
3 See Tilly (1982; 1984: 131–43) for a somewhat different appraisal of the value of Rokkan's state-building framework.
4 Admittedly, the United Provinces of the Netherlands is an awkward case from the Rokkan perspective. It does not really lie west of the European city belt.

5   There seems to be some haziness about the precise location of the central city belt. Some versions stretch as far as London to the north and Palestine in the south. We should be careful to avoid an overly Eurocentric focus in determining its boundaries. We should also be careful not to overlook other city belts in the general European–Mediterranean area or, for that matter, their comparative role outside Europe. Nevertheless, the point remains that it is difficult to overlook the zonal implications for European statemaking of a crude line drawn along the Netherlands to northern Italy axis.

6   See Brady (1985) for an analysis of the south German failure.

7   For example, Sorokin (1937) is a primary source for internal wars. Zagorin (1982: 32–35) has some highly critical things to say about this source's errors and many omissions. The general implication is that by relying heavily on Sorokin, one is apt to confuse separate events as one (or vice versa) and to undercount the frequency. If we have undercounted, however, the bias will not weaken our argument. We should also point out that we are only counting years of warfare rather than trying to catalogue individual events. Some of the errors in such sources as Sorokin can be finessed in this fashion.

8   It is interesting to speculate whether the choice primarily reflected the greater benefits perceived to lie in the east or the opportunity the decision provided to subordinate the demands of the Aragonese nobility.

9   All of the early state-building efforts had imperial overtones. Kiernan (1965: 35-36) nicely summarizes this facet of state making:

> No dynasty set out to build a nation-state; each aimed at unlimited extension . . . and the more it prospered the more the outcome was a multifarious empire instead of a nation. The nation was the empire manqué. It had to be large enough to survive and to sharpen its claws on its neighbours, but small enough to be organized from one centre and to feel itself as an entity. On the close-packed western edge of Europe, any excessive ballooning of territory was checked by competition and geographical limits.

10   The sources for figure 2.4 are Hamilton (1934), Parker (1979a), and Kamen (1980).

# Notes to Chapter 3

1   Allmand (1988: 82–87) suggests something else was afoot. He advances an intriguing but difficult to substantiate thesis on French state making in the thirteenth and fourteenth centuries that sees French rulers, initially virtually landlocked, seeking access to the coasts for military and commercial purposes. However genuine this early interest may have been, it was not maintained in later centuries.

2   Finer (1975: 154–55) argues that the centralization of the French provinces was not entirely achieved until the Napoleonic Wars forced state makers to deal with nonurban unrest and problems with military supply efforts.

3   More extensive treatments of France's early royal state financing can be found in Henneman (1971) and Wolfe (1972).

4   This observation differs in some respects from Gilpin's (1981) argument that expansion continues until costs exceed benefits. Although a stronger force will raise costs and reduce benefits, our emphasis is on the thwarting force of the opposition and not on the rationality of the expanding power.

5   Napoleon's Continental System is discussed in Heckscher (1922/1964) and Crouzet (1964).

6   See Parker (1985: 51–86) for a discussion of the German geopolitics of Mitteleuropa.

7 Our approach also puts us at odds with Rosecrance's (1986) recent interpretation of trading and military-territorial states. We make similar distinctions, but there does not seem to be much convergence on which states approximated which end of the orientation continuum.

8 Between the end of the twelfth and the fourteenth centuries, export taxes had expanded to constitute as much as one-third of England's royal revenues (Allmand 1988: 108). This factor helps explain why wool, the chief export, was so important to English royalty.

9 Wesson (1986: 4, 7) argues that the consolidation of Russia used similar methods at about the same time as France, Spain, and other western states. However, there was a major difference in the territorial expansion patterns. Western European states are said to have halted when they arrived at natural frontiers or met strong resistance. Subsequent expansion took place overseas for commercial reasons. Russia, Wesson contends, simply proceeded to annex contiguous areas in order to enhance state power. Yet this interpretation appears to understate the parallels between French and Spanish expansion efforts within Europe and Russian expansion in Eurasia. The real difference is that for centuries the Russians encountered relatively less local opposition than the western global powers. Unfortunately, we have little more to say about either Russia or the Soviet Union. Chapters 4 through 7 focus on serial data on state making—a focus that tends to sideline Russia/the Soviet Union. One explicit study of a global war's impact, however, is available in Linz (1985).

10 See Bensel (1984) for a persuasive argument on the persistence of sectoral divisions in the United States and some of their political development consequences.

## Notes to Chapter 4

1 The French advantage in total revenues continued until about 1793, although not to the same extent, according to Mathias and O'Brien (1976: 610).

2 Miskimin (1977: 163–64) notes that in 1519, the election of the Holy Roman Emperor required large sums of money for the purpose of bribing the electors. Consequently, the power struggle is said to have degenerated into a test of credit worthiness between Charles V and France's Francis I.

3 The Dutch were forced to suspend interest payments between 1572 and 1586 (Parker 1974: 573).

4 They may not have fully appreciated the function of public debt either. In 1652, Holland's debt is pegged at 132 million florins by Parker (1988: 64). Most of this debt was redeemed over the protests of the debt holders.

5 These authors note that the percentage figures are actually somewhat conservative. They are based on a comparison of wartime tax revenues with total revenues and expenditures. Because the tax revenues were designed to cover debt interest payments and peacetime military costs, the comparison of prewar, average, peacetime military costs with wartime military costs and wartime debts suggests that some 81 to 119 percent of the "extra" military expenditure was raised through loans.

6 For an introduction to the historical development of public credit in Europe, see Fryde and Fryde (1963), Lane (1966: 87–98), Miller (1970), and Tracy (1985).

7 Ardant emphasizes the capability dimension:

> Extensive use of government borrowing assumes a money economy developed to the extent that the holders of money are accustomed to lending it, and intermediate financiers are able to guide large amounts of money toward the state treasury. Just as taxation assumes a market for production, borrowing assumes a market for capital. These conditions were present in some states—the Low Countries and England. Elsewhere, at least until the eighteenth century, they were missing. (1975: 189)

8    Explicit discussions of British and U.S. national debt histories are not all that common. For the British experience, see Hamilton (1947), Peacock and Wiseman (1961), Dickson (1967), Carter (1968), Roseveare (1969), and Palmer (1977). The history of the U.S. national debt is given some attention in Ratchford (1947) and Myers (1970).

9    The sources for the GNP data are delineated in chapters 5 and 6.

10    Figure 4.4 does not reveal very well the recent rise in the U.S. relative debt position. In 1981, the level stood at .329. By 1985, it had risen to .457.

11    Another irony of global war is demonstrated by what happened to German and Japanese public debts after World War II. Between 1939 and 1945, Germany's debt increased from 31 billion to 377 billion RM (Hardach 1980: 85). Japan's debt in 1940 was close to 24 billion yen. By 1945, it had risen to about 178 billion (Cohen 1949: 89). Controlling for economic wealth and inflation, prewar public debt as a proportion of GNP (see chapter 6 for sources) was .32 for Germany and .60 for Japan. In 1945, the ratios were roughly on the order of 3.37 and 3.75, respectively (compare these figures to the peaks displayed in figure 4.4). For the most part, these debt burdens disappeared after the end of the global war. Inflation and currency reforms during the American occupations scaled back the burdens tremendously. For example, Hamada and Horiuchi (1987: 231) report government debt data indicating that the debt burden averaged less than 7 percent between 1953 and 1970. A low debt burden is important when one is seeking rapid economic growth.

12    The intervention components for models A and C are referred to as zero-order transfer functions; models B and D represent first-order transfer functions. A pulse model is distinguished from a step model by differencing the step function $(I_t)$. The resulting pulse function, $(1 - B)I_t$, equals 1 at the onset of the impact event and 0 prior to and after the impact event.

## Notes to Chapter 5

1    For Peacock and Wiseman's reaction to some of this literature's design problems, see Wiseman and Diamond (1975) and Peacock and Wiseman (1979).

2    On this point, see Porter's (1980) argument that American governmental agencies learned to use national defense rationalizations to justify expanded budgets to legislators, even when they were not directly related to the ongoing World War II effort.

3    One perhaps unexpected yet illustrative example was the impact of the 1792–1815 global war on professionalizing medicine. One reason France took the lead in medical reform was due in part to the loss of more than one-third of its army health officers between 1793 and the spring of 1794. The difficulties in obtaining qualified replacements led directly to reforms in medical education (Ramsey 1988: 75). Movement toward medical reform had been taking place prior to 1793–94, but military needs certainly encouraged it.

4    By dividing expenditures and tax revenues by GNP, we are not overlooking the probability that governmental spending and economy as a whole are likely to be subject to different inflation rates. Specialized deflationary indexes, however, are not normally available for long time series.

5    Linking taxes and war conflict has a long pedigree. According to Braun (1975: 310–11), Lang (1793) argued that all changes in the German tax system, as far back as the Carolingian era, were traceable to war and military technological change. Similarly, Goldscheid (1926) is described as viewing war as the principal motor underlying public finance development. More recently, Witte (1985: 79), writing about the American income tax, argues:

Those who model policy changes, particularly in terms of budget expenditures, often use time series data that either begin after World War II or exclude war periods as deviant events of external shocks. To do either with the income tax, or the study of taxes in general, is to ignore the single most important influence on the formation and structure of the tax code.

War also figures prominently in the historical discussion of taxes presented by Webber and Wildavsky (1986).

6  A major problem in working with Spanish revenue data is coping with the multiple currency units employed.

7  See Riley (1987) for a useful discussion and comparison of some of the possible ways to control for inflation in eighteenth-century (but not our sixteenth- to nineteenth-century period) French finances. Tits-Dievaide (1987) provides cautionary information on fluctuations in European grain prices.

8  Bean (1973: 217) and McNeill (1982: 105) see a different general pattern: a major increase in the latter part of the fifteenth century, attributable to the increases in military firepower, followed by slower increases until the second half of the seventeenth century. By that time, tax revolts (another twist on Peacock and Wiseman's perspective?) had become less likely. We do not see their pattern in our data, but the differences or interpretation may be due to Bean's attempts to control for wealth and population.

9  To subtract a least squares trend line from a series, a researcher regresses that $Y_t$ series on time $(X_t = 1, 2, 3, \ldots, N)$, estimates the least squares slope of the model, and then calculates the "detrended" $Y_t$ series. In this case, the $Y$ series is a function of the $Y_t = b_0 + b_1$ (time) $+ e_t$ equation, where $b_0$ is the intercept and represents the mean level of the $Y_t$ series; $b_1$ (time) represents the slope of the trend line or the exponential change in the level of $Y_t$ from one observation to the next. However, $b_0$ and $b_1$ are derived by minimizing the sums of the squares function

$$(Y_t - \hat{Y}_t)^2 = \Sigma [b_0 - \hat{b}_0 + (b_1 - \hat{b}_1)]^2.$$

As the independent variable $t$ (time) increases monotonically, the first and last observations of $Y_t$ usually make the greatest contribution to the sums of squares function. Consequently, the OLS estimates of $b_0$ and $b_1$ are estimated so that the OLS trendline generally passes through $Y_t$ and $Y_n$, regardless of how well the middle observations $(Y_{t+1} \ldots Y_{n-1})$ fit. This procedure represents a rather static approach to what are, after all, dynamic phenomena (McCleary and Hay 1980). Moreover, studies that do not attempt to remove trend may be subject to many of the same problems in comparing preintervention and postintervention slopes.

10 A white noise series describes a set of independent and random observations that are normally distributed about a zero mean and constant variance.

11 If a time series is the realization of an integrated process (a random walk due to drift), it can be modeled by simply differencing that $Y_t$ series. If the differenced series has a nonzero mean, it is characterized by linear trend, which is represented in the following equation as $Y_t = Y_{t-1} + \theta_0 + a_t$, where $\theta_0$ is estimated as the mean of the differenced series. To distinguish between drift and trend, $\theta_0$ is subjected to a $t$-test. If $\theta_0$ is not statistically different from zero, the series is considered to be drifting rather than trending. Whereas OLS detrending methods estimate linear trend using a time counter as the independent variable, the difference equation model uses the values of $Y_{t-1}$ as the independent variable. Because all of the $Y_{t-1}$ values influence the estimate of $\theta_0$ (the constant of the difference equation), a dynamic estimate of linear trend is produced (see Box and Jenkins 1976; McCleary and Hay 1980).

12 Significant deltas approximating or exceeding the value of one were estimated in each of the global war intervention components in table 5.6 (with the exception of the Japanese expenditure/GNP case). Substantively, this outcome may suggest that new expansionary

influences were introduced in the aftermath of war. For our immediate purposes, however, the important thing to note is that the postwar levels in the French, British, and American spending and revenues series (and the Japanese revenue series) did not return to the prewar levels, thus indicating abrupt, permanent changes. More precisely, what tends to occur is a very large temporary spike, especially in the spending series, that recedes to a level higher than that found in the prewar era. Efforts to estimate compound models (incorporating both temporary and permanent changes) were unsuccessful, we believe, due to the substantial parameter colinearity encountered and the often overwhelming size of the temporary spike. While Box-Tiao models offer certain statistical advantages, they also possess some limitations in analyzing global war-induced changes.

13  For readers who wish to pursue the percentage change conversion procedure further, McCleary and Hay (1980: 171–85) advance the following formula for translating omega parameters in log metric into percentage change intervention estimates:

$$\text{percentage change} = (e^{(\omega_0)} - 1)\,100,$$

where $e^{(\omega_0)}$ is the ratio of postintervention to preintervention equilibrium. However, in models with significant delta parameters, the incremental postintervention movement of the process requires the analyst to exponentiate the asymptotic change $(\omega_0/1 - \delta)$ in the process level.

14  This statement is not entirely true. When British global wars are examined separately (as opposed to being treated as a class of warfare, as in table 5.6), the impact of the 1701–13 Spanish Succession War on expenditures/GNP is not statistically significant, even though the same war has a significant impact on revenues/GNP. We do not regard the 1701–13 deviation as a meaningful exception, however, because we have only one year (1700) of prewar GNP data. Moreover, the 1701–13 warfare constituted only the second phase of the 1688–1713 global war.

15  See Amenta and Skocpol (1988: 99–100) for instructive criticism of the Titmuss thesis. Basically, their point of view is that the impacts of war on social policies are more complicated than the Titmuss interpretation of a single case suggests.

16  Nevertheless, we are operating at a highly aggregated level of analysis in this chapter. For less aggregated analyses of war's impact on nonmilitary spending, see Amenta and Skocpol (1988) for a comparison and explanation of the impacts of World War II on U.S. and British welfare policies. Orloff (1988) provides additional and contrasting information on U.S. welfare policies in the World War I era.

17  Intensive civil wars may also have a permanent impact on expenditures and revenues that is comparable to global war. The United States' nineteenth-century internal war is a good example.

18  Although an emphasis on global wars may not tell us much about the growth of states made independent since 1945, our findings in this chapter should at least encourage analysts of the ongoing expansion of public expenditures and revenues in industrialized states (Cameron 1978; Taylor 1981; Gould 1983; Kohl 1983; Schmidt 1983) to consider incorporating the effects of global wars in their models. In an earlier conference version of this chapter, we extended our global war impact analysis to the twentieth-century, expenditure-revenue records of some 22 nonglobal powers. Even though these data are characterized by a number of missing values that hamper serial examination, the permanent impacts of global war do not appear to be restricted to the major contenders for systemic power. The expenditures and revenues of other war participants (including minor power active belligerents and occupied states), as well as some nonparticipating states that were located near the combat theaters, appear to have been affected as well.

## Notes to Chapter 6

1   At this point, we are ignoring single-country studies, such as Dickinson (1940), Stein (1978), Nincic (1980), Hueckel (1985), and Riley (1986), that tend to examine either specific wars or different types of questions. Albert with Henderson (1988), a study of the economic impact of World War I on four Latin American states, is another type of examination beyond our immediate purview.

2   Nearly one-third of the states Barbera examines were colonial territories or nonindependent for all or most of the period studied. Certain countries, too, do quite well in rankings on the telephones per thousand indicator (Barbera 1973: 149–50). Australia, Canada, Denmark, New Zealand, Norway, Sweden, and Switzerland consistently (1913–52) rank higher than Germany, Britain, Japan, France, and the Soviet Union.

3   However, the nineteenth-century economist J. S. Mill evidently anticipated the phoenix factor when he observed in his *Principles of Political Economy*:

> The great rapidity with which countries recover from a state of devastation . . . has so often excited wonder. . . . An enemy lays waste a country by fire and sword, and destroys or carries away nearly all the moveable wealth existing in it: all the inhabitants are ruined, and yet in a few years after, everything is much as it was before. (quoted in Gordon and Walton 1982: 171)

4   The 16-year prewar periods are used prior to World War I because Organski and Kugler found that their postwar projections were more reliable after three depression years, varying somewhat per country, were dropped from the projection base.

5   The omega for the British World War I case is based on a $t_{+2}$ lag. The omega for the French Napoleonic War case is based on a $t_{+3}$ lag. In both cases, insignificant omegas were found at earlier time points. The German World War I omega and delta, however, are based on $t_0$ calculations.

6   Our estimates may be too conservative because they are based primarily on industrial output indexes and exclude agriculture fluctuations.

7   We are not overlooking the economic assistance (e.g., the Marshall Plan) the United States made available to its defeated former rivals in the aftermath of World War II. We interpret this development, however, as a nonaltruistic function of systemic leadership intended to counter possible Soviet gains after 1945.

## Notes to Chapter 7

1   McNeill (1982: 270) suggests an indirect feedback relationship as well. Suffrage extensions changed the nature of political party competitions in the late nineteenth century. If the depression of the early 1930s had occurred before the expansion of the voting rolls, the normal governmental response would have been to cut back on governmental spending. Instead, governments increased their spending on arms in part to win votes.

2   Stein (1978) also investigates the relationship between war and domestic violence. However, the issue is subsumed within the broader framework of the effects of war on government centralization, industrial productivity, unemployment, and taxation. Violence is a minor consideration and is used as an indicator, along with crime rates and strikes, to form a composite variable of social disunity. Consequently, his analysis is not included in the subsequent review.

3   Specific criticisms about the absence of intervening functions have been made by Skolnick (1974), Mack (1975), Stein (1976), and Bar-Siman-Tov (1983).

4   Other historical studies have also noted the growth in the United States' national administrative capacities and in the government's expanding role in resolving broad economic, political, and social issues during World Wars I and II (Brody 1980; Hawley 1979; Skowronek 1982; Wilensky 1975).

5   Starting in 1935, Stohl (1976) subdivides prosystem violence into government-initiated and dominant group-initiated activity. To preserve the continuity from 1890 to 1920, the distinctions are not recognized in this analysis.

6   The intervention components are coded to reflect the war years for 1898 (Spanish-American War), 1917–18 (World War I), 1941–45 (World War II), 1951–53 (Korean War), and 1965–70 (Vietnam War). Because America's entry into World War II began in December 1941, the effects on domestic violence are not expected to have full realization until 1942.

7   Therefore, the intervention components are coded to reflect the postwar years of 1899, 1919–20, 1946–49 and 1954–56. Although there are no strict theoretical guidelines for setting the parameters of postwar periods, this procedure is considered the most conservative.

8   As an aggregate measure, the total violence series will yield parameter estimates that either support the overall findings of the other violence series or show, as in table 7.1, how aggregation can distort important underlying relationships. Any further analysis of the total violence series, therefore, is unnecessary.

9   For details, see Grubbs (1968), Larson (1975), and Milton (1982).

10  The social violence data exclude lynchings.

11  In the case of World War I, there is a noticeable unstable effect on political violence. The Box-Tiao results in table 7.1 show statistically significant omega and delta parameters. Ordinarily, when values equal or exceed 1.0, the delta parameter is dropped from the equation and the omega parameter is estimated alone. However, this procedure results in a weaker and statistically insignificant omega estimate. Attempts at estimating a higher order compound model that incorporates both the temporary changes in 1917 and 1918 also yielded statistically insignificant omega estimates. An examination of figure 7.2, which plots the political violence series from 1890 to 1970, reveals that the substantial increase in 1917 is followed by a subsequent decline in 1918. This pattern contributes to the unusually large, negative delta and to a statistically insignificant estimate of omega without the presence of the parameter. Nevertheless, the magnitude of political violence in 1918 is considerably higher than any of the prewar observations from 1890 to 1916. Despite the appearance of misspecification, therefore, the earlier estimates are maintained as the appropriate findings. They probably reflect the problem of a short intervention series that has failed to establish equilibrium (McCleary and Hay 1980: 159).

12  The work stoppage statistics for the post–World War I and post–World War II eras are based on figures obtained from the U.S. Department of Commerce (1975: 179).

13  Table 7.2 also indicates that the influence of the interstate wars on social violence is associated with a large increase in level. Given the unusually large value, the separate postwar effects for the Spanish-American and Korean Wars were estimated. The only statistically significant result is the 232 percent increase that occurs with a one-year lag of the post–Korean War impact (1955–57). The substantial rise in social violence follows the 1954 Supreme Court decision in *Brown* v. *Topeka Board of Education* on the issue of public school segregation. Southern state officials enacted a flood of prosegregation legislation in reaction. When the federal government failed to enforce the Supreme Court's ruling, black political resistance gained momentum throughout the South and eventually resulted in an escalation of violence (McAdam 1982: 144; Piven and Cloward 1977: 207–08).

14  The 1930–33 years represent exceptions to this generalization. We consider these years to be crisis years (severe economic depression), even though they were not war years. Thus, the first generalization should perhaps more accurately read that the overall levels of repression are higher during the crisis-related years than in the noncrisis-related years, regardless of accommodation.

## Notes to Chapter 8

1 Parker reminds us that this process has occurred before. In the Chinese Warring States era, aristocratic charioteers gave way to large numbers of infantry conscripts. In the sixth-century B.C., armies totalled in the neighborhood of 10,000 men. Some 300 years later, army size had increased to one million. These changes affected the states that had to deal with the increasing complexities of commanding and provisioning these forces:

> And so most governments changed from something resembling a large household, with most important offices in the hands of the ruler's relatives or leading noblemen, into an autocratic state run on behalf of a despotic prince by a salaried bureaucracy, carefully indoctrinated. (Parker 1988: 3)

2 One aspect of the costs and benefits of global war that will not necessarily emerge from a relatively narrow analysis of economic growth is the way global wars facilitate the rise and fall of certain global powers. For instance, when Spain discouraged Dutch rebels from trading with the Iberian Peninsula after 1579, the Dutch were given all the more incentive to develop their own trading networks in the Mediterranean and Indian Oceans. The Portuguese had benefitted somewhat from Venetian preoccupation in the early 1500s. Certainly, the United States' trading system benefitted from Britain's problems during World Wars I and II.

3 The types of places we have in mind are areas occupied by various groups who have difficulties in coexisting but yet who have little choice except to interact within the confines of, and struggle over the price of, who will control a single state. Palestinians in Israel, Kurds in Iraq/Iran/Turkey, Eritreans in Ethiopia, Greeks and Turks in Cyprus, and Muslims of various sects and Maronite Christians in Lebanon are a few who come readily to mind.

4 Another and immensely useful source in sorting out the major approaches to analyzing states is Alford and Friedland (1985).

5 Do we go too far in suggesting that many of the most developed states became that way, in part, by participating in and surviving the system's most serious wars?

6 Wallerstein reverses some aspects of his argument on strong states:

> In the seventeenth century the strongest states were those which dominated economically: the United Provinces were in first place, England was second and France was only in third place. The English Revolution strengthened the English state, while the assertion by Louis XIV, *l'Etat cest moi*, was a sign of the relative weakness of the state. (1980: 33)

At a later point, Wallerstein (1980: 112) explains that in a capitalist world economy it is the function of the state to help owner-producers gain or maintain advantages in the marketplace. The better a state can perform this function, the stronger it is. This view seems to take us back to a variant on the weathervane model.

# References

Abrams, Philip (1982). *Historical Sociology*. Ithaca, NY: Cornell University Press.

Albert, Bill with Paul Henderson (1988). *South America and the First World War: The Impact of the War on Brazil, Argentina, Peru and Chile*. Cambridge: Cambridge University Press.

Alford, Robert R. and Roger Friedland (1985). *Powers of Theory: Capitalism, the State and Democracy*. Cambridge: Cambridge University Press.

Allmand, Christopher (1988). *The Hundred Years War: England and France at War, c. 1300–c. 1450*. Cambridge: Cambridge University Press.

Almond, Gabriel, Scott Flanigan, and Robert Mundt, eds. (1973). *Crisis, Choice and Change*. Boston: Little, Brown.

Almond, Gabriel and G. Bingham Powell, Jr. (1966). *Comparative Politics: A Developmental Approach*. Boston: Little, Brown.

Amenta, Edwin and Theda Skocpol (1988). "Redefining the New Deal: World War II and the Development of Social Provision in the United States." In Margaret Weir, Ann S. Orloff, and Theda Skocpol, eds., *The Politics of Social Policy in the United States*. Princeton: Princeton University Press.

Ames, E. and R. T. Rapp (1977). "The Birth and Death of Taxes: A Hypothesis." *Journal of Economic History*, 37, 161–78.

Anderson, Perry (1974). *Lineages of the Absolutist State*. London: New Left Books.

Andre, C. and R. Delorme (1978). "The Long-Run Growth of Public Expenditure in France." *Public Finance*, 33, 42–67.

Ardant, Gabriel (1975). "Financial Policy and Economic Infrastructure of Modern States and Nations." In Charles Tilly, ed., *The Formation of National States in Western Europe*. Princeton: Princeton University Press.

Badie, Bertrand and Pierre Birnbaum (1983). *The Sociology of the State*, translated by Arthur Goldhammer. Chicago: University of Chicago Press.

Banks, Arthur S. (1971). *Cross-Polity Times Series*. Cambridge: MIT Press.

Barbera, H. (1973). *Rich Nations and Poor in Peace and War*. Lexington, MA: Lexington Books.

Bar-Siman-Tov, Yaacov (1983). *Linkage Politics in the Middle East: Syria between Domestic and External Conflict, 1961–1970*. Boulder: Westview Press.

Baulant, M. (1968). "Le Prix des Grains à Paris de 1431 à 1788." *Annales: Economies, Societes, Civilisations*, 23, 520–40.

Bean, R. (1973). "War and the Birth of the Nation State." *Journal of Economic History*, 33, 203–21.

Bennett, J. T. and M. H. Johnson (1980). *The Political Economy of Federal Government: 1959–1978*. College Station, TX: Center for Education and Research in Free Enterprise, Texas A & M University.

Bensel, Richard F. (1984). *Sectionalism and American Political Development: 1880–1980*. Madison: University of Wisconsin Press.

Berman, William (1974). "Civil Rights and Political Centrism." In Alonzo Hamby, ed., *Harry S Truman and the Fair Deal*. Lexington, MA: D. C. Heath.

Bernstein, Barton (1974). "America in War and Peace: The Test of Liberalism." In Alonzo Hamby, ed., *Harry S Truman and the Fair Deal*. Lexington, MA: D. C. Heath.

Bernstein, Irving (1960). *A History of the American Worker, 1920–1933: The Lean Years*. Boston: Houghton Mifflin.

———— (1970). *A History of the American Worker, 1933–1941: Turbulent Years*. Boston: Houghton Mifflin.

Berry, Thomas S. (1978). *Revised Annual Estimates of American Gross National Product: Preliminary Estimates of Four Major Components of Demand, 1789–1889*. Richmond, VA: Bostwick Press.

Best, Geoffrey (1986). *War and Society in Revolutionary Europe, 1770–1870*. New York: Oxford University Press.

Binder, Leonard, James S. Coleman, Joseph LaPalombara, Lucien W. Pye, Sidney Verba, and Myron Weiner (1971). *Crises and Sequences in Political Development*. Princeton: Princeton University Press.

Bird, R. M. (1971). "Wagner's 'Law' of Expanding State Activity." *Public Finance*, 26, 1–26.

Bisson, T. N. (1986). *The Medieval Crown of Aragon: A Short History*. New York: Oxford University Press.

Block, Fred (1977). "The Ruling Class Does Not Rule: Notes on the Marxist Theory of the State." *Socialist Revolution*, 7, 6–28.

———— (1980). "Beyond Relative Autonomy: State Managers as Historical Subjects." In Ralph Miliband and J. Saville, eds., *The Socialist Register*. London: Merlin Press.

———— (1981). "Beyond Relative Autonomy: State Managers as Historical Subjects." *New Political Science*, 2, 33–49.

Blondal, G. (1969). "The Growth of Public Expenditure in Iceland." *Scandinavian Economic History Review*, 17, 1–22.

Blum, John M. (1976). *V Was for Victory: Politics and American Culture during World War II*. San Diego: Harcourt Brace Jovanovich.

Bond, Brian (1986). *War and Society in Europe, 1870–1970*. New York: Oxford University Press.

Bonin, J. M., B. W. Finch, and J. B. Waters (1967). "Alternative Tests of the 'Displacement Effect' Hypothesis." *Public Finance*, 24, 440–56.

Bonney, Richard J. (1978). *Political Change in France under Richelieu and Mazarin, 1624–1661*. London: Oxford University Press.

———— (1981). *The King's Debts: Finance and Politics in France, 1589–1661*. Oxford: Clarendon Press.

Borcherding, Thomas E. (1977a). "One Hundred Years of Public Spending, 1870–1970." In Thomas E. Borcherding, ed., *Budgets and Bureaucrats: The Sources of Government Growth*. Durham, NC: Duke University Press.

———— (1977b). "The Sources of Growth of Public Expenditures in the United States, 1902–1970." In Thomas E. Borcherding, ed., *Budgets and Bureaucrats: The Sources of Government Growth*. Durham, NC: Duke University Press.

Bosher, J. F. (1970). *French Finances, 1770–1795: From Business to Bureaucracy*. Cambridge: Cambridge University Press.

Box, George and Gwilyn Jenkins (1976). *Time Series Analysis: Forecasting and Control*, rev. ed. San Francisco: Holden-Day.

Box, George, and E. P. and G. C. Tiao (1975). "Intervention Analysis with Applications to Economic and Environmental Problems." *Journal of the American Statistical Association*, 70, 70–92.

Brady, Thomas A., Jr. (1985). *Turning Swiss: Cities and Empire, 1450–1550*. Cambridge: Cambridge University Press.

Braudel, Fernand (1984). *The Perspective of the World: Civilization and Capitalism in the 15th–18th Centuries*, vol. 3. New York: Harper and Row.

Braun, R. (1975). "Taxation, Socio-Political Structure, and State-Building: Great Britain and Brandenburg-Prussia." In Charles Tilly, ed., *The Formation of National States in Western Europe*. Princeton: Princeton University Press.

Bridbury, A. R. (1976). "The Hundred Years' War: Costs and Profits." In D. C. Coleman and A. H. John, eds., *Trade, Government and Economy in Pre-Industrial England*. London: Weidenfeld and Nicolson.

Brody, David (1980). *Workers in Industrial America: Essays on the Twentieth Century Struggle*. New York: Oxford University Press.

Brooks, Robin (1979). 'Domestic Violence and America's Wars." In Hugh Graham and Ted Gurr, eds., *Violence in America: Historical and Comparative Perspectives*. Beverly Hills: Sage.

Burke, K., ed. (1982). *War and the State: The Transformation of British Government, 1914–1919*. London: George Allen and Unwin.

Cameron, D. R. (1978). "The Expansion of the Public Economy: A Comparative Analysis." *American Political Science Review*, 72, 1243–61.

Campbell, Donald T. and Julian C. Stanley (1966). *Experimental and Quasi-Experimental Designs for Research*. Chicago: Rand McNally.

Caron, Francois (1979). *An Economic History of Modern France*, translated by Barbara Bray. New York: Columbia University Press.

Carre, J. J., P. Dubois, and E. Malinvaud (1975). *French Economic Growth*, translated by J. P. Hatfield. Stanford: Stanford University Press.

Carter, Alice C. (1968). *The English Public Debt in the Eighteenth Century*. London: The Historical Association.

Central Statistical Office, United Kingdom (multiple volumes). *Annual Abstract of Statistics*. London: HMSO.

Chan, Steve (1987). "Growth with Equality: A Test of Olson's Theory for the Asian-Pacific Rim Countries." *Journal of Peace Research*, 24, 135–49.

Chandaman, C. D. (1975). *The English Public Revenue, 1660–88*. Oxford: Clarendon Press.

Chejne, Anwar G. (1974). *Muslim Spain: Its History and Culture*. Minneapolis: University of Minnesota Press.

Clark, John G. (1981). *La Rochelle and the Atlantic Economy during the Eighteenth Century*. Baltimore: Johns Hopkins University Press.

Cohen, Jerome B. (1949). *Japan's Economy in War and Reconstruction*. Minneapolis: University of Minnesota Press.

Cole, W. A. (1981). "Factors in Demand, 1700–80." In R. Floud and D. McCloskey, eds., *The Economic History of Britain since 1700, Vol. 1: 1700–1860*. London: Cambridge University Press.

Contamine, Philippe (1984). *War in the Middle Ages*, translated by Michael Jones. New York: Basil Blackwell.

Cooper, J. P. (1970). "General Introduction." In J. P. Cooper, ed., *The New Cambridge Modern History, Vol. 4: The Decline of Spain and the Thirty Years War*. London: Cambridge University Press.

Coxe, William (1813). *Memoirs of the Kings of Spain*, vol. 1. London: Longman.

Crouzet, Francois (1964). "Wars, Blockade and Economic Change in Europe, 1792–1815." *Journal of Economic History*, 24, 567–88.

Dalfiume, Richard (1974). "The Achievement of Military Desegregation." In Alonzo Hamby, ed., *Harry S Truman and the Fair Deal*. Lexington, MA: D. C. Heath.

Davies, R. Trevor (1937). *The Golden Century of Spain, 1501–1621*. London: Macmillan.

Davis, Ralph (1973). *The Rise of the Atlantic Economies*. Ithaca, NY: Cornell University Press.

Deane, Phyllis (1955). "The Implications of Early National Income Estimates for the Measurement of Long-Term Economic Growth in the United Kingdom." *Economic Development and Cultural Change*, 4, 3–38.

——— (1968). "New Estimates of GNP for the United Kingdom, 1830–1914." *Review of Income and Wealth*, 14, 95–112.

——— (1975). "War and Industrialization." In J. M. Winter, ed., *War and Economic Development*. Cambridge: Cambridge University Press.

Deane, Phyllis and W. A. Cole (1962). *British Economic Growth, 1688–1959*. London: Cambridge University Press.

deKaufman, R. (1884). *Les Finances de la France*. Paris: Guillaumin et Cie.

Dent, Julian (1973). *Crisis in Finance: Crown, Financiers and Society in Seventeenth-Century France*. New York: St. Martin's Press.

Denton, Frank (1966). "Some Regularities in International Conflict, 1820–1949." *Background*, 9, 283–96.

Denton, Frank and Warren Phillips (1968). "Some Patterns in the History of Violence." *Journal of Conflict Resolution*, 12, 182–95.

DeVries, Jan (1976). *Economy of Europe in an Age of Crisis, 1600–1750*. Cambridge: Cambridge University Press.

Dickinson, F. G. (1940). "An Aftercost of the World War to the United States." *American Economic Review*, 30 (supplement, part 2), 326–39.

Dickson, P. G. M. (1967). *The Financial Revolution in England: A Study in the Development of Public Credit, 1688–1756*. London: Macmillan.

Dickson, P. G. M. and John Sperling (1970). "War Finance, 1689–1714." In J. S. Bromley, ed., *The New Cambridge Modern History: The Rise of Great Britain and Russia, 1688–1725*. London: Cambridge University Press.

Dietz, F. C. (1923). "The Exchequer in Elizabeth's Reign." *Smith College Studies in History*, 8.

——— (1928). "The Receipts and Issues of the Exchequer during the Reigns of James I and Charles I." *Smith College Studies in History*, 13.

——— (1964). *English Government Finance, 1485–1588*. London: Cass.

Diffie, Bailey W. (1960). *Prelude to Empire: Portugal Overseas before Henry the Navigator*. Lincoln: University of Nebraska Press.

Diffie, Bailey W. and George Winius (1977). *Foundations of the Portuguese Empire, 1415–1580*. Minneapolis: University of Minnesota Press.

Dominguez Ortiz, Antonio (1971). *The Golden Age of Spain, 1516–1659*, translated by James Casey. New York: Basic Books.

Dubofsky, Melvyn (1975). *Industrialism and the American Worker, 1865–1920*. Arlington Heights, IL: Harlan Davidson.

Dunleavy, Patrick and Brendan O'Leary (1987). *Theories of the State: The Politics of Liberal Democracy*. London: Macmillan.

Dupuy, R. E. and T. N. Dupuy (1977). *The Encyclopedia of Military History*, rev. ed. New York: Harper and Row.

The Economist (1982). *World Business Cycles*. London: The Economist Newspaper.

Eichenberg, Richard C. (1983). "Problems in Using Public Employment Data." In Charles L. Taylor, ed., *Why Governments Grow*. Beverly Hills: Sage.

Elliott, John H. (1961). "The Decline of Spain." *Past and Present*, 20, 52–75.

——— (1963). *Imperial Spain, 1469–1716*. New York: St. Martin's Press.

——— (1970). *The Old World and the New, 1492–1650*. Cambridge: Cambridge University Press.

―――― (1977). "Self-Perception and Decline in Early Seventeenth-Century Spain." *Past and Present*, 74, 41–61.

Emi, K. (1963). *Government Fiscal Activity and Economic Growth in Japan, 1868–1960*. Tokyo: Kinokuniya.

―――― (1979). "Expenditure." In K. Ohkawa and M. Shinohara with L. Meissner, eds., *Patterns of Japanese Economic Development: A Quantitative Appraisal*. New Haven: Yale University Press.

Emsley, Clive (1979). *British Society and the French Wars, 1793–1815*. London: Macmillan.

Evans, Peter B., Dietrich Rueschemeyer, and Theda Skocpol, eds. (1985). *Bringing the State Back In*. Cambridge: Cambridge University Press.

Farmer, D. C. (1956). "Some Price Fluctuations in Angevin England." *Economic History Review*, 9.

―――― (1957). "Some Grain Prices Movements in 13th Century England." *Economic History Review*, 10.

Feige, Edgar L. and Douglas K. Pearce (1979). "The Causal Relations between Money and Income: Some Caveats for the Time Series Analysis." *Review of Economics and Statistics*, 61, 521–33.

Feinstein, C. H. (1972). *National Income Expenditure and Output of the United Kingdom, 1855–1965*. London: Cambridge University Press.

Finer, Samuel E. (1975). "State- and Nation-Building in Europe: The Role of the Military." In Charles Tilly, ed., *The Formation of National States in Western Europe*. Princeton: Princeton University Press.

Fishel, Leslie and Benjamin Quarles (1970). "In the New Deal's Wake: The Negro American." In Allen Weinstein and Frank Gatell, eds., *The Segregation Era, 1863–1954: A Modern Reader*. New York: Oxford University Press.

Flanigan, William and Edwin Fogelman (1970). "Patterns of Political Violence in Comparative Historical Perspective." *Comparative Politics*, 3, 1–20.

Foner, Philip (1982). *Organized Labor and the Black Worker, 1619–1981*, 2d ed. New York: International Publishers.

Fox, Edward W. (1971). *History in Geographic Perspective*. New York: W. W. Norton.

France, Ministere de l'Economie (multiple volumes). *Annuaire Statistique de la France*. Paris: Republique Francaise.

France, Ministere des Finances (1946). *Inventaire de la Situation Financiere, 1913–1946*. Paris: Imprimerie Nationale.

France, Ministere du Travail (1966). *Annuaire Statistique de la France*. Paris: Republique Francaise.

Freeland, Richard (1972). *The Truman Doctrine and the Origins of McCarthyism*. New York: Alfred A. Knopf.

Fryde, E. B. and M. M. Fryde (1963). "Public Credit with Special Reference to North-Western Europe." In M. M. Postan and E. E. Rich, eds., *The Cambridge Economic History of Europe: Economic Organization and Policies in the Middle Ages*, vol. 3. London: Cambridge University Press.

Germany (multiple volumes). *Statistisches Jahrbuch fur die Bundesrepublik Deutschland*. Bonn: Bundesrepublik Deutschland.

Gillis, John R. (1978). "Germany." In Raymond Grew, ed., *Crises of Political Development in Europe and the United States*. Princeton: Princeton University Press.

Gilpin, Robert (1981). *War and Change in World Politics*. London: Cambridge University Press.

Ginsberg, Benjamin (1986). *The Captive Public: How Mass Opinion Promotes State Power*. New York: Basic Books.

Godson, Roy (1976). *American Labor and European Politics*. New York: Crane, Russak.

Goetz, C. J. (1977). "Fiscal Illusion in State and Local Finance." In Thomas E. Borcherding, ed., *Budgets and Bureaucracy: The Sources of Government Growth*. Durham, NC: Duke University Press.

Goffman, I. J. and D. J. Mahar (1971). "The Growth of Public Expenditures in Selected Developing Nations: Six Caribbean Countries, 1940–65." *Public Finance*, 26, 57–74.

Goldscheid, Rudolf (1926). "Staat, Offentlichen Haushalt und Gesellschaft." In *Hanbuch der Finanzwissenschaft*. Tubingen: Mohr, 1, 146–84.

Goldstone, Jack A. (1988). "East and West in the Seventeenth Century: Political Crises in Stuart England, Ottoman Turkey, and Ming China." *Comparative Studies in Society and History*, 30, 103–42.

Good, David F. (1984). *The Economic Rise of the Habsburg Empire, 1750–1914*. Berkeley: University of California Press.

Gordon, Donald F. and Gary M. Walton (1982). "A Theory of Regenerative Growth and the Experience of Post-World War II West Germany." In Roger Ransom, Richard Sutch, and Gary M. Walton, eds., *Explorations in the New Economic History*. New York: Academic Press.

Gottman, James M. (1981). *Time-Series Analysis*. New York: Cambridge University Press.

Gould, G. (1983). "The Growth of Public Expenditures: Theory and Evidence from Six Advanced Democracies." In Charles L. Taylor, ed., *Why Governments Grow*. Beverly Hills: Sage.

Gould, Jay D. (1972). *Economic Growth in History: Survey and Analysis*. London: Methuen.

Gourevitch, Peter (1986). *Politics in Hard Times: Comparative Response to International Economic Crises*. Ithaca, NY: Cornell University Press.

Graham, Gerald S. (1950). *Empire of the North Atlantic: The Maritime Struggle for North America*. Toronto: University of Toronto Press.

Grew, Raymond, ed. (1978). *Crises of Political Development in Europe and the United States*. Princeton: Princeton University Press.

Grubbs, Frank (1968). *The Struggle for Labor Loyalty: Gompers, the A. F. of L. and the Pacifists, 1917–1920*. Durham, NC: Duke University Press.

Guenee, Bernard (1971). *L'Occident aux XIVe et XVe Siecles: Les Etats*. Paris: Presses Universitaires de France.

Guery, Alain (1978). "Les Finances de la Monarchie Francaise sous L'Ancien Regime." *Annales Economies, Societies, Civilisations*, 36, 216–39.

Gupta, S. P. (1967). "Public Expenditure and Economic Growth: A Time Series Analysis." *Public Finance*, 22, 423–61.

Gurr, Ted (1970). *Why Men Rebel*. Princeton: Princeton University Press.

—— (1988). "War, Revolution, and the Growth of the Coercive State." *Comparative Political Studies*, 21, 45–65.


Hale, J. R. (1985). *War and Society in Renaissance Europe, 1450–1620*. Baltimore: Johns Hopkins University Press.

Hamada, Koichi and Akiyoshi Horiuchi (1987). "The Political Economy of the Financial Market." In Kozo Yamamura and Yasukichi Yasuba, eds., *The Political Economy of Japan: The Domestic Transformation*. Stanford: Stanford University Press.

Hamby, Alonzo (1974). "The Vital Center, the Fair Deal, and Quest for a Liberal Political Economy." In Alonzo Hamby, ed., *Harry S Truman and the Fair Deal*. Lexington, MA: D. C. Heath.

Hamilton, Earl J. (1934). *American Treasure and the Price Revolution in Spain, 1501–1650*. Cambridge: Harvard University Press.

—— (1947). "Original Growth of National Debt in Western Europe." *American Economic Review*, 37, 118–30.

Hardach, Karl (1980). *The Political Economy of Germany in the Twentieth Century*. Berkeley: University of California Press.

Hawley, Ellis (1979). *The Great War and the Search for a Modern Order: A History of the American People and Their Institutions, 1917–1923*. New York: St. Martin's Press.

Hechter, Michael (1975). *Internal Colonialism: The Celtic Fringe in British National Development, 1536–1966*. Berkeley: University of California Press.

Hechter, Michael and William Brustein (1980). "Regional Modes of Production and Patterns of State Formation in Western Europe." *American Journal of Sociology*, 85, 1061–94.

Heckscher, Eli F. (1922/1964). *The Continental System: An Economic Interpretation*, Harold Westergaard, ed. Gloucester, MA: Peter Smith.

Henneman, John B. (1971). *Royal Taxation in Fourteenth Century France: The Development of War Financing, 1322–1356*. Princeton: Princeton University Press.

Hibbs, Douglas A., Jr. (1974). "Problem of Statistical Estimation and Causal Inference in Time Series Regression Models." In Herbert L. Costner, ed., *Sociological Methodology, 1973–1974*. San Francisco: Jossey-Bass.

Higgs, Robert (1987). *Crisis and Leviathan: Critical Episodes in the Growth of the American Government*. New York: Oxford University Press.

Hillgarth, J. N. (1978). *The Spanish Kingdoms, 1250–1516*, 2 vols. Oxford: Clarendon Press.

Hintze, Otto (1975). "Military Organization and the Organization of the State." In Felix Gilbert, ed., *The Historical Essays of Otto Hintze*. New York: Oxford University Press.

Hoffman, Walter G. (1965). *Das Wachstum der Deutsche Wirtschaft seit der Mitte des 19. Jahrhunderts*. Berlin: Springer-Verlag.

Howard, Michael (1976). *War in European History*. London: Oxford University Press.

Hueckel, Glenn R. (1985). *The Napoleonic Wars and Their Impact on Factor Returns and Output Growth in England, 1793–1815*. New York: Garland Publishing.

Huntington, Samuel P. (1968). *Political Order in Changing Societies*. New Haven: Yale University Press.

Israel, Jonathan (1981). "Debate—The Decline of Spain: A Historical Myth." *Past and Present*, 91, 170–85.

*Japan Statistical Yearbook* (various years). Tokyo: Executive Office of the Statistics Commission and Statistics Bureau of the Prime Minister's Office.

Jeze, G. (1927). *Les Depenses de Guerre de la France*. Paris: Les Presses Universitaires de France.

John, A. H. (1954–55). "War and the English Economy, 1700–1763." *Economic History Review*, 2d ser., 7. Cambridge: Cambridge University Press.

Jones, Archer (1987). *The Art of War in the Western World*. Urbana: University of Illinois Press.

Kamen, Henry (1969). *The War of Succession in Spain, 1700–15*. Bloomington: Indiana University Press.

—— (1978). "The Decline of Spain: A Historical Myth?" *Past and Present*, 81, 24–50.

—— (1980). *Spain in the Later Seventeenth Century, 1665–1700*. New York: Longman.

—— (1983). *Spain, 1469–1714*. London: Longman.

Kaufman, J. P. (1983). "The Social Consequences of War: The Social Development of Four Nations." *Armed Forces and Society*, 9, 245–64.

Kennedy, David M. (1980). *Over Here: The First World War and American Society*. Oxford: Oxford University Press.

Kennedy, Paul (1987). *The Rise and Fall of the Great Powers*. New York: Random House.

Kiernan, V. G. (1965). "State and Nation in Western Europe." *Past and Present*, 31, 20–38.

Kimmel, Michael S. (1983). "War, State Finance and Revolution: Foreign Policy and Domestic Opposition in the Sixteenth- and Seventeenth-Century World-Economy." In Patrick J. McGowan and Charles W. Kegley, Jr., eds., *Foreign Policy and the Modern World-System*. Beverly Hills: Sage.

Kochan, Lionel and Richard Abraham (1983). *The Making of Modern Russia*. London: Macmillan.
Kohl, J. (1983). "The Functional Structure of Public Expenditures: Long-Term Changes." In Charles L. Taylor, ed., *Why Governments Grow*. Beverly Hills: Sage.
Kohn, George C. (1987). *Dictionary of Wars*. Garden City, NY: Anchor Books.
Krasner, Stephen D. (1984). "Approaches to the State: Alternative Conceptions and Historical Dynamics." *Comparative Politics*, 16, 223–46.
—— (1988). "Sovereignty: An Institutional Perspective." *Comparative Political Studies*, 21, 66–94.
Kuznets, Simon S. (1964). *Postwar Economic Growth*. Cambridge: Harvard University Press.
—— (1971). *Economic Growth of Nations: Total Output and Production Structure*. Cambridge: Harvard University Press.

Lachman, Richard (1987). *From Manor to Market: Structural Change in England, 1536–1640*. Madison: University of Wisconsin Press.
Ladd, Everett and Charles Hadley (1978). *Transformations of the American Party System*, 2d ed. New York: W. W. Norton.
Ladero Quesada, Miguel Angel (1970). "Les Finances Royales de Castille a la Veille des Temps Modernes." *Annales: Economies, Societies, Civilisations*, 26, 775–88.
Lane, Frederic D. (1966). "The Economic Meaning of War and Protection." In *Venice and History: The Collected Papers of Frederic C. Lane*. Baltimore: Johns Hopkins University Press.
Lang, Karl H. (1793). *Historische Entwicklung der Deutschen Steuerur fassungen seit der Karolinger bis aufunsere Zeit*. Berlin and Stettin: F. Nicolai.
Larson, Simeon (1975). *Labor and Foreign Policy: Gompers, the AFL and the First World War, 1914–1918*. London: Associated University Press.
Leff, N. H. (1982). *Underdevelopment and Development in Brazil*, vol. 2. London: George Allen and Unwin.
Legoherel, H. (1965). *Les Tresoriers Generaux de la Marine (1517–1788)*. Paris: Editions Cujas.
Levi, Margaret (1988). *Of Rule and Revenue*. Berkeley: University of California Press.
Levy, Jack S. (1983). *War in the Modern Great Power System, 1494–1975*. Lexington: University of Kentucky Press.
—— (1985). "Theories of General War." *World Politics*, 37, 344–74.
Linz, Susan J. (1985). *The Impact of World War II on the Soviet Union*. Totowa, NJ: Rowman and Allanheld.
Lomax, Derek W. (1978). *The Reconquest of Spain*. London: Longman.
Lopez, Robert S. (1987). "The Trade and Medieval Europe: the South." In Michael M. Postan and Edward Miller, with Cynthia Postan, eds., *The Cambridge Economic History of Europe: Trade and Industry in the Middle Ages*, vol. 2, 2d ed. Cambridge: Cambridge University Press.
Lovett, A. W. (1986). *Early Habsburg Spain, 1517–1598*. Oxford: Oxford University Press.
Lynch, John (1984). *Spain under the Habsburgs*, 2d ed., 2 vols. New York: New York University Press.

McAdam, Doug (1982). *Political Process and the Development of Black Insurgency, 1930–1970*. Chicago: University of Chicago Press.
McCleary, Richard and Richard A. Hay, Jr. (1980). *Applied Time Series Analysis for the Social Sciences*. Beverly Hills: Sage.
McClure, Arthur (1969). *The Truman Administration and the Problems of Post-War Labor, 1945–1948*. New Jersey: Associated University Presses.
McEvedy, Colin and Richard Jones (1978). *Atlas of World Population History*. New York: Facts on File.
Mack, Andrew (1975). "Numbers Are Not Enough." *Comparative Politics*, 7, 597–618.

Mackay, Angus (1981). *Money, Prices and Politics in Fifteenth Century Castile*. London: Royal Historical Society.

McNeill, William H. (1982). *The Pursuit of Power*. Chicago: University of Chicago Press.

Maddison, Angus (1982). *Phases of Capitalist Development*. New York: Oxford University Press.

—— (1987). "Growth and Slowdown in Advanced Capitalist Economies: Techniques of Quantitative Assessment." *Journal of Economic Literature*, 25, 649–98.

Mahan, Alfred T. (1890). *The Influence of Sea Power upon History, 1660–1783*. New York: Wang Hill.

Mahar, D. J. and F. A. Rezende (1975). "The Growth and Pattern of Public Expenditure in Brazil, 1920–1969." *Public Finances Quarterly*, 3, 380–99.

Maier, Charles (1978). "The Politics of Productivity: Foundations of American International Economic Policy after World War II." In Peter Katzenstein, ed., *Between Power and Plenty*. Madison: University of Wisconsin Press.

Mallez, P. (1927). *La Restauration des Finances Francaises apres 1814*. Paris: Librarie Delloz.

Mann, Michael (1986). *The Sources of Social Power*, vol. 1. Cambridge: Cambridge University Press.

Marczewski, J. (1961). "Some Aspects of the Economic Growth of France, 1660–1958." *Economic Development and Cultural Change*, 9, 369–86.

Marion, M. (1914). *Histoire Financiere de la France depuis 1715*, 6 vols. Paris: Arthur Rousseau.

Marwick, Arthur (1965). *The Deluge: British Society and the First World War*. New York: W. W. Norton.

—— (1974). *War and Social Change in the Twentieth Century: A Comparative Study of Britain, France, Germany, Russia, and the United States*. New York: St. Martin's Press.

Mathias, Peter and Patrick O'Brien (1976). "Taxation in Britain and France, 1715–1810: A Comparison of Social and Economic Incidence of Taxes Collected for the Central Government." *Journal of European Economic History*, 5, 601–49.

Meltzer, A. H. and S. F. Richard (1978). "Why Government Grows (and Grows) in a Democracy." *Public Interest*, 52, 111–18.

Merriman, Roger B. (1918). *The Rise of the Spanish Empire in the Old World and in the New*. New York: Macmillan.

Miller, Edward (1970). "Government Economic Policies and Public Finance, 1000–1500." In Carlo M. Cipolla, ed., *The Fontana Economic History of Europe: The Middle Ages*. New York: Harper and Row.

Milton, David (1982). *The Politics of U.S. Labor: From the Great Depression to the New Deal*. New York: Monthly Review Press.

Milward, Alan S. (1979). *War, Economy and Society, 1939–1945*. Berkeley: University of California Press.

Milward, Alan S. and S. B. Saul (1973). *The Economic Development of Continental Europe, 1780–1870*. Totowa, NJ: Rowan and Littlefield.

Miskimin, H. A. (1977). *The Economy of Later Renaissance Europe, 1460–1600*. London: Cambridge University Press.

Mitchell, Brian R. (1981). *European Historical Statistics, 1750–1975*, 2d rev. ed. New York: Facts on File.

—— (1982). *International Historical Statistics, Africa and Asia*. New York: New York University Press.

Mitchell, Brian R. with Phyllis Deane (1962). *Abstract of British Historical Statistics*. London: Cambridge University Press.

Mitchell, Brian R. and H. G. Jones (1971). *Second Abstract of British Historical Statistics*. London: Cambridge University Press.

Modelski, George (1972). *Principles of World Politics*. New York: Free Press.

—— (1978). "The Long Cycle of Global Politics and the Nation-State." *Comparative Studies in Society and History*, 20, 214–35.

—— (1984). "Global Wars and World Leadership Selection." Paper presented at the Second World Peace Science Society Congress, Rotterdam, the Netherlands.

—— (1987a). "A Bibliography of Long Cycles Research, 1975–1985." In George Modelski, ed., *Exploring Long Cycles*. Boulder, CO: Lynne Rienner.

—— (1987b). *Long Cycles in World Politics*. Seattle: University of Washington Press.

Modelski, George and William R. Thompson (1988). *Sea Power in Global Politics, 1494-1993*. Seattle: University of Washington Press.

Moore, Barrington (1966). *Social Origins of Dictatorship and Democracy*. Boston: Beacon Press.

Musgrave, R. A. (1969). *Fiscal Systems*. New Haven: Yale University Press.

Myers, M. G. (1970). *A Financial History of the United States*. New York: Columbia University Press.

Myrdal, Gunnar (1970). "America Again at the Crossroads." In R. Y. Young, ed., *Roots of Rebellion: The Evolution of Black Politics and Protest since World War II*. New York: Harper and Row.

Nagarajan, P. (1979). "Econometric Testing of the 'Displacement Effect' Associated with a 'Non-Global' Social Disturbance in India." *Public Finance*, 34, 100–13.

Nef, John U. (1950). *War and Human Progress: An Essay on the Rise of Industrial Civilization*. Cambridge: Harvard University Press.

Nincic, Miroslav (1980). "Capital, Labor and the Spoils of War." *Journal of Peace Research*, 17, 103–17.

North, Douglas C. and Robert P. Thomas (1973). *The Rise of the Western World: A New Economic History*. New York: Cambridge University Press.

O'Brien, Patrick and Calgar Keyder (1978). *Economic Growth in Britain and France, 1780–1914*. London: George Allen and Unwin.

O'Callaghan, Joseph F. (1975). *A History of Medieval Spain*. Ithaca, NY: Cornell University Press.

Ohkawa, K. and H. Rosovsky (1973). *Japanese Economic Growth*. Palo Alto: Stanford University Press.

Oliveira Marques, Antonio H. de (1976). *History of Portugal*, 2d ed. New York: Columbia University Press.

Organski, A. F. K. and Jacek Kugler (1977). "The Cost of Major Wars: The Phoenix Factor." *American Political Science Review*, 71, 1347–66.

Organski, A. F. K. and Jacek Kugler (1980). *The War Ledger*. Chicago: University of Chicago Press.

Orloff, Ann S. (1988). "The Political Origins of America's Belated Welfare State." In Margaret Weir, Ann S. Orloff, and Theda Skocpol, eds., *The Politics of Social Policy in the United States*. Princeton: Princeton University Press.

Paige, Jeffrey (1975). *Agrarian Revolution: Social Movements and Export Agriculture in the Underdeveloped World*. New York: Free Press.

Palmer, Stanley H. (1977). *Economic Arithmetic: A Guide to the Statistical Sources of English Commerce, Industry, and Finance, 1700–1850*. New York: Garland Publishing.

Parker, David (1983). *The Making of French Absolutism*. New York: St. Martin's Press.

Parker, G. (1985). *Western Geopolitical Thought in the Twentieth Century*. London: Croom Helm.

Parker, Geoffrey (1974). "The Emergence of Modern Finance in Europe, 1500–1730." In Carlo M. Cipolla, ed., *The Fontana Economic History of Europe: The Sixteenth and Seventeenth Centuries*. Glasgow: William Collins Sons.

—— (1975). "War and Economic Change: The Economic Costs of the Dutch Revolt." In J. M. Winter, ed., *War and Economic Development*. Cambridge: Cambridge University Press.

———— (1979a). "Warfare." In Peter Burke, ed., *The New Cambridge Modern History: Companion Volume*, vol. 13. London: Cambridge University Press.

———— (1979b). *Spain and the Netherlands, 1559–1659: Ten Studies*. London: Collins.

———— (1979c). *Europe in Crisis, 1598–1648*. Ithaca, NY: Cornell University Press.

———— (1988). *The Military Revolution: Military Innovation and the Rise of the West, 1500–1800*. Cambridge: Cambridge University Press.

Peacock, Alan T. and Jack Wiseman (1961). *The Growth of Public Expenditures in the United Kingdom*. Princeton: Princeton University Press.

Peacock, Alan T. and Jack Wiseman (1979). "Approaches to the Analysis of Government Expenditure Growth." *Public Finance Quarterly*, 7, 3–23.

Peterson, H. C. and Gilbert Fite (1957). *Opponents of War, 1917–1918*. Madison: University of Wisconsin Press.

Phelps-Brown, E. H. and S. V. Hopkins (1956). "Seven Centuries of the Price of Consumables." *Economica*, 23.

Phillips, Carla R. (1987). "Time and Duration: A Model for the Economy of Early Modern Spain." *American Historical Review*, 92, 531–62.

Pierce, David A. and Larry D. Haugh (1977). "Causality in Temporal Systems: Characterizations and a Survey." *Journal of Econometrics*, 5, 265–93.

Pintner, Walter M. (1978). "Russia." In Raymond Grew, ed., *Crises of Political Development in Europe and the United States*. Princeton: Princeton University Press.

Piven, Frances and Richard Cloward (1977). *Poor People's Movements*. New York: Random House.

Poggi, Gianfranco (1978). *The Development of the Modern State: A Sociological Introduction*. Stanford: Stanford University Press.

Polenberg, Richard (1972). *War and Society: The United States, 1941–1945*. New York: J. B. Lippincott.

Porter, B. D. (1980). "Parkinson's Law Revised: War and the Growth of American Government." *Public Interest*, 60, 50–68.

Postan, Michael M. (1973). *Essays on Medieval Agriculture and General Problems of the Medieval Economy*. Cambridge: Cambridge University Press.

———— (1987). "The Trade of Medieval Europe: the North." In Michael M. Postan, Edward Miller, with Cynthia Postan, eds., *The Cambridge Economic History of Europe: Trade and Industry in the Middle Ages*, vol. 2, 2d ed. Cambridge: Cambridge University Press.

Pryor, Frederick L. (1968). *Public Expenditures in Communist and Capitalist Nations*. Homewood, IL: Richard D. Irwin.

Ramsey, J. H. (1925). *A History of the Revenues of the Kings of England, 1066–1399*, 2 vols. Oxford: Clarendon Press.

Ramsey, John (1973). *Spain: The Rise of the First World Power*. University: University of Alabama Press.

Ramsey, Matthew (1988). *Professional and Popular Medicine in France, 1770–1830: The Social World of Medical Practice*. Cambridge: Cambridge University Press.

Ratchford, Benjamin U. (1947). "History of the Federal Debt in the United States." *American Economic Review*, 37, 131–41.

Ray, James L. and J. David Singer (1973). "Measuring the Concentration of Power in the International Systems." *Sociological Methods and Research*, 1, 403–37.

Reddy, K. N. (1970). "Growth of Government Expenditure and National Income in India: 1872–1966." *Public Finance*, 25, 81–97.

Riley, James C. (1980). *International Government Finance and the Amsterdam Capital Market, 1740–1815*, New York: Cambridge University Press.

———— (1986). *The Seven Years War and the Old Regime in France: The Economic and Financial Toll*. Princeton: Princeton University Press.

——— (1987). "French Finances, 1727–1768." *Journal of Modern History*, 59, 209–43.

Ringrose, David R. (1983). *Madrid and the Spanish Economy, 1560–1850*. Berkeley: University of California Press.

Rogowski, R. (1986). "War, Trade, and Domestic Politics in Advanced Economies." Paper presented at the annual meeting of the American Political Science Association, Washington, DC, August.

Rokkan, Stein (1975). "Dimensions of State Formation and Nation-Building: A Possible Paradigm for Research on Variations Within Europe." In Charles Tilly, ed., *The Formation of National States in Western Europe*. Princeton: Princeton University Press.

——— (1980). "Territories, Centres and Peripheries: Toward a Geoethnic-Geoeconomic-Geopolitical Model of Differentiation within Western Europe." In Jean Gottman, ed., *Centre and Periphery: Spatial Variation in Politics*. Beverly Hills: Sage.

——— (1981). "Territories, Nations, Parties: Towards a Geoeconomic-Geopolitical Model for the Explanation of Variations within Western Europe." In Richard L. Merritt and Bruce M. Russett, eds., *From National Development to Global Community: Essays in Honor of Karl W. Deutsch*. London: Allen and Unwin.

Ropp, Theodore (1962). *War in the Modern World*, rev. ed. New York: Collier Books.

Rosecrance, Richard (1986). *The Rise of the Trading State: Commerce and Conquest in the Modern World*. New York: Basic Books.

Rosenau, James N. (1988). "The State in an Era of Cascading Politics: Wavering Concept, Widening Competence, Withering Colossus or Weathering Change?" *Comparative Political Studies*, 21, 13–44.

Rosenfeld, B. D. (1973). "The Displacement-Effect in the Growth of Canadian Government Expenditures." *Public Finance*, 28, 301–14.

Roseveare, H. (1969). *The Treasury: The Evolution of a British Institution*. New York: Columbia University Press.

Rostow, Walt W. (1962). *The Process of Economic Growth*, 2d ed. New York: Norton.

Rowen, Herbert H. (1988). *The Princes of Orange: The Stadholders in the Dutch Republic*. Cambridge: Cambridge University Press.

Russell, Conrad (1973). "Parliament and the King's Finances." In Conrad Russell, ed., *The Origins of the English Civil War*. New York: Harper and Row.

Saelen, Kirsti T. (1981). "Stein Rokkan: A Bibliography." In Per Torsvik, ed., *Mobilization, Center-Periphery Structures and Nation-Building*. Oslo: Universtetsforlaget.

Scheiber, Jane and Harry Scheiber (1969). "The Wilson Administration and the Wartime Mobilization of Black Americans, 1917–1918." *Labor History*, 10, 433–58.

Schmidt, M. G. (1983). "The Growth of the Tax State: The Industrial Democracies, 1950–1978." In Charles L. Taylor, ed., *Why Governments Grow*. Beverly Hills: Sage.

Shneidman, Jerome L. (1970). *The Rise of the Aragonese-Catalonian Empire, 1200–1350*, 2 vols. New York: New York University Press.

Singer, J. David and Melvin Small (1972). *The Wages of War, 1816–1965*. New York: Wiley.

Siverson, Randolph M. (1980). "War and Change in the International System." In Ole R. Holsti, Randolph M. Siverson, and Alexander L. George, eds., *Change in the International System*. Boulder, CO: Westview.

Skocpol, Theda (1979). *States and Social Revolutions: A Comparative Analysis of France, Russia and China*. Cambridge: Cambridge University Press.

——— (1980). "Political Response to Capitalist Crisis: Neo-Marxist Theories of the State and the Case of the New Deal." *Politics and Society*, 10, 155–202.

——— (1985). "Bringing the State Back In: Strategies of Analysis in Current Research." In Peter D. Evans, D. Rueschemeyer, and Theda Skocpol, eds., *Bringing the State Back In*. Cambridge: Cambridge University Press.

Skolnick, Joseph (1974). "An Appraisal of Studies of the Linkage between Domestic and International Conflict." *Comparative Political Studies*, 6, 485–509.

Skowronek, Stephen (1982). *Building a New American State: The Expansion of National Administrative Capacities, 1877–1920*. Cambridge: Cambridge University Press.

Small, Melvin and J. David Singer (1982). *Resort to Arms*. Beverly Hills: Sage.

Snyder, David and Charles Tilly (1972). "Hardship and Collective Violence in France, 1830–1960." *American Sociological Review*, 37, 320–32.

Sombart, Werner (1913). *Krieg und Kapitalismus*. Leipzig: Duncker and Humblot.

Sorokin, Pitrim (1937). *Social and Cultural Dynamics: Fluctuations of Social Relationships, War and Revolution*, 3 vols. New York: Bedminster.

Steel, A. (1954). *The Receipt of the Exchequer, 1377–1485*. Cambridge: Cambridge University Press.

Stein, Arthur (1976). "Conflict and Cohesion: A Review of the Literature." *Journal of Conflict Resolution*, 20, 143–72.

—— (1978). *The Nation at War*. Baltimore: Johns Hopkins University Press.

Stein, Arthur and Bruce Russett (1980). "Evaluating War: Outcome and Consequences." In Ted R. Gurr, ed., *Handbook of Political Conflict: Theory and Research*. New York: Free Press.

Stohl, Michael (1975). "War and Domestic Violence: The Case of the United States, 1890–1970." *Journal of Conflict Resolution*, 19, 379–416.

—— (1976). *War and Domestic Political Violence: The American Capacity for Repression and Reaction*. Beverly Hills: Sage.

—— (1980). "The Nexus of Civil and International Conflict." In Ted Gurr, ed., *Handbook of Political Conflict: Theory and Research*. New York: Free Press.

Stradling, R. A. (1981). *Europe and the Decline of Spain: A Study of the Spanish System, 1580–1720*. London: Allen and Unwin.

Strayer, Joseph (1970). *On the Medieval Origins of the Modern State*. Princeton: Princeton University Press.

Strickland, Julie (1983). " 'The Second Image Reversed' Revisited: The Concept of the State, War, and the Enhancement of American National Administrative Capacities, 1916–1920." Paper presented at the annual meeting of the International Studies Association, Mexico City, Mexico, March.

Sudre, F. C. (1883). *Les Finances de la France au XIXe Siecle*, vol. 1. Paris: Librarie E. Plon et Cie.

Tanter, Raymond (1969). "International War and Domestic Turmoil: Some Contemporary Evidence." In Hugh Graham and Ted Gurr, eds., *The History of Violence in America: A Report to the National Commission on the Causes and Prevention of Violence*. New York: Praeger.

Taylor, Charles L. (1981). "Limits to Governmental Growth." In Richard L. Merritt and Bruce Russett, eds., *From National Development to Global Community*. London: George Allen and Unwin.

Taylor, Robert H. (1987). *The State in Burma*. Honolulu: University of Hawaii Press.

Theoharis, Athan (1970). "The Rhetoric of Politics: Foreign Policy, Internal Security, and Domestic Politics in the Truman Era, 1945–1950." In Barton Bernstein, ed., *Politics and Policies of the Truman Administration*. Chicago: Quadrangle Books.

Thompson, I. A. A. (1976). *War and Government in Hapsburg Spain, 1560–1620*. London: Athlone Press.

Thompson, William R. (1988). *On Global War: Historical-Structural Approaches to World Politics*. Columbia: University of South Carolina Press.

Thompson, William R. and Karen A. Rasler (1988). "War and Systemic Capability Reconcentration." *Journal of Conflict Resolution*, 32, 335–66.

Tilly, Charles (1975). "Reflections on the History of European State Making." In Charles Tilly, ed., *The Formation of National States in Western Europe*. Princeton: Princeton University Press.

——— (1978). *From Mobilization to Revolution*. Reading, MA: Addison-Wesley.

——— (1979). "Sinews of War." Paper presented at the Council of European Studies Conference of Europeanists, Washington, DC, March.

——— (1982). "Sinews of War." In P. Torsvik, ed., *Mobilization, Center-Periphery Structures and Nation Building*. Oslo: Universtetsforlaget.

——— (1984). *Big Structures, Large Processes, Huge Comparisons*. New York: Russell Sage Foundation.

——— (1985). "War Making and State Making as Organized Crime." In Peter B. Evans, D. Rueschemeyer, and Theda Skocpol, eds., *Bringing the State Back In*. Cambridge: Cambridge University Press.

——— (1986). *The Contentious French*. Cambridge: Harvard University Press.

Titmuss, R. M. (1969). *Essays on the Welfare State*, 2d ed. Boston: Beacon Press.

Tits-Dievaide, Marie-Jeanne (1987). "L'Evolution du Prix des Ble dans Quelques Villes D'Europe Occidentale du XVe au XVIIIe Siecle." *Annales, ESC*, 42, 529–48.

Tracy, James D. (1985). *A Financial Revolution in the Habsburg Netherlands: Renten and Renteniers in the County of Holland, 1515–1565*. Berkeley: University of California Press.

Trimberger, Ellen (1978). *Revolution from Above: Military Bureaucrats and Development in Japan, Turkey, Egypt and Peru*. New Brunswick, NJ: Transaction Books.

Tussing, A. D. and J. A. Henning (1974). "Long-Run Growth of Non-Defense Government Expenditures in the United States." *Public Finance Quarterly*, 2, 202–22.

United Kingdom, Central Statistical Office (multiple volumes). *Annual Abstract of Statistics*. London: HMSO.

United States Department of Commerce (1975). *Historical Statistics of the United States: Colonial Times to 1970*. Washington, DC: GPO.

United States Office of the President (multiple volumes). *Economic Report of the President*. Washington, DC: GPO.

Van der Wee, H. (1977). "Monetary, Credit and Banking Systems." In E. E. Rich and Charles H. Wilson, eds., *The Cambridge Economic History of Europe: The Economic Organization of Early Modern Europe*, vol. 5. London: Cambridge University Press.

Vicens Vives, Jaime with Jorge Nadal Oller (1969). *An Economic History of Spain*, 3d ed. rev., translated by Francis M. Lopez-Morillas. Princeton: Princeton University Press.

Wagner, R. E. and W. E. Weber (1977). "Wagner's Law, Fiscal Institutions and the Growth of Government." *National Tax Journal*, 30, 59–67.

Wallerstein, Immanuel (1974). *The Modern World-System: Capitalist Agriculture and the Origins of the European World-Economy in the Sixteenth Century*. New York: Academic Press.

——— (1980). *The Modern World-System: Mercantilism and the Consolidation of the European World-Economy, 1600–1750*. New York: Academic Press.

Webber, Carolyn and Aaron Wildavsky (1986). *A History of Taxation and Expenditure in the Western World*. New York: Simon and Schuster.

Wernham, Richard B. (1966). *Before the Armada: The Emergence of the English Nation, 1485–1588*. New York: Harcourt, Brace and World.

Wesson, Robert (1986). *The Russian Dilemma*, rev. ed. New York: Praeger.

Wheeler, Hugh G. (1975). "Effects of War on Industrial Growth." *Society*, 12, 48–52.

——— (1980). "Postwar Industrial Growth." In J. David Singer, ed., *The Correlates of War II: Testing Some Realpolitik Models*. New York: Free Press.

White, James W. (1988). "State Growth and Popular Protest in Tokugawa Japan." *Journal of Japanese Studies*, 14, 1–25.

White, Lynn, Jr. (1962). *Medieval Technology and Social Change*. London: Oxford University Press.

Wilensky, Harold (1975). *The Welfare State and Equality: Structural and Ideological Roots of Public Expenditures*. Berkeley: University of California Press.

Wilson, Charles H. (1965). *England's Apprenticeship, 1603–1763*. New York: St. Martin's Press.

Winter, J. M. (1975). "Select Bibliography of Works on War and Economic Development." In J. M. Winter, ed., *War and Economic Development*. Cambridge: Cambridge University Press.

———— (1986). *The Great War and the British People*. Cambridge: Harvard University Press.

Wiseman, J. and J. Diamond (1975). "Comment: On Long-Run Growth of Nondefense Government Expenditures in the United States." *Public Finance Quarterly*, 3, 411–14.

Witte, John F. (1985). *The Politics and the Development of the Federal Income Tax*. Madison: University of Wisconsin Press.

Wolf, Eric (1969). *Peasant Wars of the Twentieth Century*. New York: Harper and Row.

Wolfe, Martin (1972). *The Fiscal System of Renaissance France*. New Haven: Yale University Press.

Wolffe, B. P. (1971). *The Royal Demesne in English History*. London: Allen and Unwin.

Wonnacott, Ronald J. and Thomas H. Wonnacott (1979). *Econometrics*, 2d ed. New York: John Wiley.

Wright, Quincy (1965). *A Study of War*. Chicago: University of Chicago Press.

Wynn, Neil A. (1986). *From Progressivism to Prosperity: World War I and American Society*. New York: Holmes and Meier.

Zagorin, Perez (1982). *Rebels and Rulers, 1500–1660: Society, States, and Early Modern Revolution*, vol. 1. Cambridge: Cambridge University Press.

Zimmerman, Ekkart (1983). *Political Violence, Crises, and Revolutions: Theories and Research*. Cambridge: Schenckman.

———— (1985). "The 1930s World Economic Crisis in Six European Countries: A First Report on the Causes of Political Instability and Reactions to Crisis." In Paul M. Johnson and William R. Thompson, eds., *Rhythms in Politics and Economics*. New York: Praeger.

Zolberg, Aristide R. (1980). "Strategic Interactions and the Formation of Modern States: France and England." *International Social Science Journal*, 32, 687–716.

———— (1981). "Origins of the Modern World System: A Missing Link." *World Politics*, 33, 253–81.

# Index

Printed in the United States
by Baker & Taylor Publisher Services